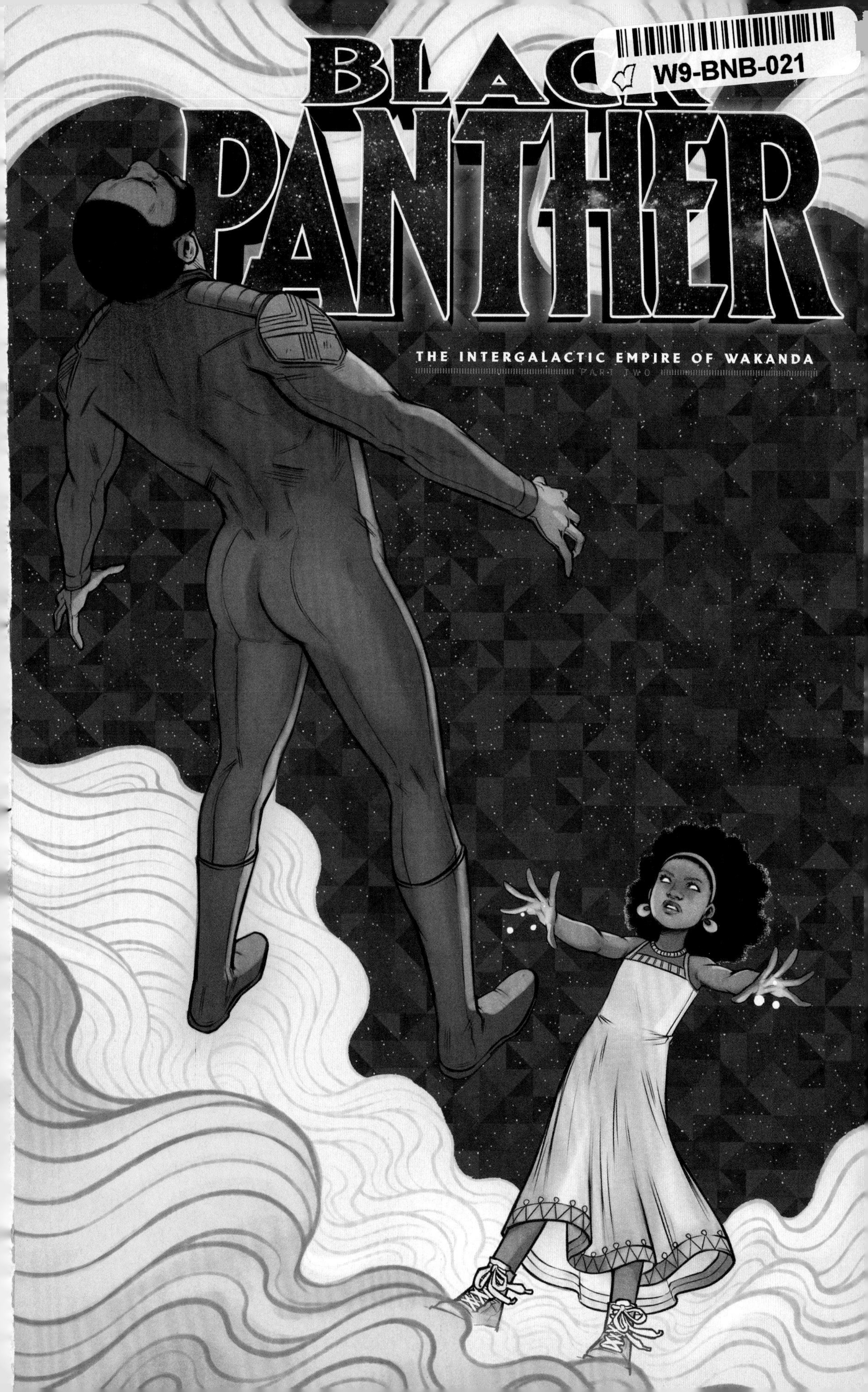
BLAC
PANTHER
THE INTERGALACTIC EMPIRE OF WAKANDA
PART TWO

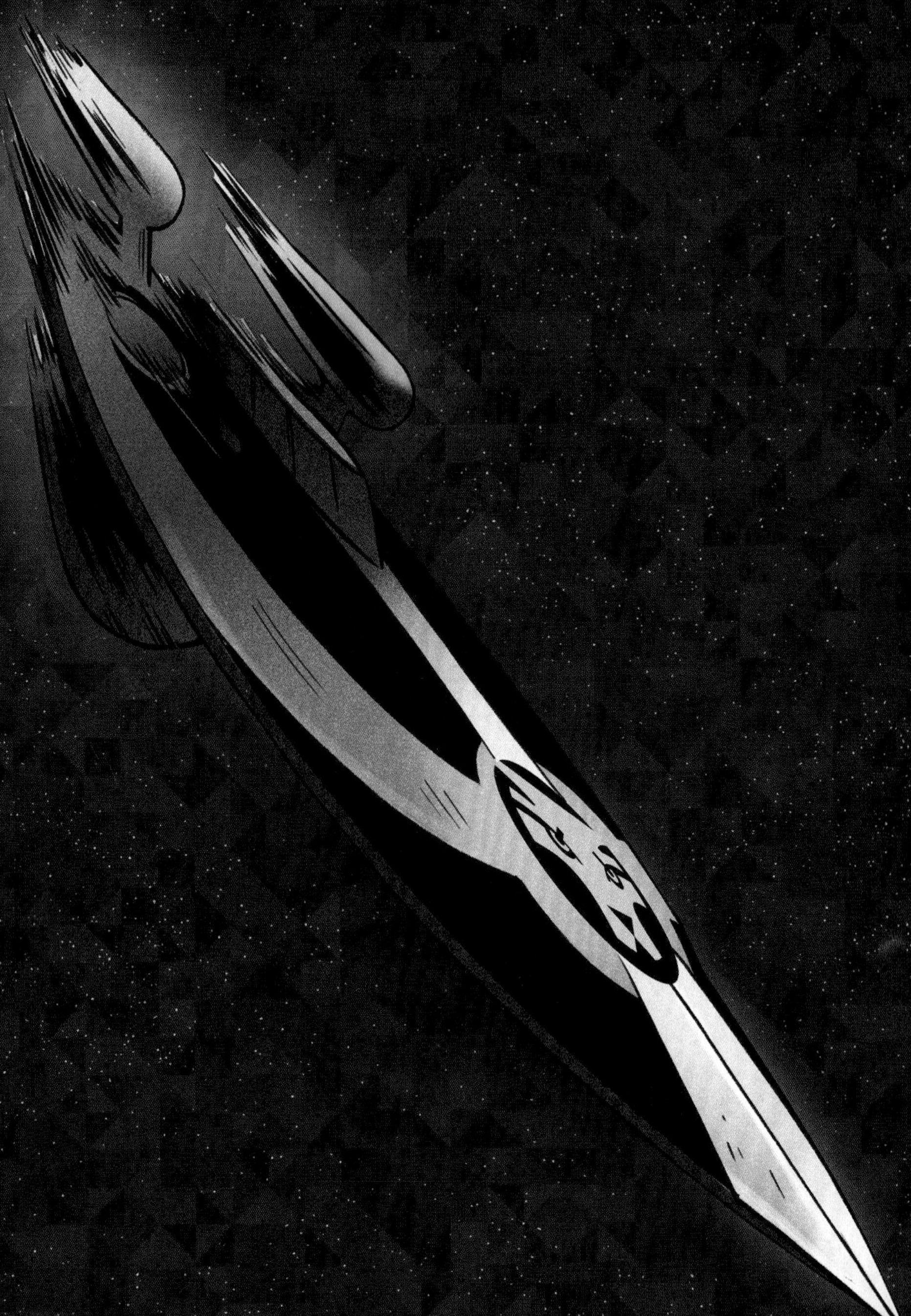

COLLECTION EDITOR **JENNIFER GRÜNWALD**
ASSISTANT EDITOR **CAITLIN O'CONNELL**
ASSOCIATE MANAGING EDITOR **KATERI WOODY**
EDITOR, SPECIAL PROJECTS **MARK D. BEAZLEY**
VP PRODUCTION & SPECIAL PROJECTS **JEFF YOUNGQUIST**
BOOK DESIGNERS **SALENA MAHINA** & **ADAM DEL RE**

SVP PRINT, SALES & MARKETING **DAVID GABRIEL**
DIRECTOR, LICENSED PUBLISHING **SVEN LARSEN**
EDITOR IN CHIEF **C.B. CEBULSKI**
CHIEF CREATIVE OFFICER **JOE QUESADA**
PRESIDENT **DAN BUCKLEY**
EXECUTIVE PRODUCER **ALAN FINE**

BLACK PANTHER BOOK 7: THE INTERGALACTIC EMPIRE OF WAKANDA PART TWO. Contains material originally published in magazine form as BLACK PANTHER #7-12. First printing 2019. ISBN 978-1-302-91294-9. Published by MARVEL WORLDWIDE, INC., a subsidiary of MARVEL ENTERTAINMENT, LLC. OFFICE OF PUBLICATION: 135 West 50th Street, New York, NY 10020. © 2019 MARVEL No similarity between any of the names, characters, persons, and/or institutions in this magazine with those of any living or dead person or institution is intended, and any such similarity which may exist is purely coincidental. **Printed in Canada.** DAN BUCKLEY, President, Marvel Entertainment; JOHN NEE, Publisher; JOE QUESADA, Chief Creative Officer; TOM BREVOORT, SVP of Publishing; DAVID BOGART, Associate Publisher & SVP of Talent Affairs; DAVID GABRIEL, SVP of Sales & Marketing, Publishing; JEFF YOUNGQUIST, VP of Production & Special Projects; DAN CARR, Executive Director of Publishing Technology; ALEX MORALES, Director of Publishing Operations; DAN EDINGTON, Managing Editor; SUSAN CRESPI, Production Manager; STAN LEE, Chairman Emeritus. For information regarding advertising in Marvel Comics or on Marvel.com, please contact Vit DeBellis, Custom Solutions & Integrated Advertising Manager, at vdebellis@marvel.com. For Marvel subscription inquiries, please call 888-511-5480. **Manufactured between 5/31/2019 and 7/2/2019 by SOLISCO PRINTERS, SCOTT, QC, CANADA.**

10 9 8 7 6 5 4 3 2 1

BLACK PANTHER

THE INTERGALACTIC EMPIRE OF WAKANDA

PART TWO

Ta-Nehisi Coates
WRITER

ISSUES #7-11

Kev Walker
ARTIST

Marc Deering
INKER

Stéphane Paitreau (#7-10) & Java Tartaglia (#10-11)
COLOR ARTISTS

ISSUE #12

Jen Bartel
ARTIST

Kris Anka
LAYOUTS

Tríona Farrell
COLOR ARTIST

VC's Joe Sabino
LETTERER

Paolo Rivera & Daniel Acuña (#7, #10, #12); Paolo Rivera (#8) & Daniel Acuña (#9, #11)
COVER ART

Sarah Brunstad
ASSOCIATE EDITOR

Wil Moss
EDITOR

BLACK PANTHER CREATED BY
Stan Lee & Jack Kirby

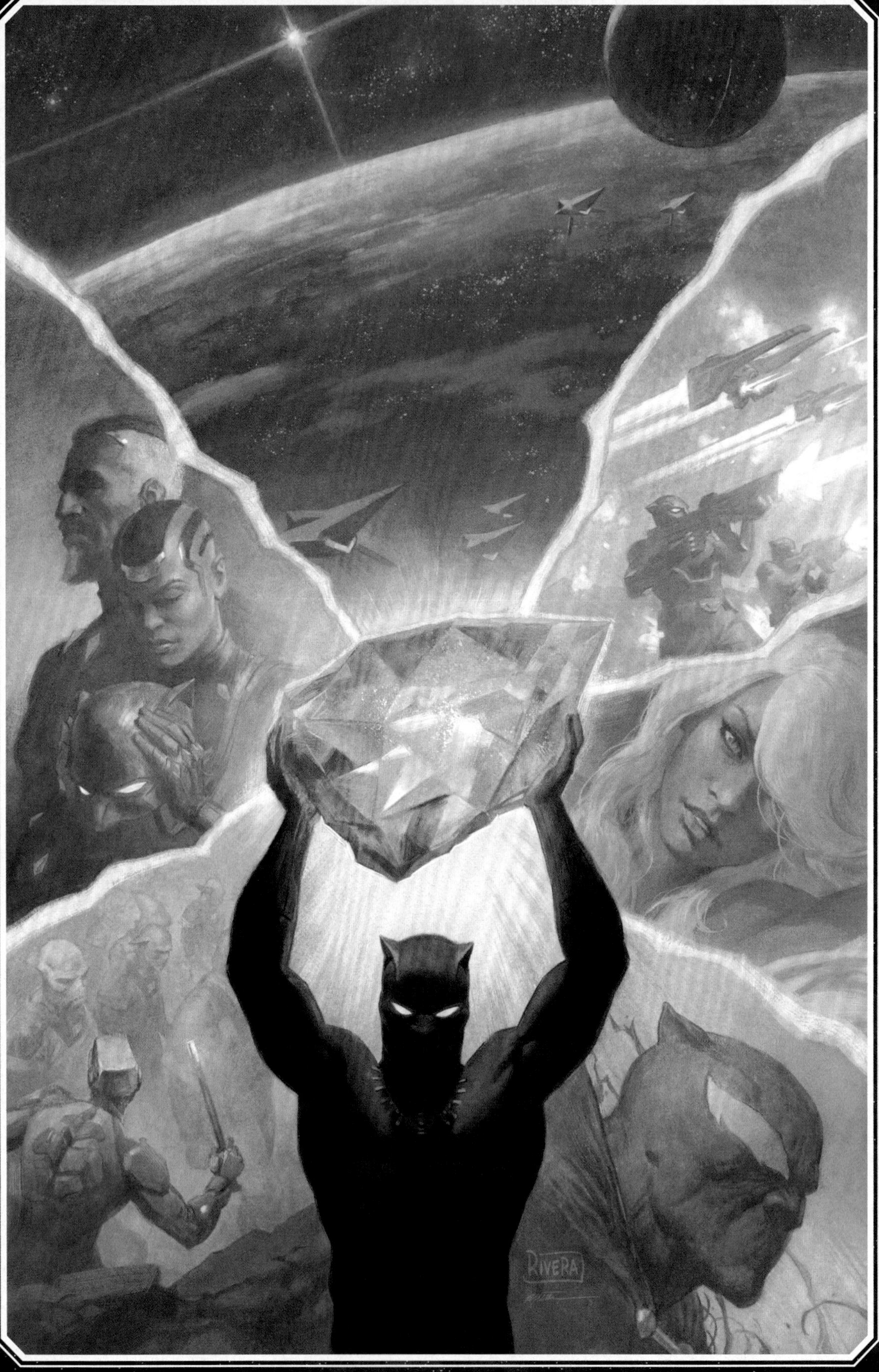
RIVERA

THE INTERGALACTIC EMPIRE OF WAKANDA

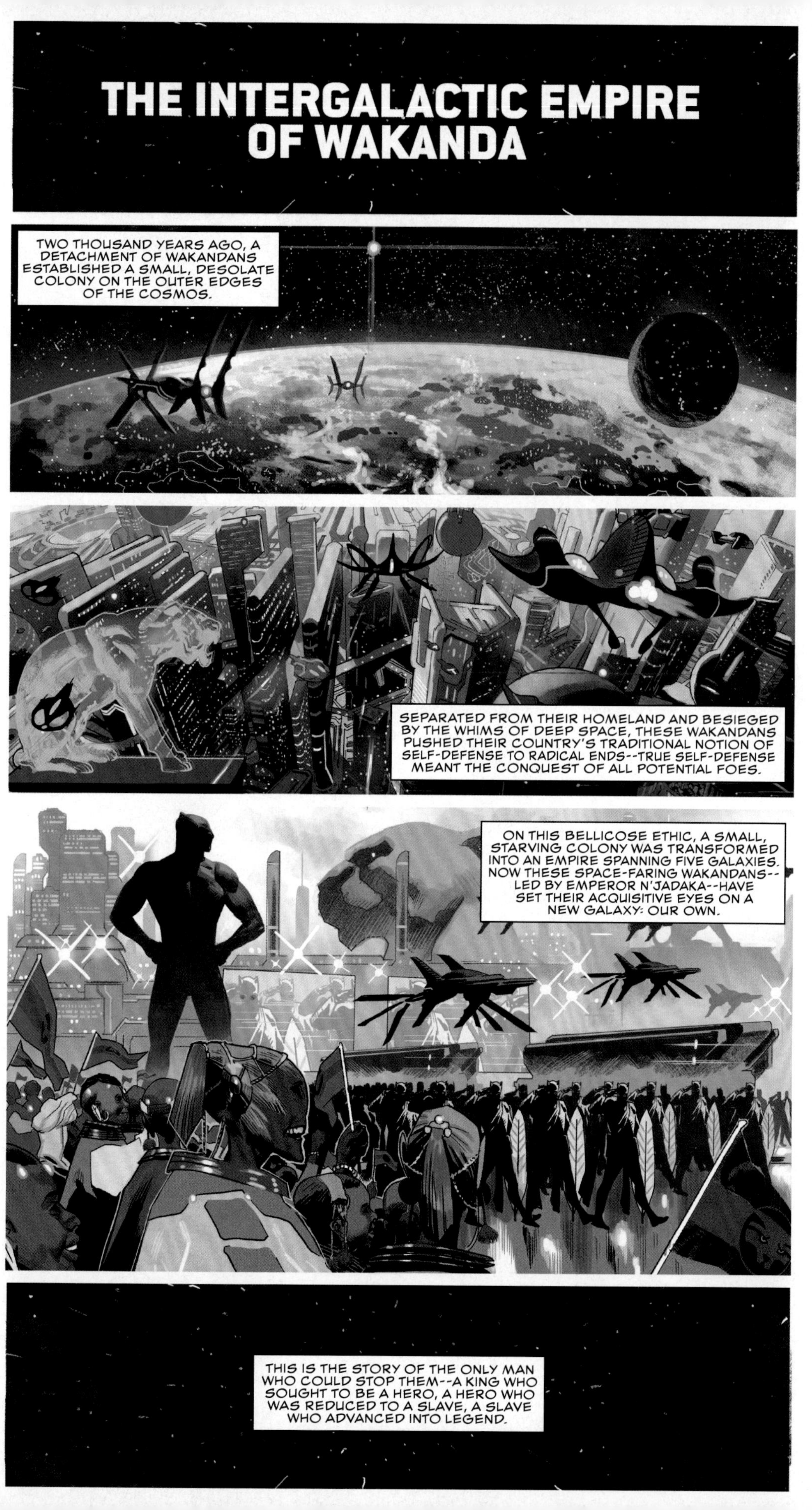
TWO THOUSAND YEARS AGO, A DETACHMENT OF WAKANDANS ESTABLISHED A SMALL, DESOLATE COLONY ON THE OUTER EDGES OF THE COSMOS.
SEPARATED FROM THEIR HOMELAND AND BESIEGED BY THE WHIMS OF DEEP SPACE, THESE WAKANDANS PUSHED THEIR COUNTRY'S TRADITIONAL NOTION OF SELF-DEFENSE TO RADICAL ENDS--TRUE SELF-DEFENSE MEANT THE CONQUEST OF ALL POTENTIAL FOES.
ON THIS BELLICOSE ETHIC, A SMALL, STARVING COLONY WAS TRANSFORMED INTO AN EMPIRE SPANNING FIVE GALAXIES. NOW THESE SPACE-FARING WAKANDANS--LED BY EMPEROR N'JADAKA--HAVE SET THEIR ACQUISITIVE EYES ON A NEW GALAXY: OUR OWN.

THIS IS THE STORY OF THE ONLY MAN WHO COULD STOP THEM--A KING WHO SOUGHT TO BE A HERO, A HERO WHO WAS REDUCED TO A SLAVE, A SLAVE WHO ADVANCED INTO LEGEND.

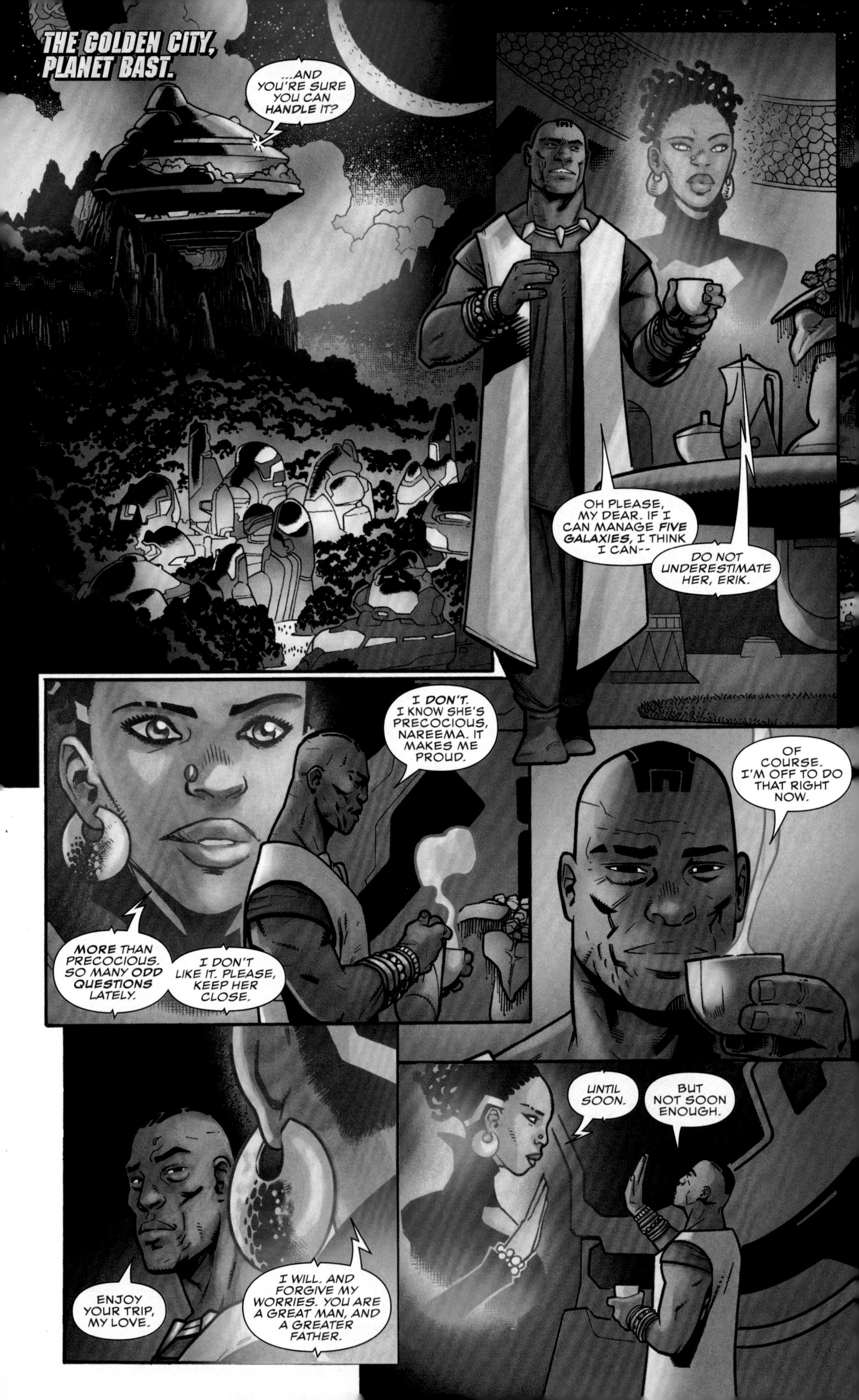
THE GOLDEN CITY, PLANET BAST.
...AND YOU'RE SURE YOU CAN HANDLE IT?
OH PLEASE, MY DEAR. IF I CAN MANAGE FIVE GALAXIES, I THINK I CAN--
DO NOT UNDERESTIMATE HER, ERIK.
I DON'T. I KNOW SHE'S PRECOCIOUS, NAREEMA. IT MAKES ME PROUD.
MORE THAN PRECOCIOUS. SO MANY ODD QUESTIONS LATELY.
I DON'T LIKE IT. PLEASE, KEEP HER CLOSE.
OF COURSE. I'M OFF TO DO THAT RIGHT NOW.
ENJOY YOUR TRIP, MY LOVE.
I WILL. AND FORGIVE MY WORRIES. YOU ARE A GREAT MAN, AND A GREATER FATHER.
UNTIL SOON.
BUT NOT SOON ENOUGH.

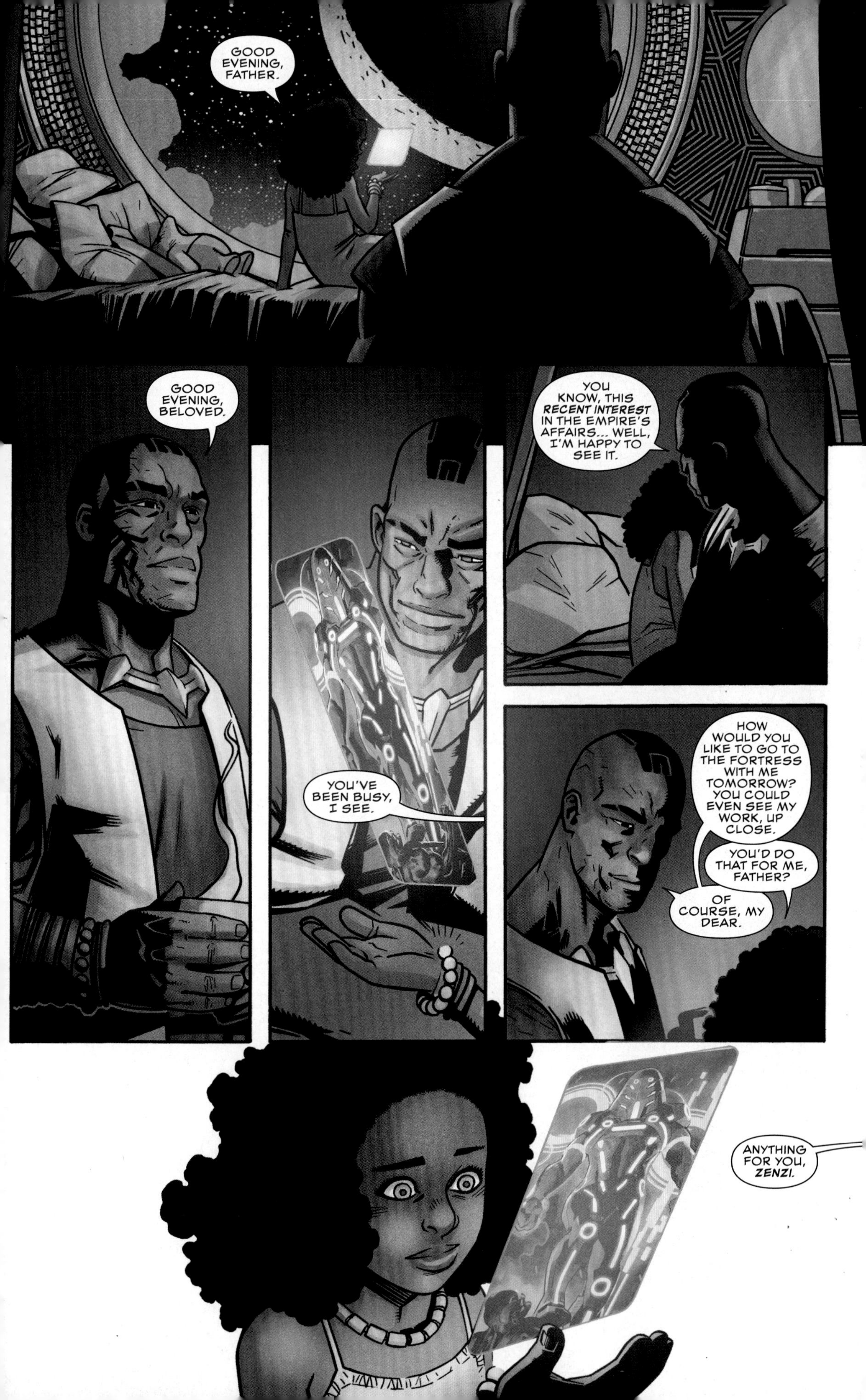
GOOD EVENING, FATHER.
GOOD EVENING, BELOVED.
YOU'VE BEEN BUSY, I SEE.
YOU KNOW, THIS *RECENT INTEREST* IN THE EMPIRE'S AFFAIRS... WELL, I'M HAPPY TO SEE IT.
HOW WOULD YOU LIKE TO GO TO THE FORTRESS WITH ME TOMORROW? YOU COULD EVEN SEE MY WORK, UP CLOSE.
YOU'D DO THAT FOR ME, FATHER?
OF COURSE, MY DEAR.
ANYTHING FOR YOU, *ZENZI*.

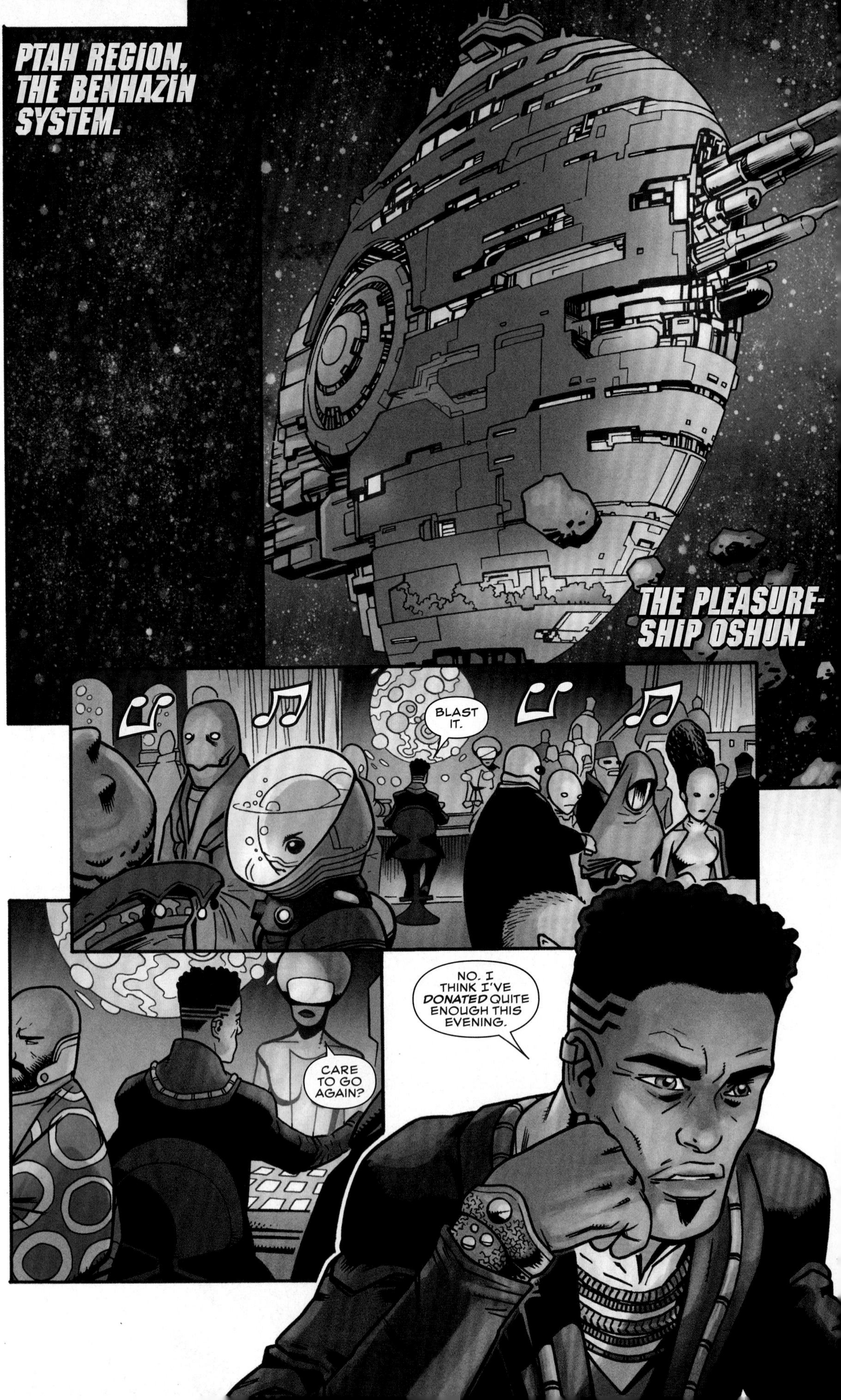
PTAH REGION, THE BENHAZIN SYSTEM.
THE PLEASURE-SHIP OSHUN.
BLAST IT.
CARE TO GO AGAIN?
NO. I THINK I'VE DONATED QUITE ENOUGH THIS EVENING.

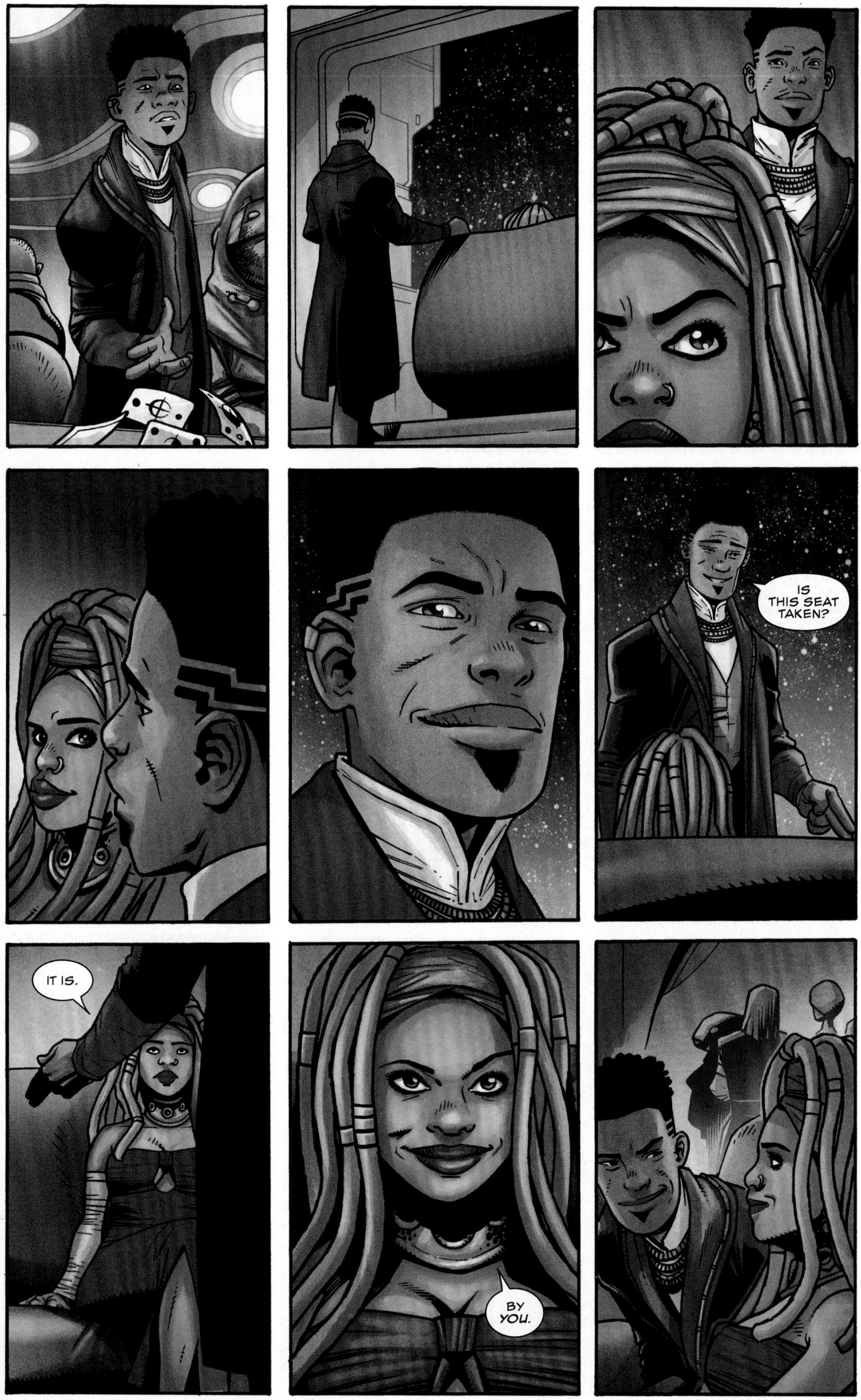
IS THIS SEAT TAKEN?
IT IS.
BY YOU.

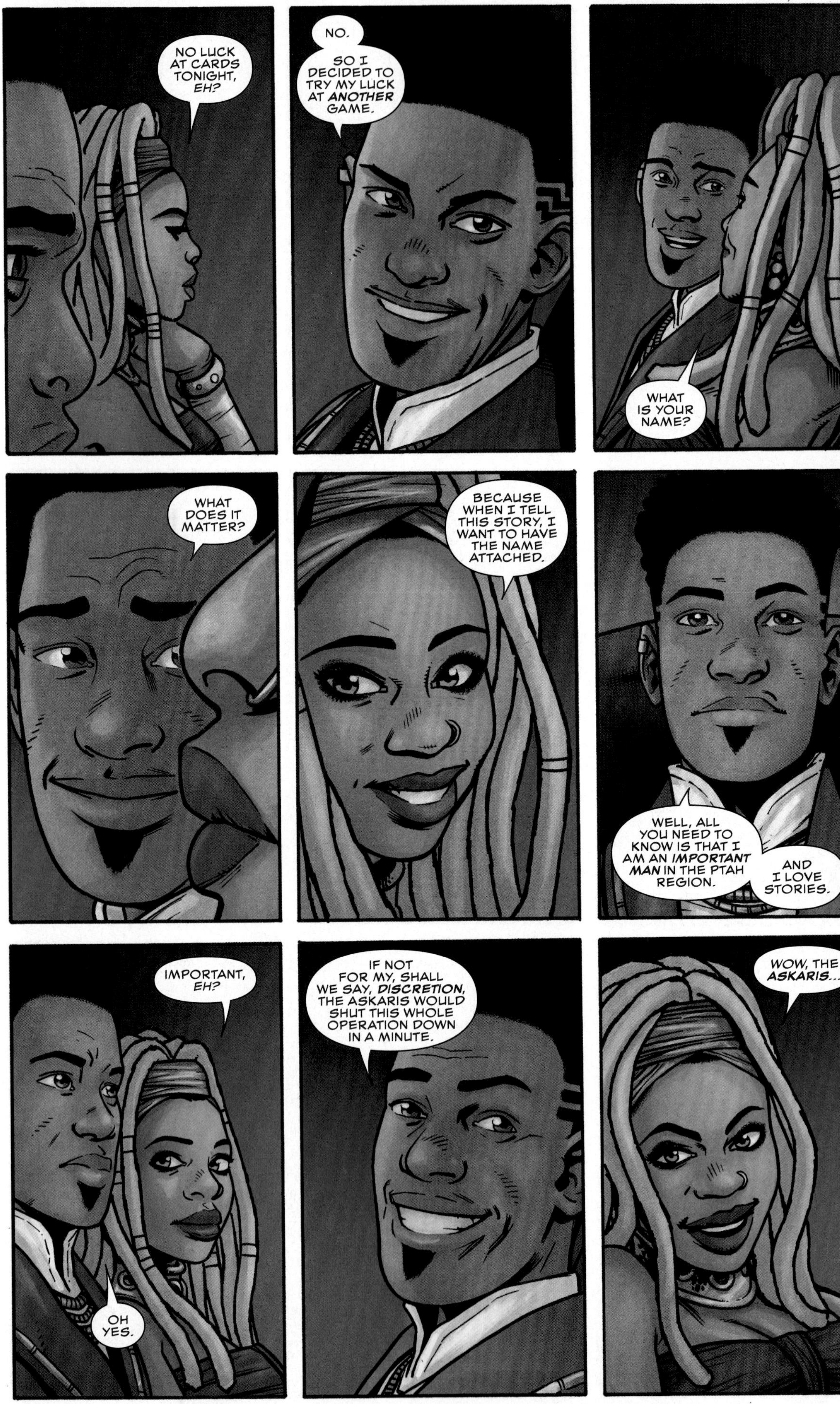
NO LUCK AT CARDS TONIGHT, EH?
NO.
SO I DECIDED TO TRY MY LUCK AT ANOTHER GAME.
WHAT IS YOUR NAME?
WHAT DOES IT MATTER?
BECAUSE WHEN I TELL THIS STORY, I WANT TO HAVE THE NAME ATTACHED.
WELL, ALL YOU NEED TO KNOW IS THAT I AM AN IMPORTANT MAN IN THE PTAH REGION.
AND I LOVE STORIES.
IMPORTANT, EH?
OH YES.
IF NOT FOR MY, SHALL WE SAY, DISCRETION, THE ASKARIS WOULD SHUT THIS WHOLE OPERATION DOWN IN A MINUTE.
WOW, THE ASKARIS...

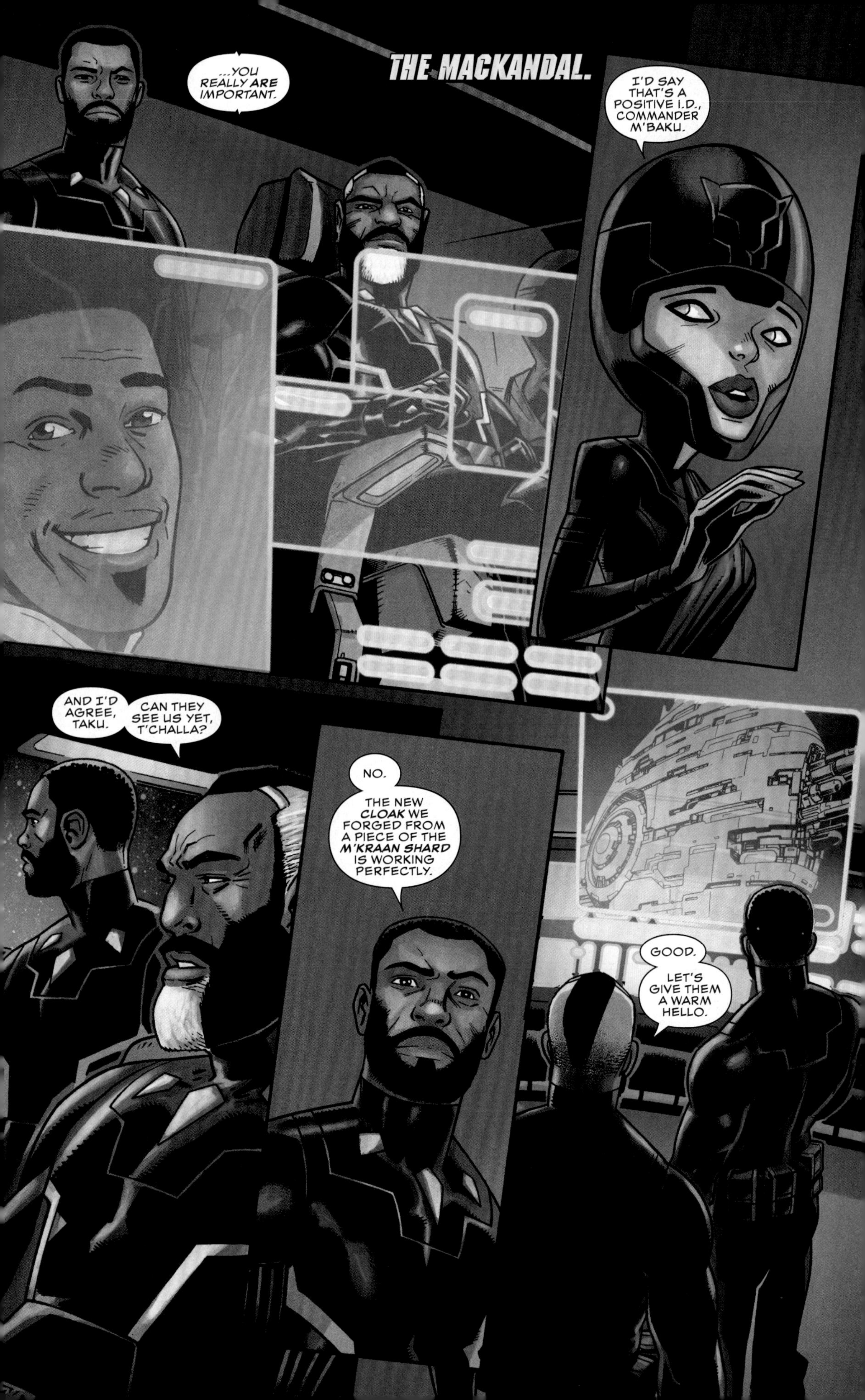
...YOU REALLY ARE IMPORTANT.
THE MACKANDAL.
I'D SAY THAT'S A POSITIVE I.D., COMMANDER M'BAKU.
AND I'D AGREE, TAKU.
CAN THEY SEE US YET, T'CHALLA?
NO.
THE NEW CLOAK WE FORGED FROM A PIECE OF THE M'KRAAN SHARD IS WORKING PERFECTLY.
GOOD.
LET'S GIVE THEM A WARM HELLO.

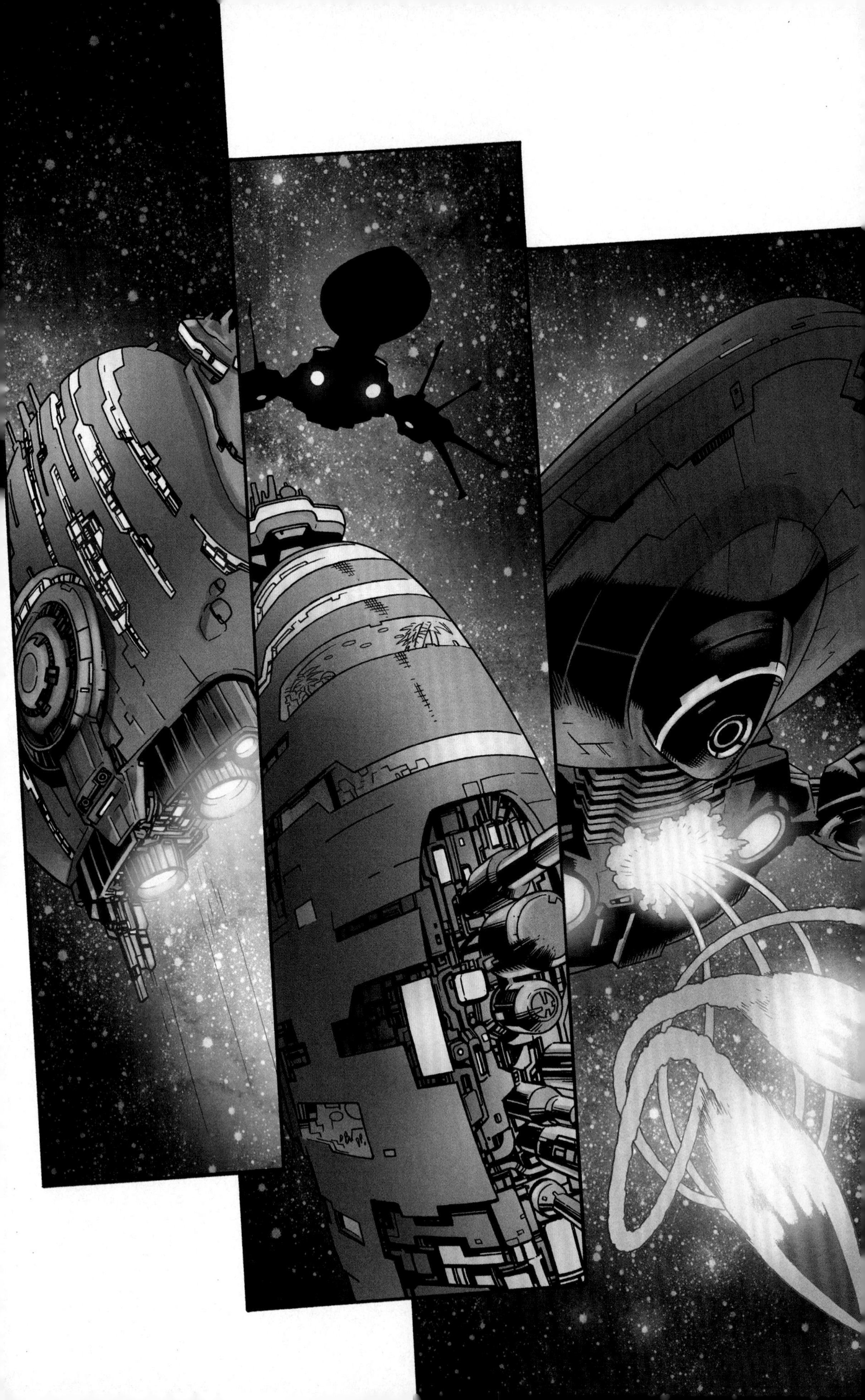

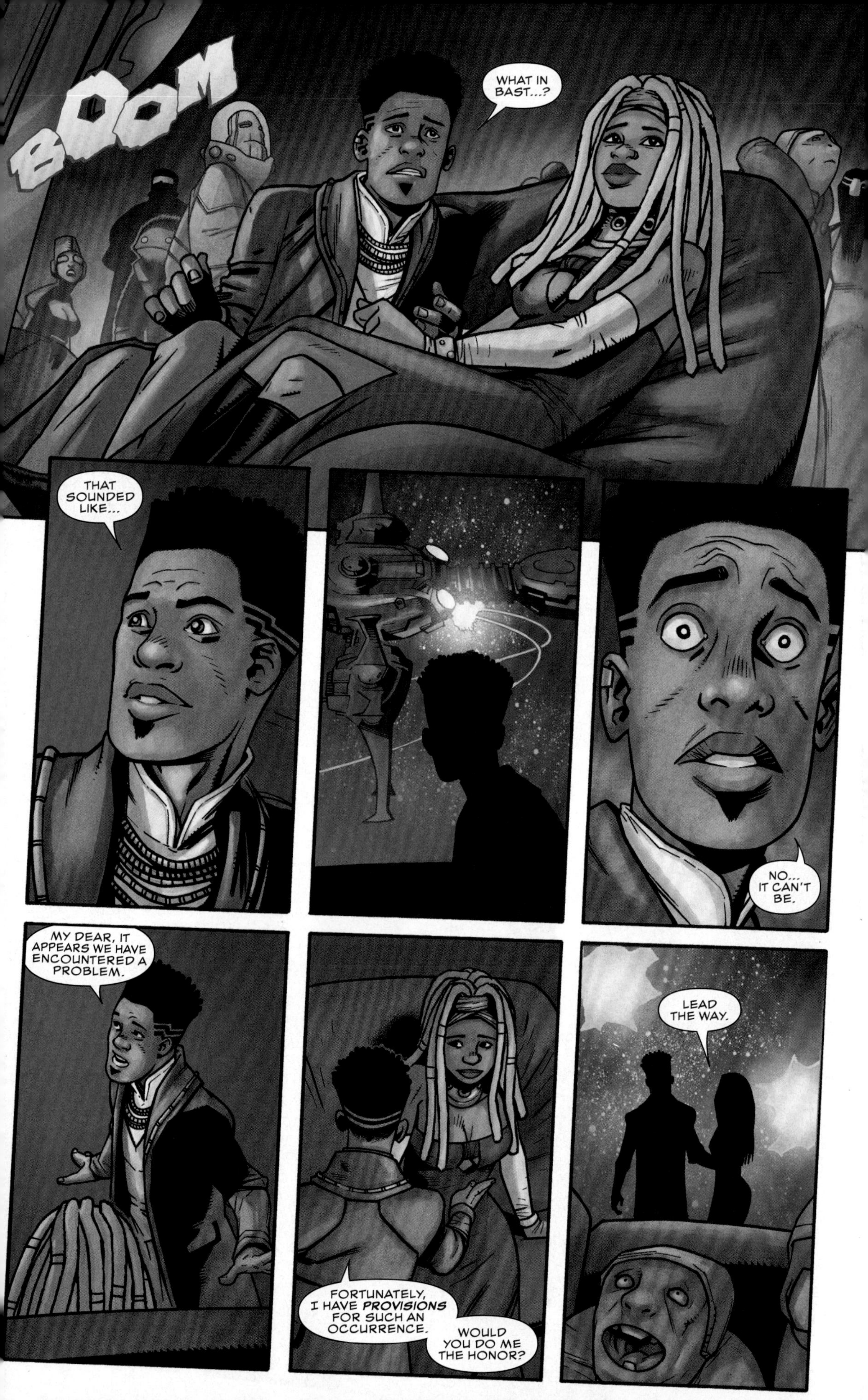
BOOM
WHAT IN BAST...?
THAT SOUNDED LIKE...
NO... IT CAN'T BE.
MY DEAR, IT APPEARS WE HAVE ENCOUNTERED A PROBLEM.
FORTUNATELY, I HAVE PROVISIONS FOR SUCH AN OCCURRENCE.
WOULD YOU DO ME THE HONOR?
LEAD THE WAY.

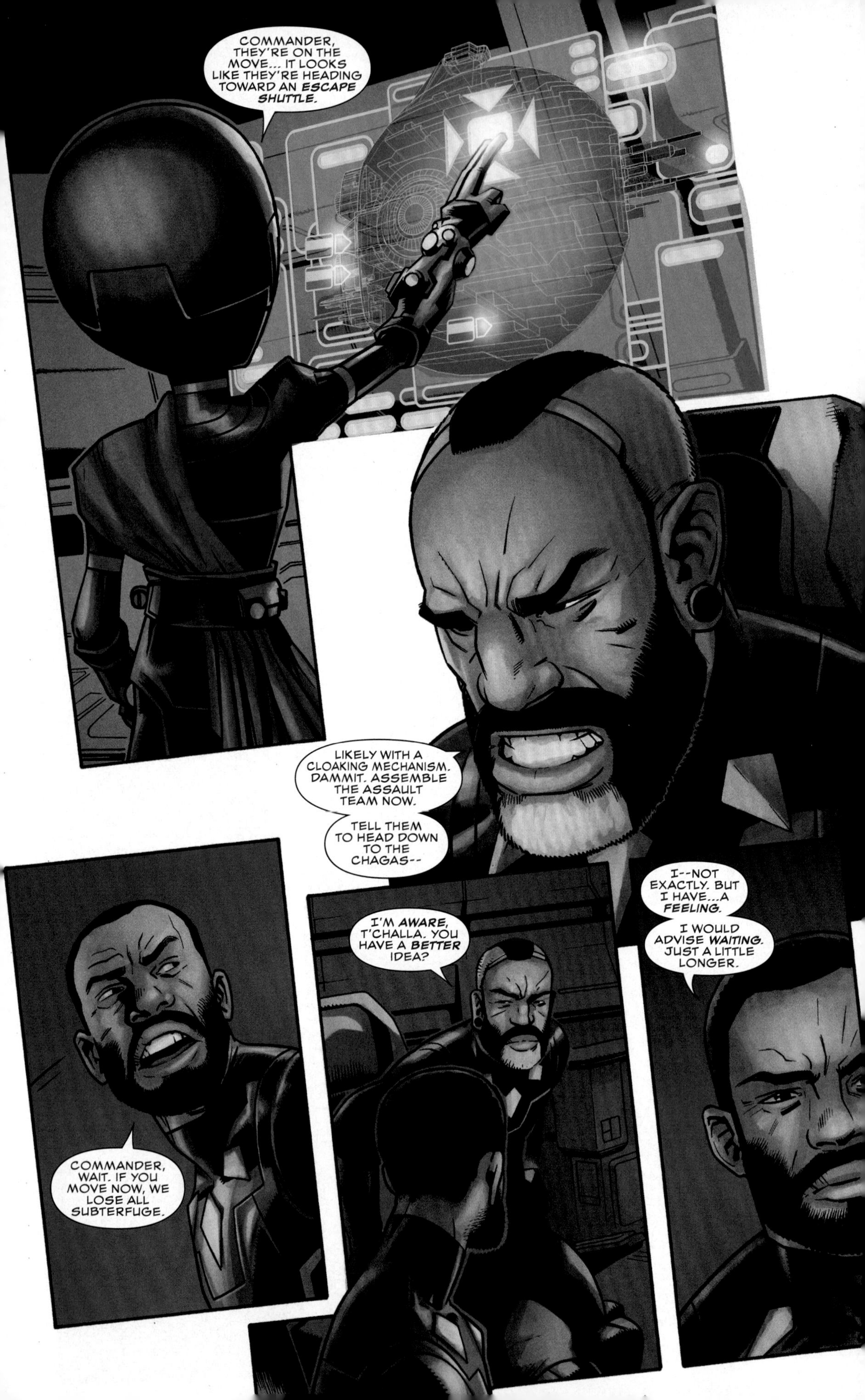

COMMANDER, THEY'RE ON THE MOVE... IT LOOKS LIKE THEY'RE HEADING TOWARD AN ESCAPE SHUTTLE.
LIKELY WITH A CLOAKING MECHANISM. DAMMIT. ASSEMBLE THE ASSAULT TEAM NOW.
TELL THEM TO HEAD DOWN TO THE CHAGAS--
COMMANDER, WAIT. IF YOU MOVE NOW, WE LOSE ALL SUBTERFUGE.
I'M AWARE, T'CHALLA. YOU HAVE A BETTER IDEA?
I--NOT EXACTLY. BUT I HAVE...A FEELING.
I WOULD ADVISE WAITING. JUST A LITTLE LONGER.

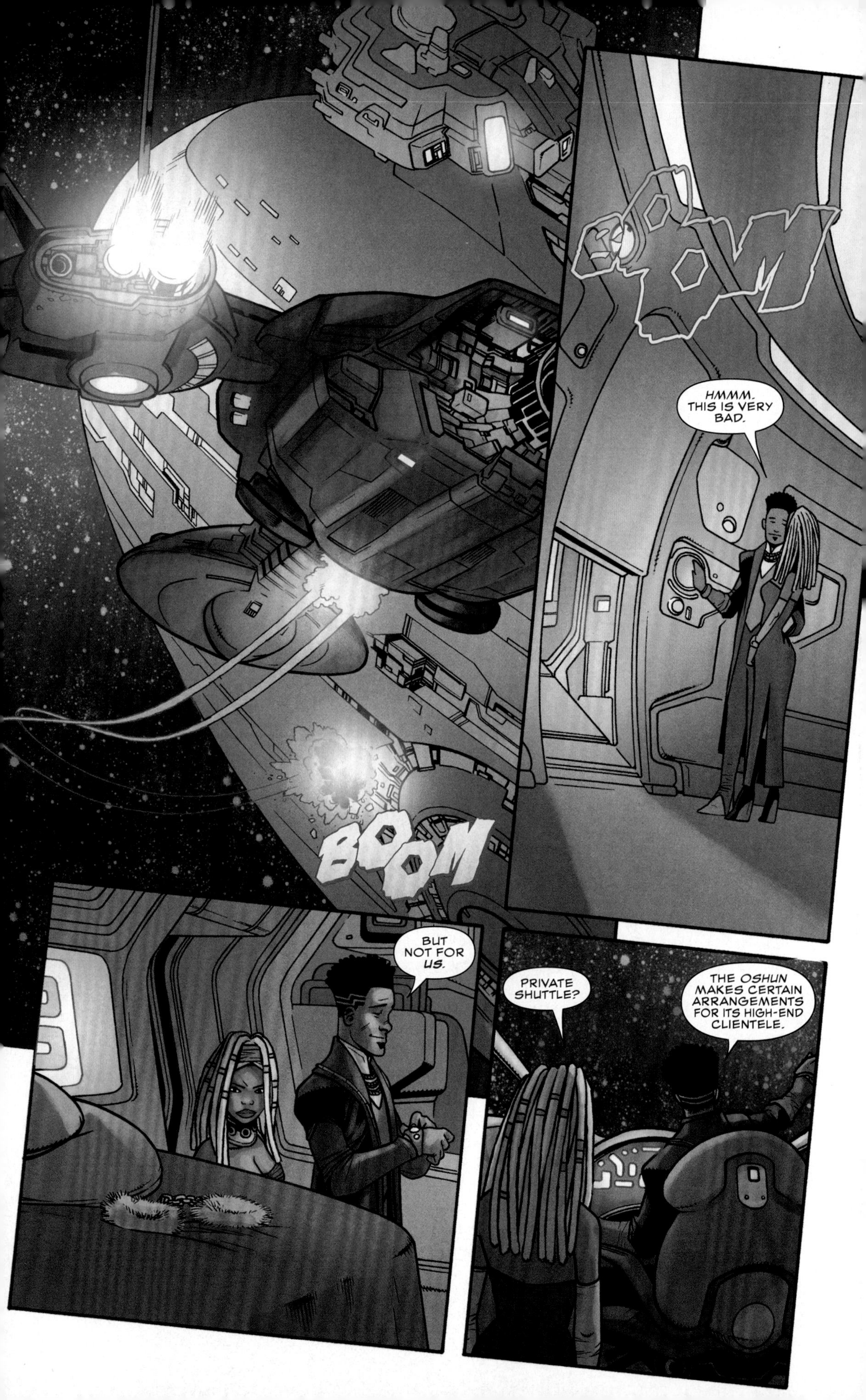
BOOM
HMMM. THIS IS VERY BAD.
BOOM
BUT NOT FOR US.
PRIVATE SHUTTLE?
THE OSHUN MAKES CERTAIN ARRANGEMENTS FOR ITS HIGH-END CLIENTELE.

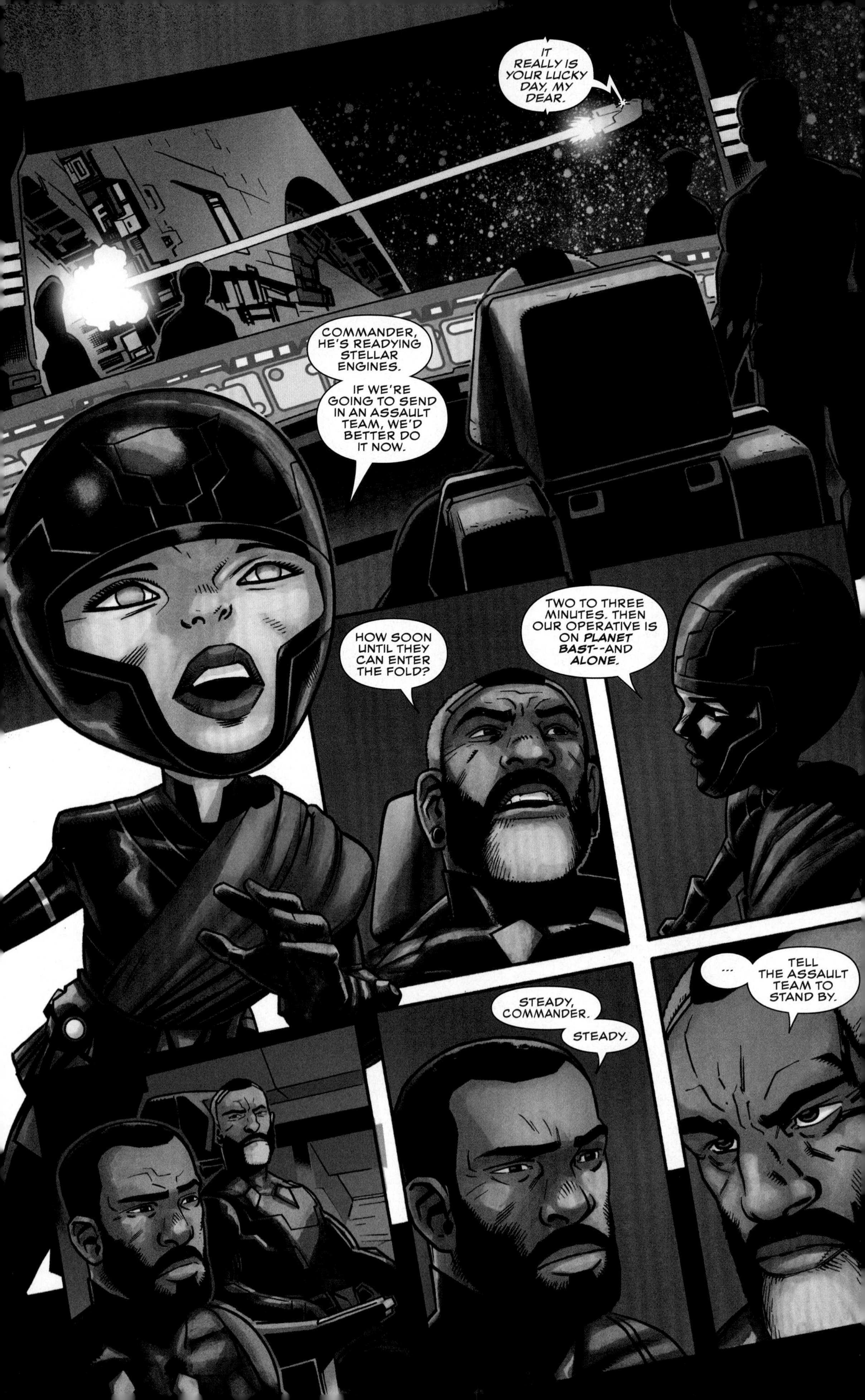
IT REALLY IS YOUR LUCKY DAY, MY DEAR.
COMMANDER, HE'S READYING STELLAR ENGINES.
IF WE'RE GOING TO SEND IN AN ASSAULT TEAM, WE'D BETTER DO IT NOW.
HOW SOON UNTIL THEY CAN ENTER THE FOLD?
TWO TO THREE MINUTES. THEN OUR OPERATIVE IS ON PLANET BAST--AND ALONE.
STEADY, COMMANDER.
STEADY.
...
TELL THE ASSAULT TEAM TO STAND BY.

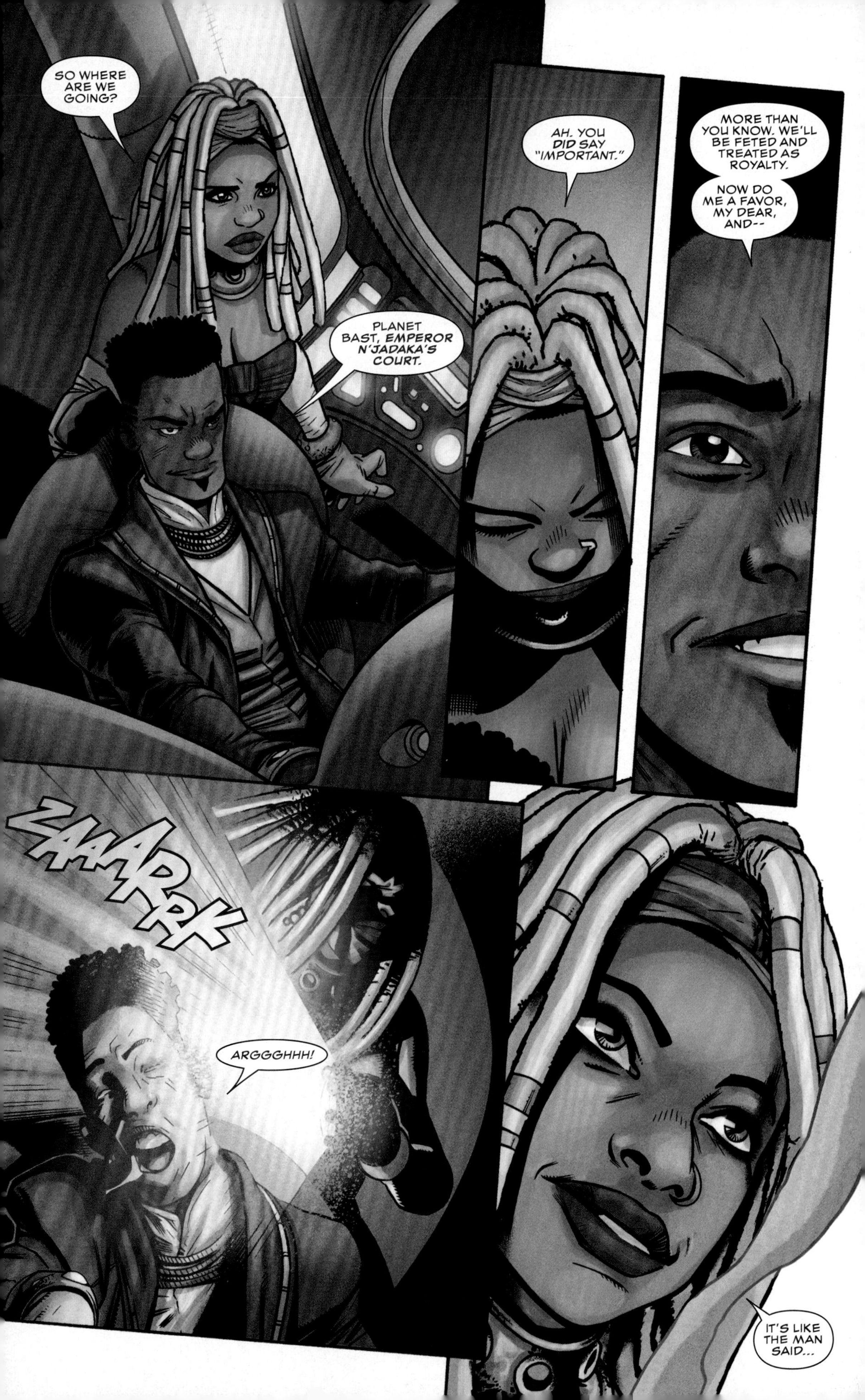
SO WHERE ARE WE GOING?
PLANET BAST, EMPEROR N'JADAKA'S COURT.
AH. YOU DID SAY "IMPORTANT."
MORE THAN YOU KNOW. WE'LL BE FETED AND TREATED AS ROYALTY.
NOW DO ME A FAVOR, MY DEAR, AND--
ZAAARRK
ARGGGHHH!
IT'S LIKE THE MAN SAID...

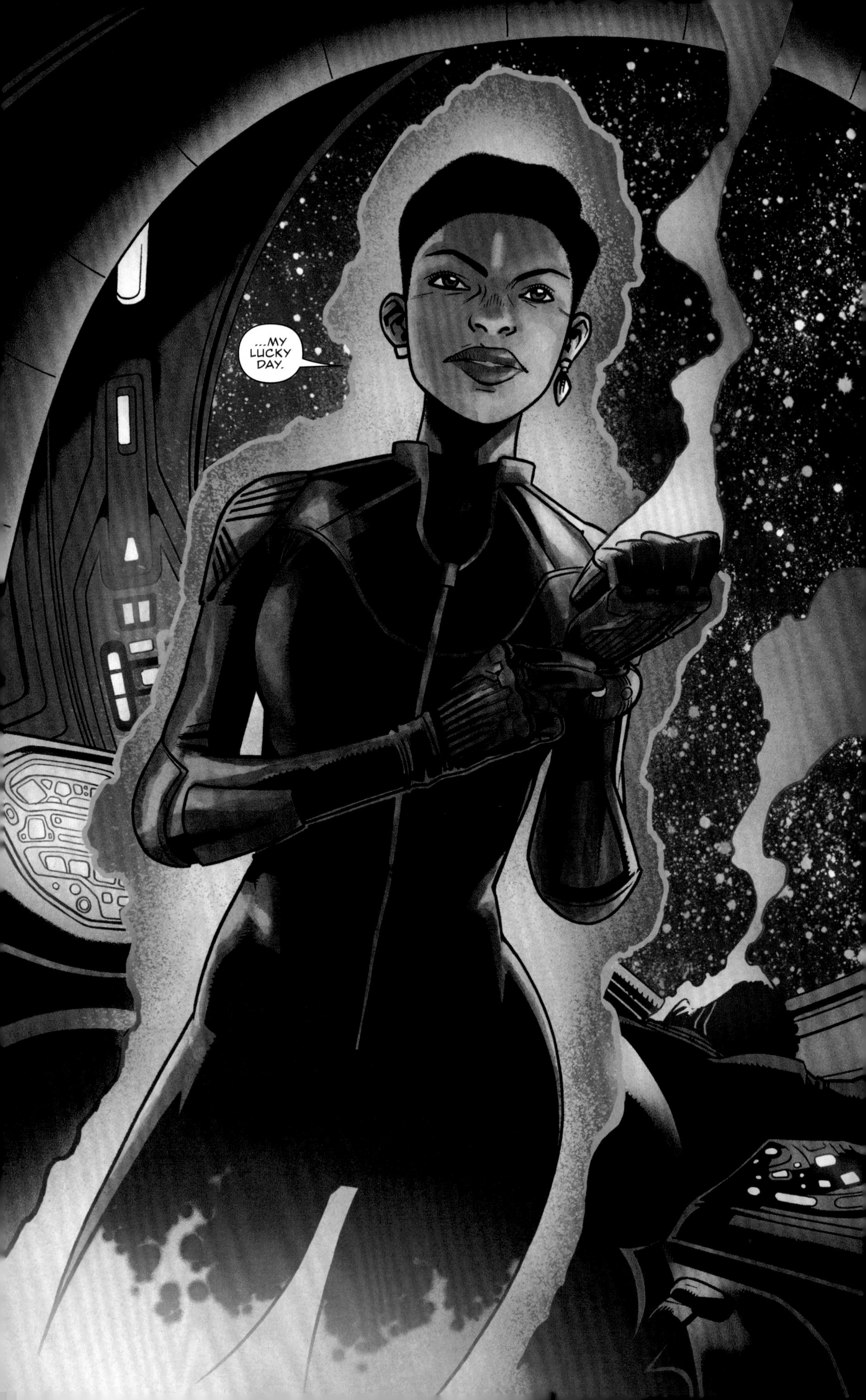
...MY LUCKY DAY.

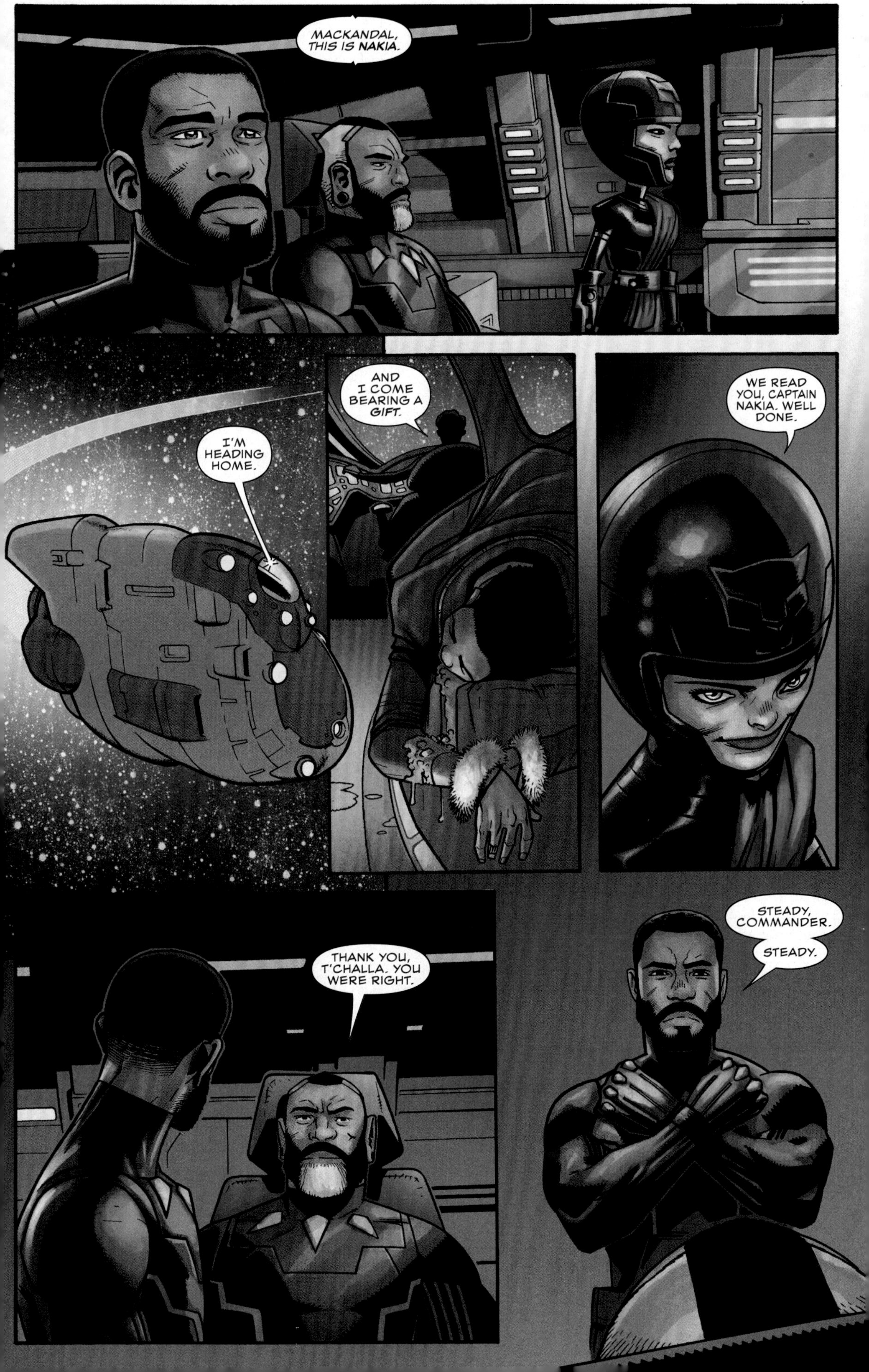
MACKANDAL, THIS IS NAKIA.
I'M HEADING HOME.
AND I COME BEARING A GIFT.
WE READ YOU, CAPTAIN NAKIA. WELL DONE.
THANK YOU, T'CHALLA. YOU WERE RIGHT.
STEADY, COMMANDER.
STEADY.

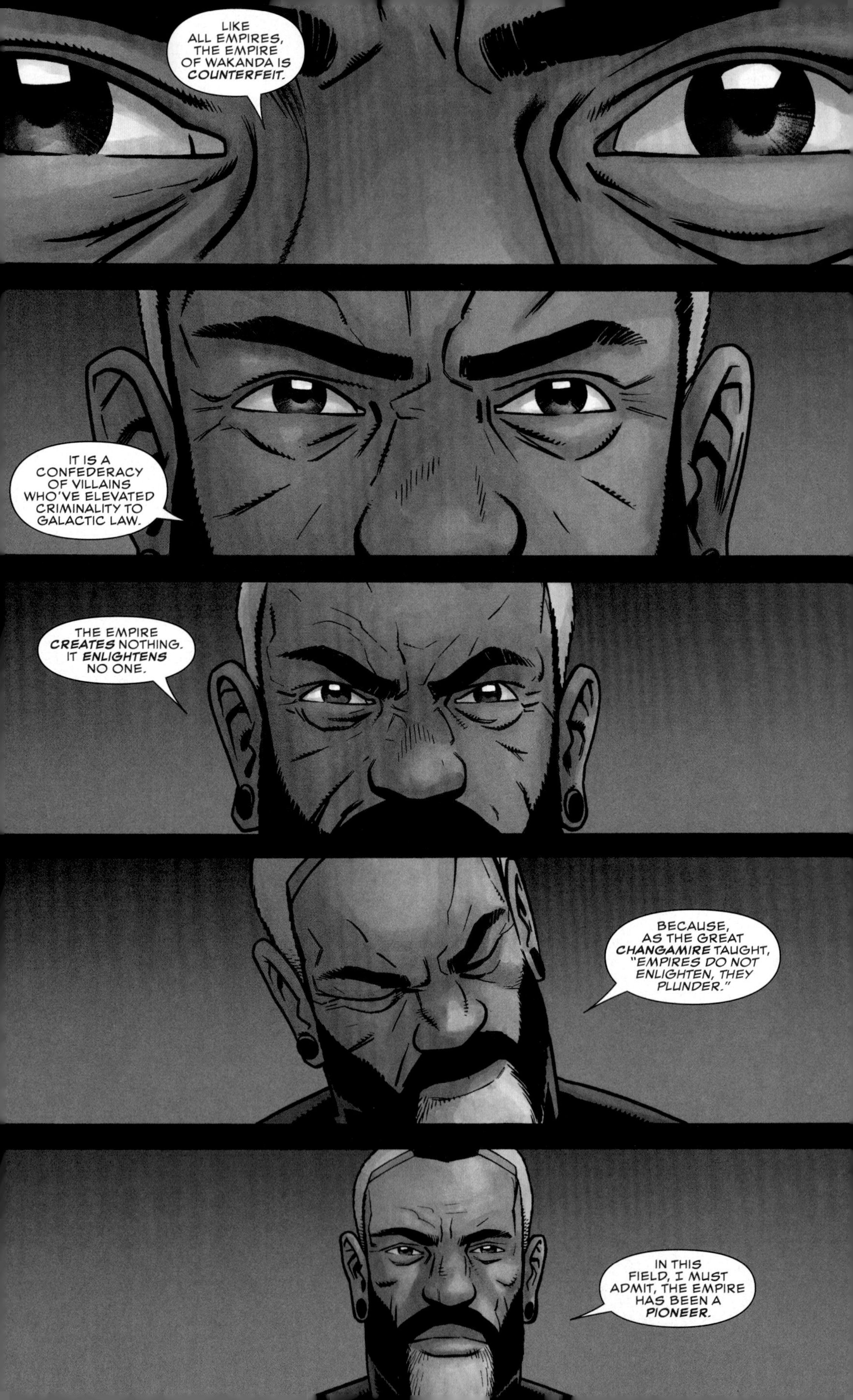
LIKE ALL EMPIRES, THE EMPIRE OF WAKANDA IS COUNTERFEIT.
IT IS A CONFEDERACY OF VILLAINS WHO'VE ELEVATED CRIMINALITY TO GALACTIC LAW.
THE EMPIRE CREATES NOTHING. IT ENLIGHTENS NO ONE.
BECAUSE, AS THE GREAT CHANGAMIRE TAUGHT, "EMPIRES DO NOT ENLIGHTEN, THEY PLUNDER."
IN THIS FIELD, I MUST ADMIT, THE EMPIRE HAS BEEN A PIONEER.

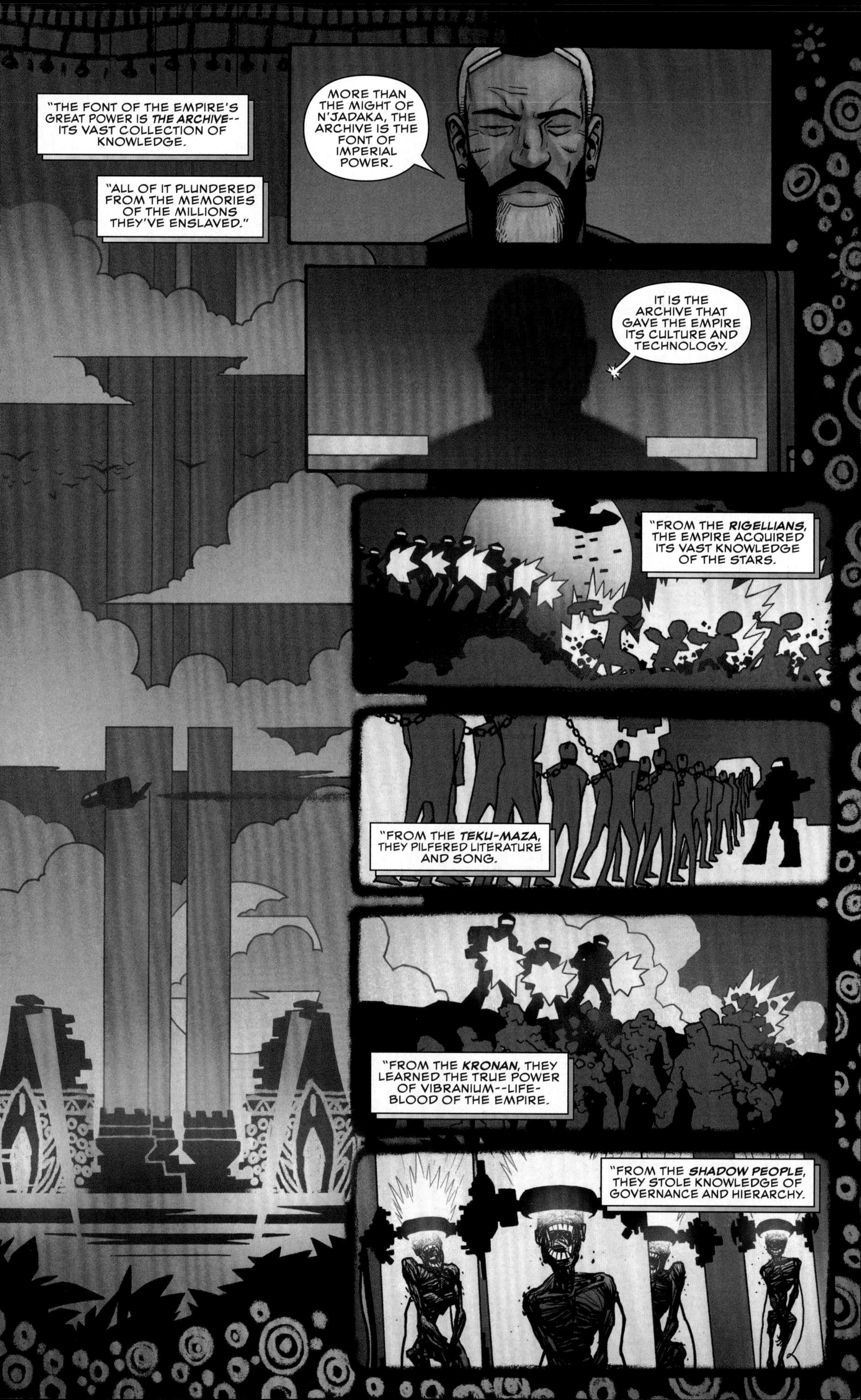
"THE FONT OF THE EMPIRE'S GREAT POWER IS *THE ARCHIVE*-- ITS VAST COLLECTION OF KNOWLEDGE.
"ALL OF IT PLUNDERED FROM THE MEMORIES OF THE MILLIONS THEY'VE ENSLAVED."
MORE THAN THE MIGHT OF N'JADAKA, THE ARCHIVE IS THE FONT OF IMPERIAL POWER.
IT IS THE ARCHIVE THAT GAVE THE EMPIRE ITS CULTURE AND TECHNOLOGY.
"FROM THE *RIGELLIANS,* THE EMPIRE ACQUIRED ITS VAST KNOWLEDGE OF THE STARS.
"FROM THE *TEKU-MAZA,* THEY PILFERED LITERATURE AND SONG.
"FROM THE *KRONAN,* THEY LEARNED THE TRUE POWER OF VIBRANIUM--LIFE-BLOOD OF THE EMPIRE.
"FROM THE *SHADOW PEOPLE,* THEY STOLE KNOWLEDGE OF GOVERNANCE AND HIERARCHY.

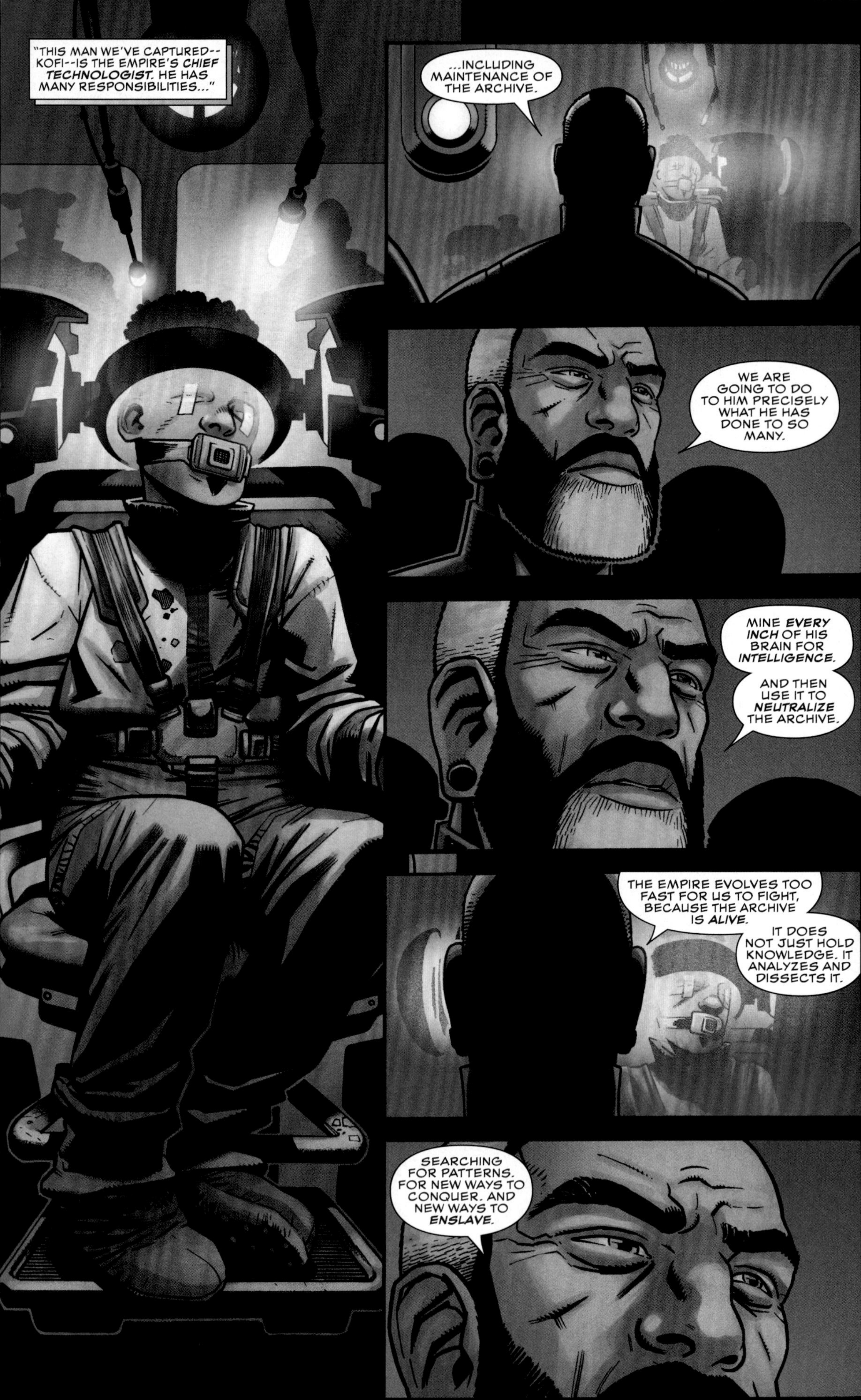
"THIS MAN WE'VE CAPTURED--KOFI--IS THE EMPIRE'S *CHIEF TECHNOLOGIST.* HE HAS MANY RESPONSIBILITIES..."
...INCLUDING MAINTENANCE OF THE ARCHIVE.
WE ARE GOING TO DO TO HIM PRECISELY WHAT HE HAS DONE TO SO MANY.
MINE ***EVERY*** INCH OF HIS BRAIN FOR ***INTELLIGENCE.***
AND THEN USE IT TO ***NEUTRALIZE*** THE ARCHIVE.
THE EMPIRE EVOLVES TOO FAST FOR US TO FIGHT, BECAUSE THE ARCHIVE IS ***ALIVE.***
IT DOES NOT JUST HOLD KNOWLEDGE. IT ANALYZES AND DISSECTS IT.
SEARCHING FOR PATTERNS. FOR NEW WAYS TO CONQUER. AND NEW WAYS TO ***ENSLAVE.***

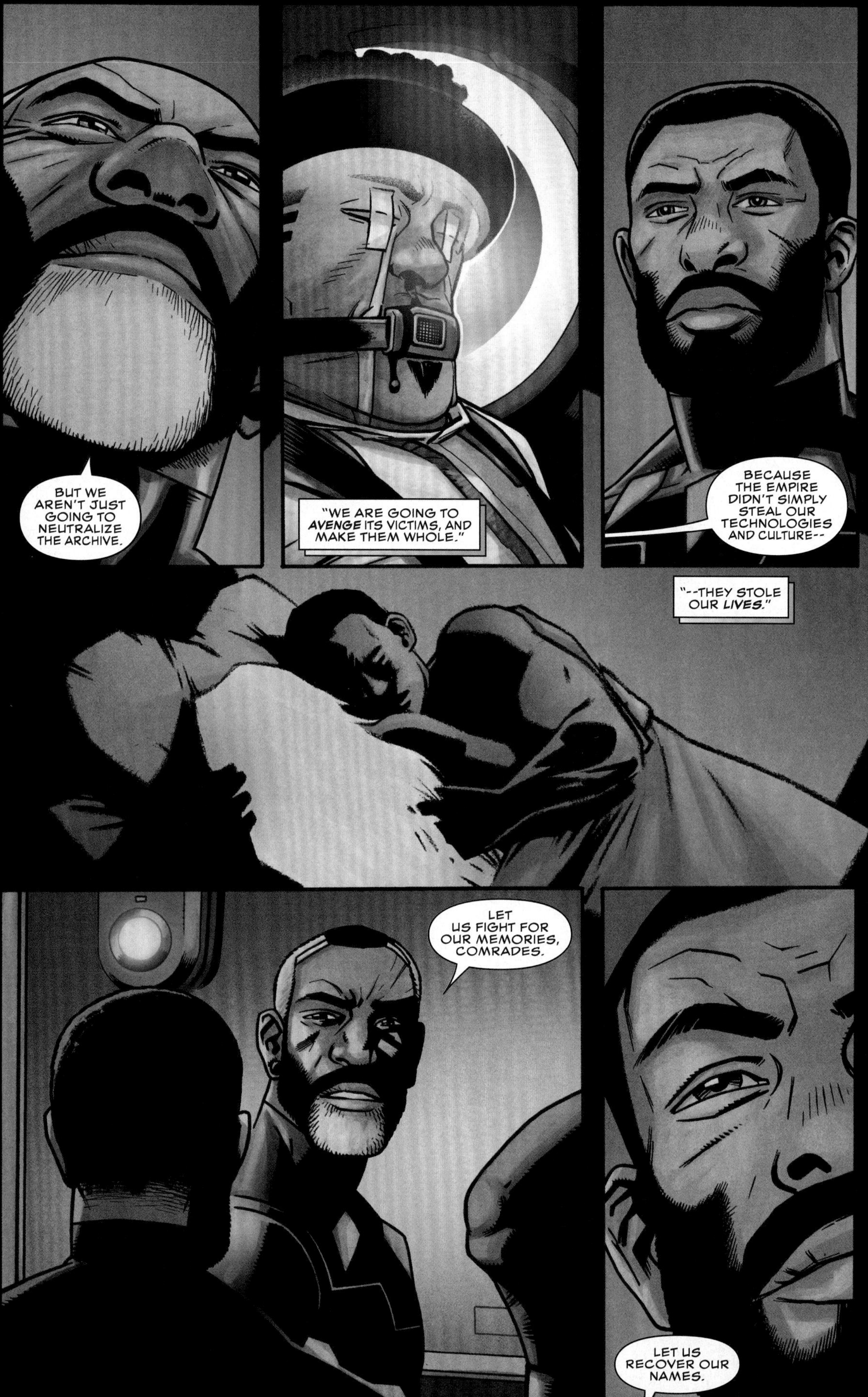
BUT WE AREN'T JUST GOING TO NEUTRALIZE THE ARCHIVE.
"WE ARE GOING TO *AVENGE* ITS VICTIMS, AND MAKE THEM WHOLE."
BECAUSE THE EMPIRE DIDN'T SIMPLY STEAL OUR TECHNOLOGIES AND CULTURE--
"--THEY STOLE OUR *LIVES*."
LET US FIGHT FOR OUR MEMORIES, COMRADES.
LET US RECOVER OUR NAMES.

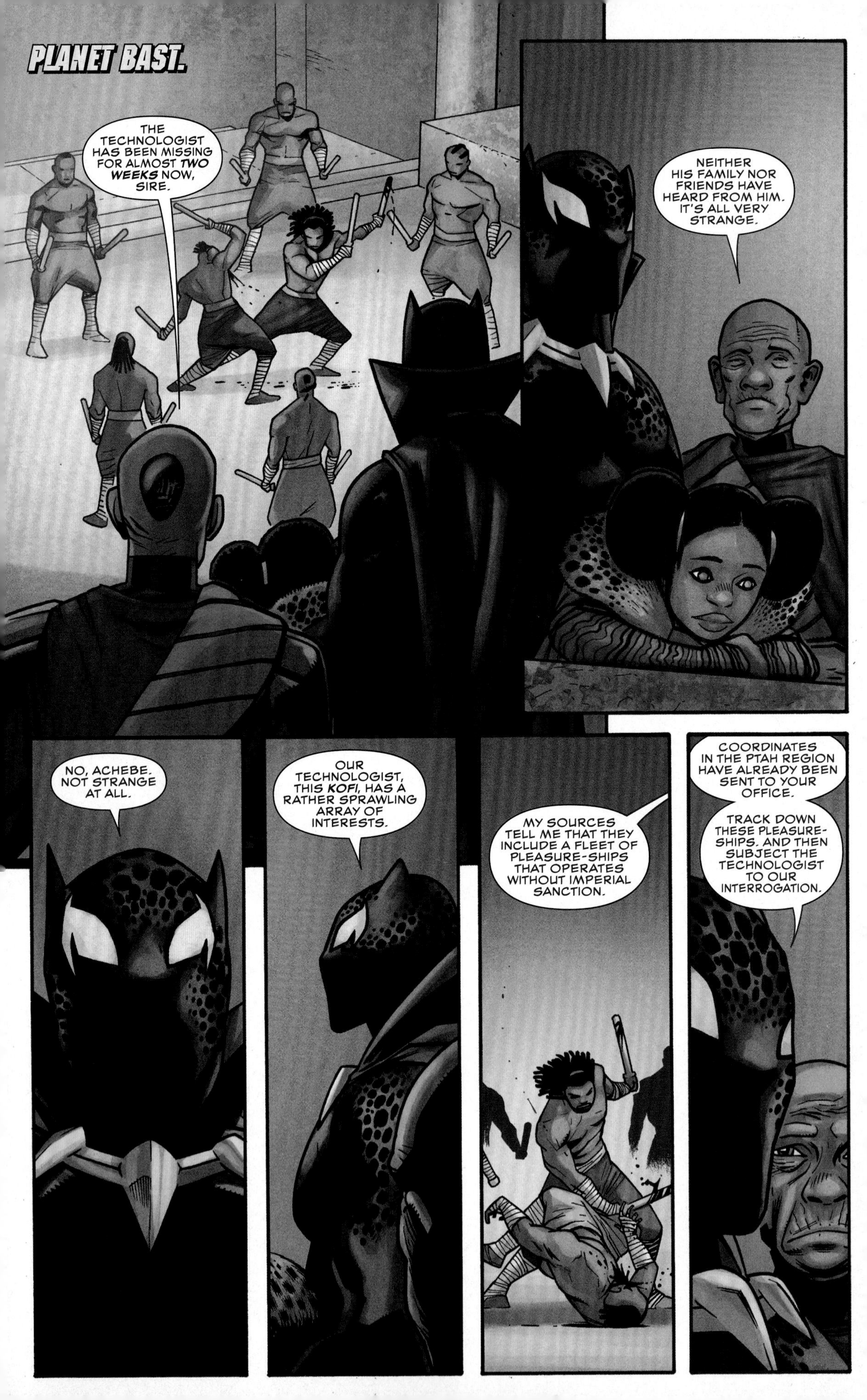
PLANET BAST.
THE TECHNOLOGIST HAS BEEN MISSING FOR ALMOST TWO WEEKS NOW, SIRE.
NEITHER HIS FAMILY NOR FRIENDS HAVE HEARD FROM HIM. IT'S ALL VERY STRANGE.
NO, ACHEBE. NOT STRANGE AT ALL.
OUR TECHNOLOGIST, THIS KOFI, HAS A RATHER SPRAWLING ARRAY OF INTERESTS.
MY SOURCES TELL ME THAT THEY INCLUDE A FLEET OF PLEASURE-SHIPS THAT OPERATES WITHOUT IMPERIAL SANCTION.
COORDINATES IN THE PTAH REGION HAVE ALREADY BEEN SENT TO YOUR OFFICE.
TRACK DOWN THESE PLEASURE-SHIPS. AND THEN SUBJECT THE TECHNOLOGIST TO OUR INTERROGATION.

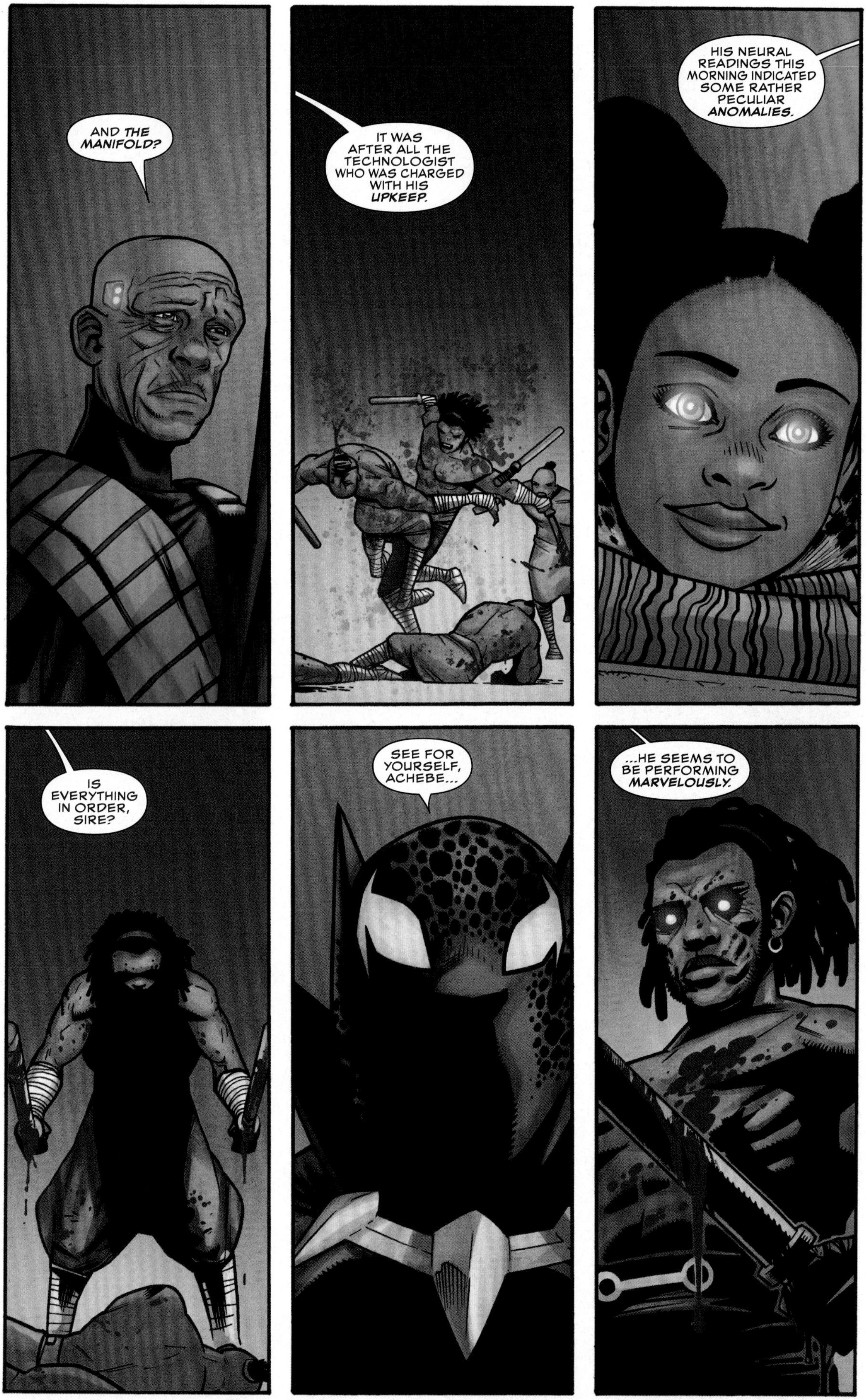
AND THE MANIFOLD?
IT WAS AFTER ALL THE TECHNOLOGIST WHO WAS CHARGED WITH HIS UPKEEP.
HIS NEURAL READINGS THIS MORNING INDICATED SOME RATHER PECULIAR ANOMALIES.
IS EVERYTHING IN ORDER, SIRE?
SEE FOR YOURSELF, ACHEBE...
...HE SEEMS TO BE PERFORMING MARVELOUSLY.

THE INTERGALACTIC EMPIRE OF WAKANDA

OCCUPYING THE FAR REACHES OF THE UNIVERSE, THE INTERGALACTIC EMPIRE OF WAKANDA IS A SPRAWLING IMPERIUM MADE UP OF FIVE STAR CLUSTERS.

THE EARLY WAKANDAN SETTLERS OF THE BENHAZIN SYSTEM WERE INITIALLY PEACEFUL, PREFERRING TO REMAIN AMONG THEIR OWN, AS WAS THE WAY OF THEIR FOREFATHERS. BUT A SERIES OF ATTEMPTED INVASIONS CONVINCED THE SETTLERS THAT SELF-DEFENSE WOULD NOT BE ENOUGH FOR THIS BARBARIC PORTION OF SPACE -- PREVENTIVE STRIKES MUST BE MADE. THEN, AFTER THE WAKANDANS MASTERED THE TECHNOLOGY OF DEEP-SPACE PASSAGE, THOSE PREVENTIVE STRIKES BECAME PREVENTIVE OCCUPATION AND FINALLY PREVENTIVE CONQUEST.

ARMED WITH SUPERIOR TECHNOLOGY AND A TYPICAL WAKANDAN FEROCITY IN BATTLE, THE CONQUERORS QUICKLY BECAME MASTERS OF THEIR CORNER OF THE UNIVERSE -- AND THERE IS NO REASON TO BELIEVE THEY WILL SIMPLY SETTLE FOR THAT CORNER.

THIS ISSUE YOU LEARNED ABOUT THE ARCHIVE, WHERE THE COLLECTIVE MEMORIES OF MANY SUBJECTED RACES ARE STORED. HERE'S A LITTLE MORE INFORMATION FROM TA-NEHISI COATES ABOUT THE RACES CONQUERED BY THE INTERGALACTIC EMPIRE -- AND THEIR CURRENT FATES.

THE TEKU-MAZA

ONE OF THE EARLIEST PEOPLES TO BE INCORPORATED INTO THE WAKANDAN EMPIRE, THE TEKU-MAZA HAIL FROM A JOVIAN PLANET WHOSE MASS CONSISTS MAINLY OF LIQUID. THE TEKU-MAZA WERE ORIGINALLY AQUATIC, BUT AFTER CERTAIN GENETIC MODIFICATIONS, THEY HAVE BECOME AMPHIBIOUS. THE TEKU-MAZA ARE DISTANT RELATIVES OF THE ATLANTEANS OF EARTH, AND LIKE THE ATLANTEANS THEY HAVE PALE GREENISH SKINS. BOTH MEN AND WOMEN WEAR THEIR HAIR IN ELABORATE STYLES: THE WOMEN TEND TO WEAR THEIR HAIR UP OFF THEIR HEADS, DECORATED WITH VARIOUS BANDS OF METAL, WHILE THE MEN TEND TO BRAID THEIRS AND DECORATE THEM WITH JEWELRY AND PRECIOUS STONES. FALLEN MAROON COMMANDER N'YAMI WAS A TEKU-MAZA.

N'YAMI ART BY DANIEL ACUÑA

THE KRONAN

WELL-KNOWN TO THE MARVEL UNIVERSE, THE KRONAN ARE A RACE MADE OF NEAR SOLID ROCK. LIKE THE IMPERIAL WAKANDANS, THE KRONAN CAME TO THE BENHAZIN STAR SYSTEM THROUGH A WORMHOLE BUT LANDED FAR FROM PLANET BAST. WITHIN THE PAST TWO CENTURIES, THESE KRONAN WERE CONQUERED BY IMPERIAL WAKANDA AND SUBJECTED TO THEIR RULE.

THE RIGELLIANS

A RACE KNOWN TO THE MARVEL UNIVERSE, A RIGELLIAN EMPIRE SPRUNG UP IN T'CHAKA'S REACH; ONE DISCONNECTED FROM THE KNOWN RIGELLIAN PEOPLE. THE PROSPEROUS RIGELLIAN EMPIRE WAS THE FIRST TO FALL TO THE INTERGALATIC EMPIRE. RIGELLIANS CAN BE FOUND THROUGHOUT THE EMPIRE NOW AND ARE OVERREPRESENTED AMONG THE LOWER CLASSES, THE SLAVES AND THE NAMELESS. THE MAROONS' CHIEF INTELLIGENCE OFFICER, TAKU, IS A RIGELLIAN.

THE SHADOW PEOPLE

ANOTHER RACE KNOWN TO THE MARVEL UNIVERSE, A DETACHMENT OF SHADOW PEOPLE MADE THEIR WAY INTO IMPERIAL AIRSPACE IN THE EARLY DAYS OF THE EMPIRE. THEY MULTIPLIED ACROSS THE CENTURIES AND COLONIZED MOST OF A SOLAR SYSTEM. DESPITE THEIR SUCCESS AT COLONIZATION, THE SHADOW PEOPLE PROVED NO MATCH FOR IMPERIAL WAKANDA AND WERE QUICKLY SUBJUGATED. SHADOW PEOPLE CAN NOW BE FOUND THROUGHOUT THE HIERARCHY OF THE INTERGALACTIC EMPIRE.

KRONAN, RIGELLIAN & SHADOW PEOPLE ART BY KEV WALKER & STÉPHANE PAITREAU

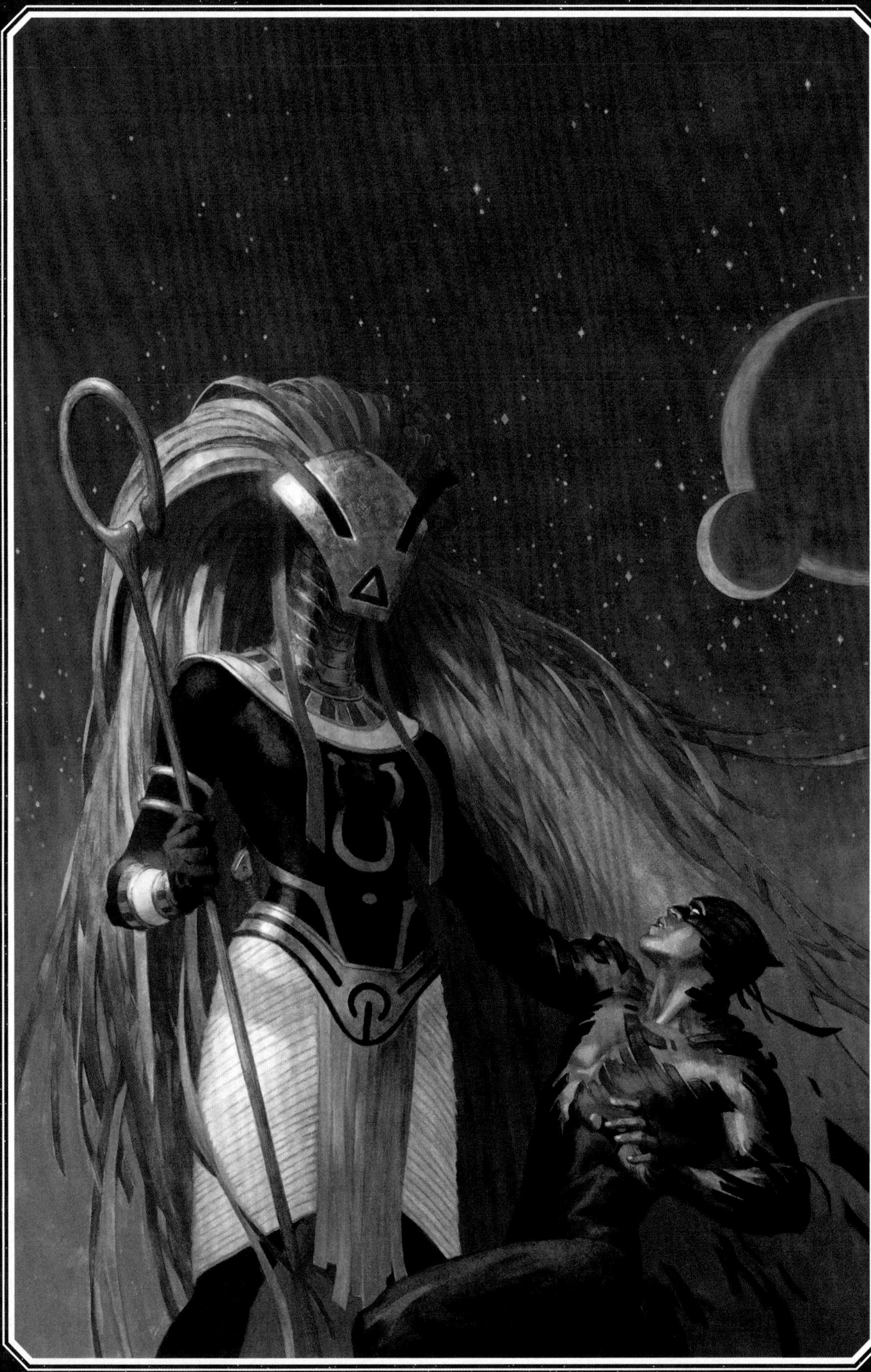

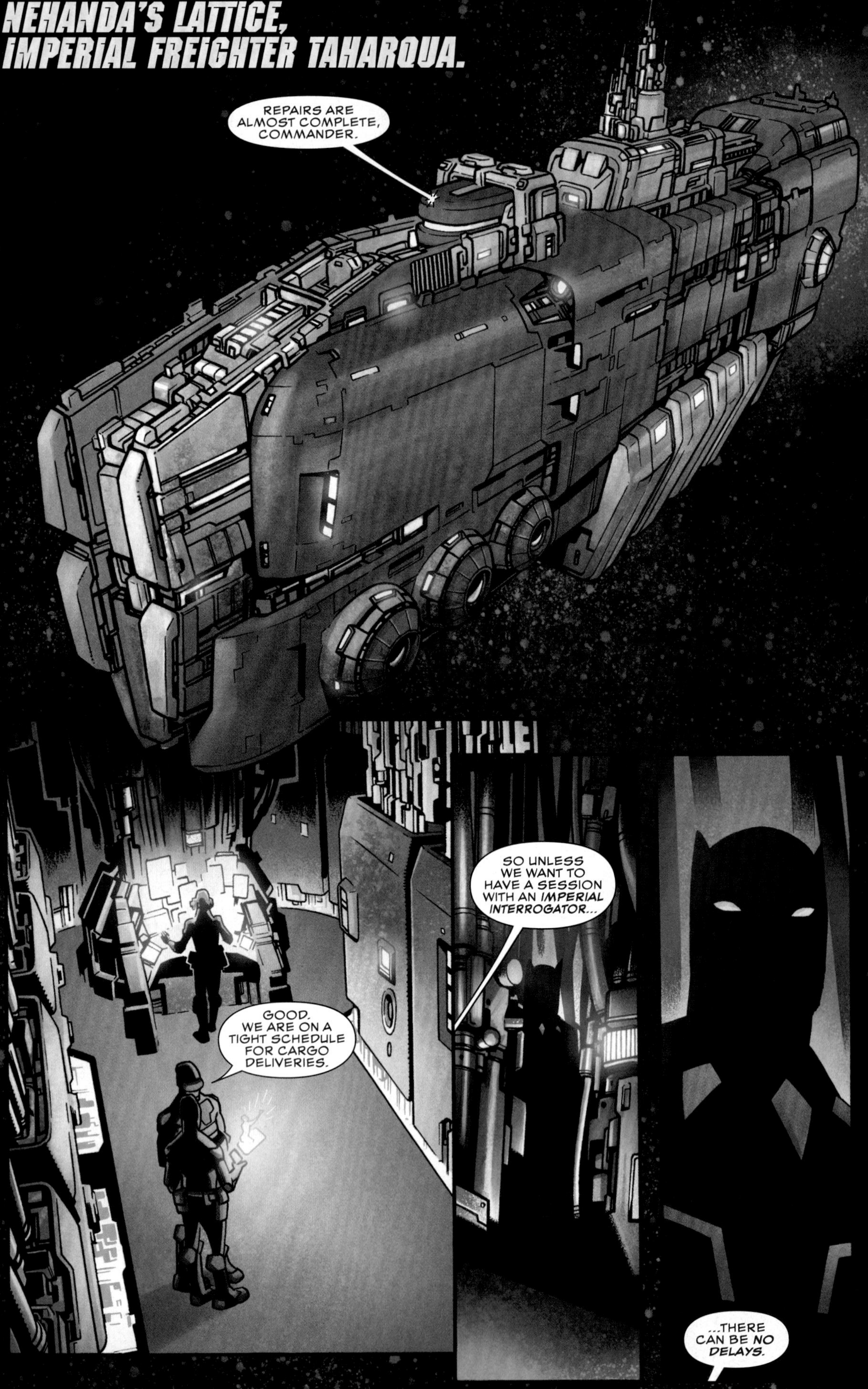
NEHANDA'S LATTICE, IMPERIAL FREIGHTER TAHARQUA.
REPAIRS ARE ALMOST COMPLETE, COMMANDER.
GOOD. WE ARE ON A TIGHT SCHEDULE FOR CARGO DELIVERIES.
SO UNLESS WE WANT TO HAVE A SESSION WITH AN IMPERIAL INTERROGATOR...
...THERE CAN BE NO DELAYS.

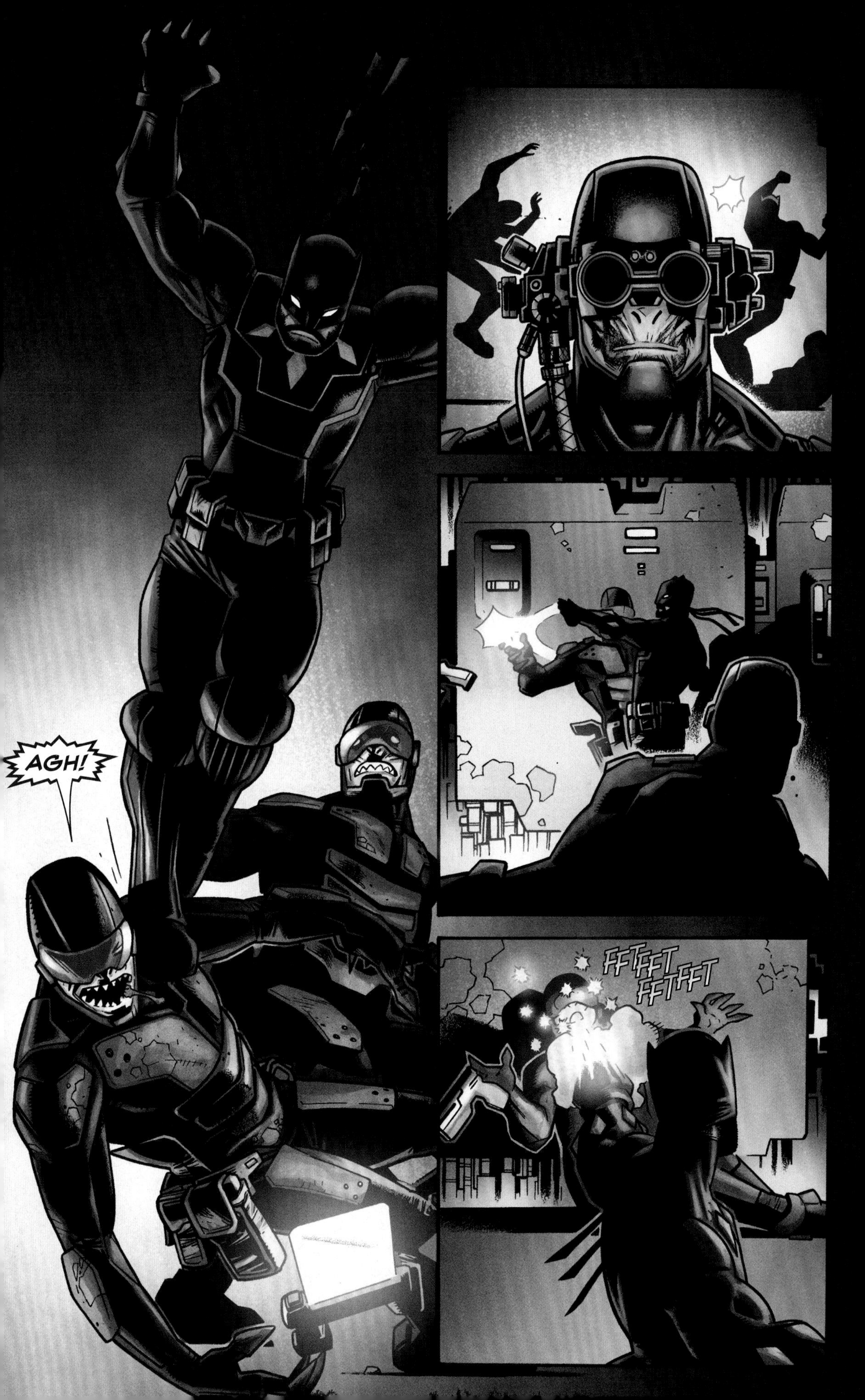
AGH!
FFT FFT
FFT FFT

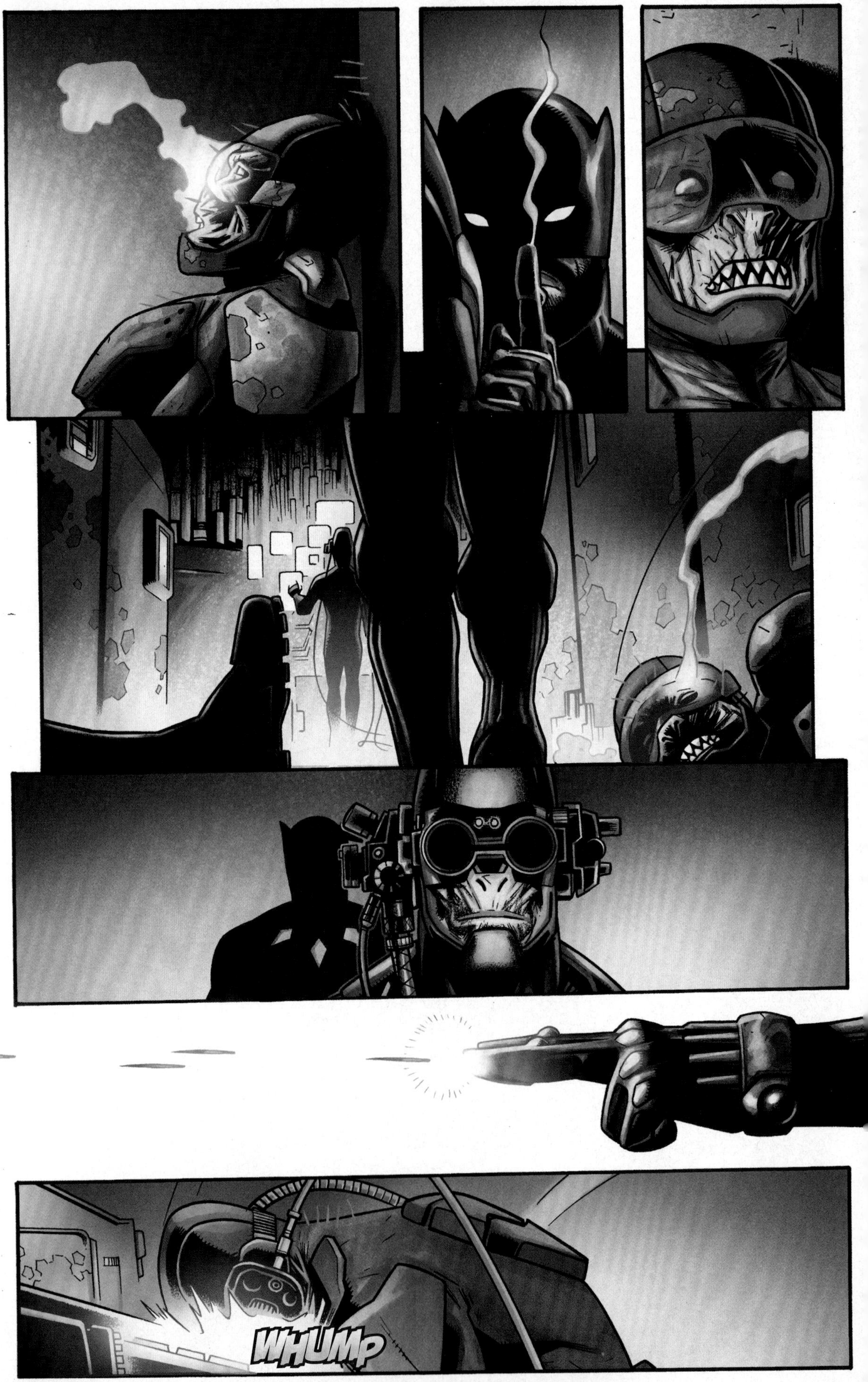
WHUMP

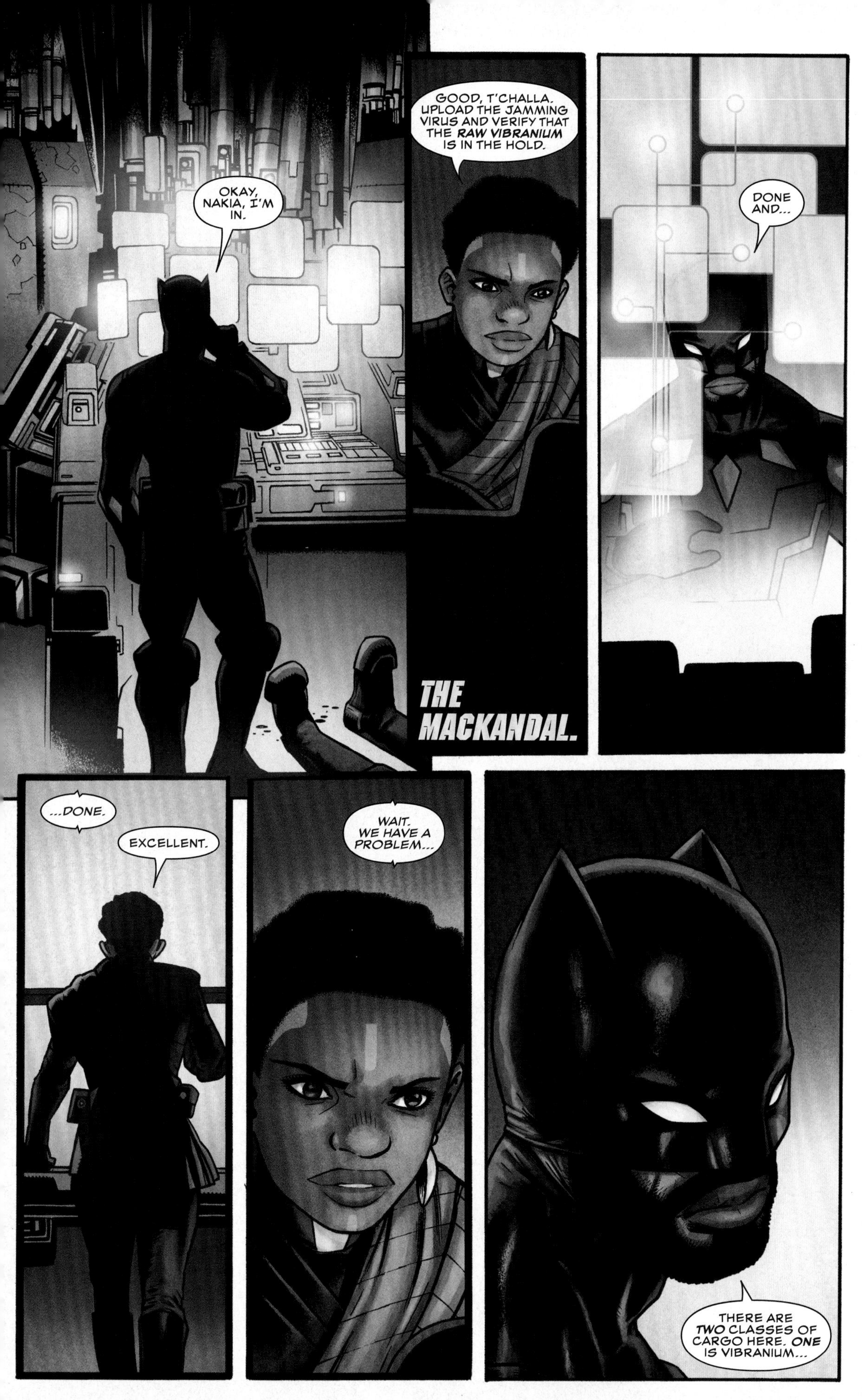
OKAY, NAKIA, I'M IN.
GOOD, T'CHALLA. UPLOAD THE JAMMING VIRUS AND VERIFY THAT THE RAW VIBRANIUM IS IN THE HOLD.
THE MACKANDAL.
DONE AND...
...DONE.
EXCELLENT.
WAIT. WE HAVE A PROBLEM...
THERE ARE TWO CLASSES OF CARGO HERE. ONE IS VIBRANIUM...

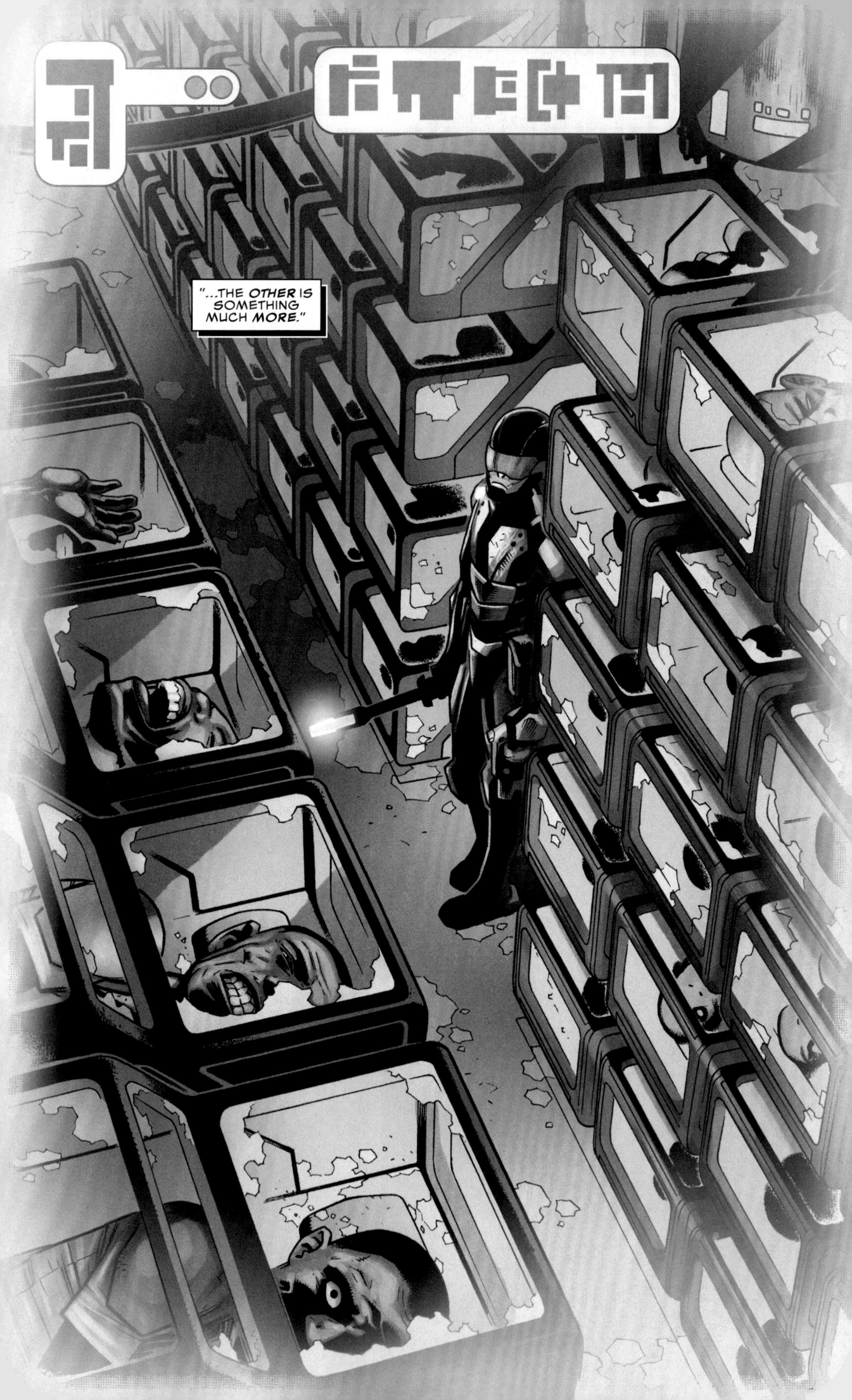
"...THE OTHER IS SOMETHING MUCH MORE."

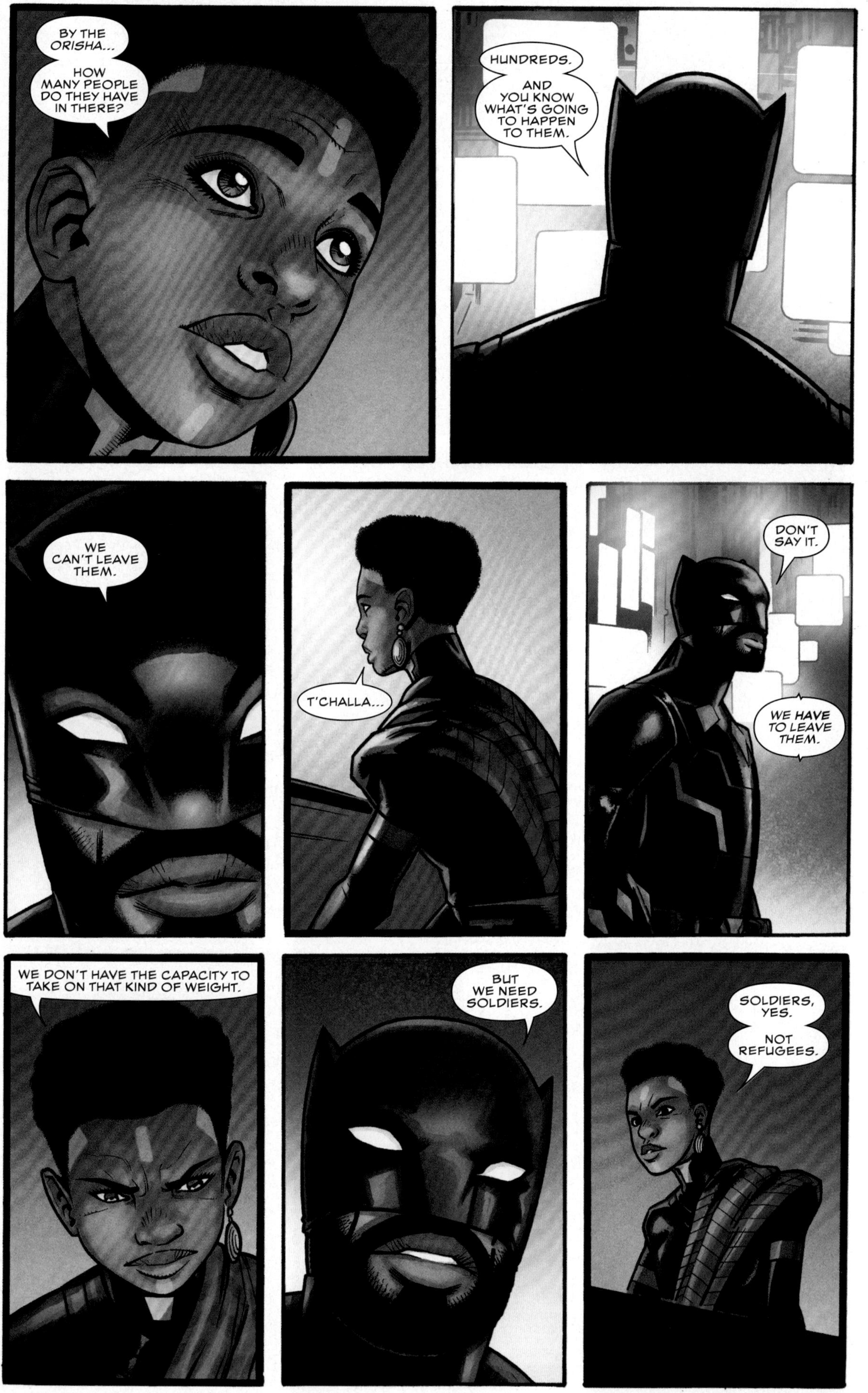
BY THE ORISHA...
HOW MANY PEOPLE DO THEY HAVE IN THERE?
HUNDREDS.
AND YOU KNOW WHAT'S GOING TO HAPPEN TO THEM.
WE CAN'T LEAVE THEM.
T'CHALLA...
DON'T SAY IT.
WE HAVE TO LEAVE THEM.
WE DON'T HAVE THE CAPACITY TO TAKE ON THAT KIND OF WEIGHT.
BUT WE NEED SOLDIERS.
SOLDIERS, YES.
NOT REFUGEES.

I WAS ONE OF THOSE REFUGEES.

NO, T'CHALLA.

YOU...YOU WERE...

...AN ASSET.

WE CHOSE TO RAID THAT MINE BECAUSE WE KNEW *YOU* WERE THERE AND WE HAD SEEN WHAT YOU COULD DO.

WE HAVE NO SUCH ASSURANCES HERE.

THE RAW VIBRANIUM IS THE FIRST ELEMENT FOR THE *DJALIA DEVICE.*

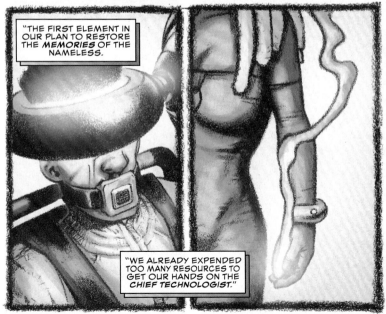

"THE FIRST ELEMENT IN OUR PLAN TO RESTORE THE *MEMORIES* OF THE NAMELESS."

"WE ALREADY EXPENDED TOO MANY RESOURCES TO GET OUR HANDS ON THE *CHIEF TECHNOLOGIST.*"

WE CAN'T CHANGE THE PLAN NOW. THE VIBRANIUM IS THE PRIORITY.

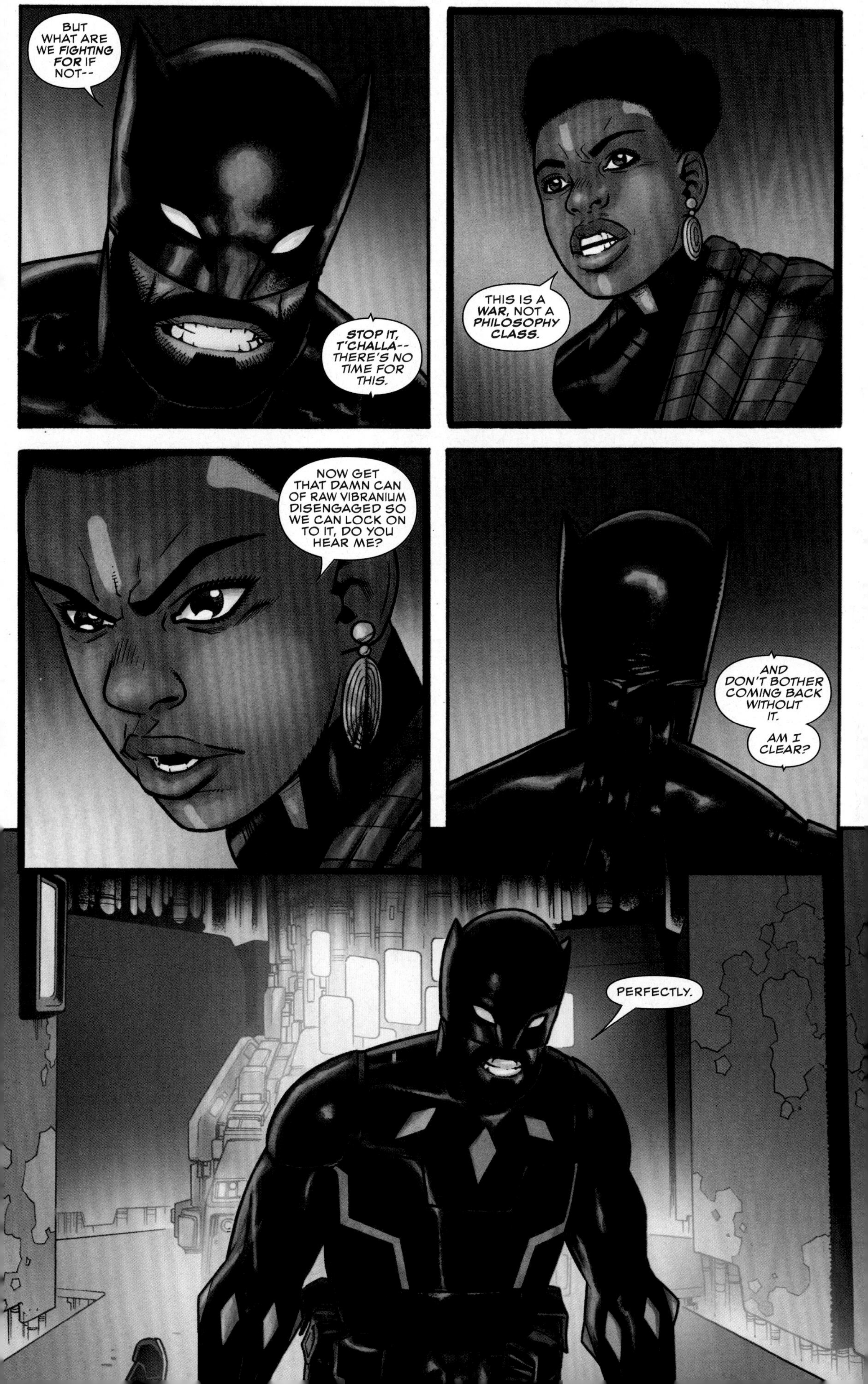
BUT WHAT ARE WE *FIGHTING FOR* IF NOT--
STOP IT, T'CHALLA-- THERE'S NO TIME FOR THIS.
THIS IS A *WAR*, NOT A *PHILOSOPHY CLASS.*
NOW GET THAT DAMN CAN OF RAW VIBRANIUM DISENGAGED SO WE CAN LOCK ON TO IT, DO YOU HEAR ME?
AND DON'T BOTHER COMING BACK WITHOUT IT.
AM I CLEAR?
PERFECTLY.

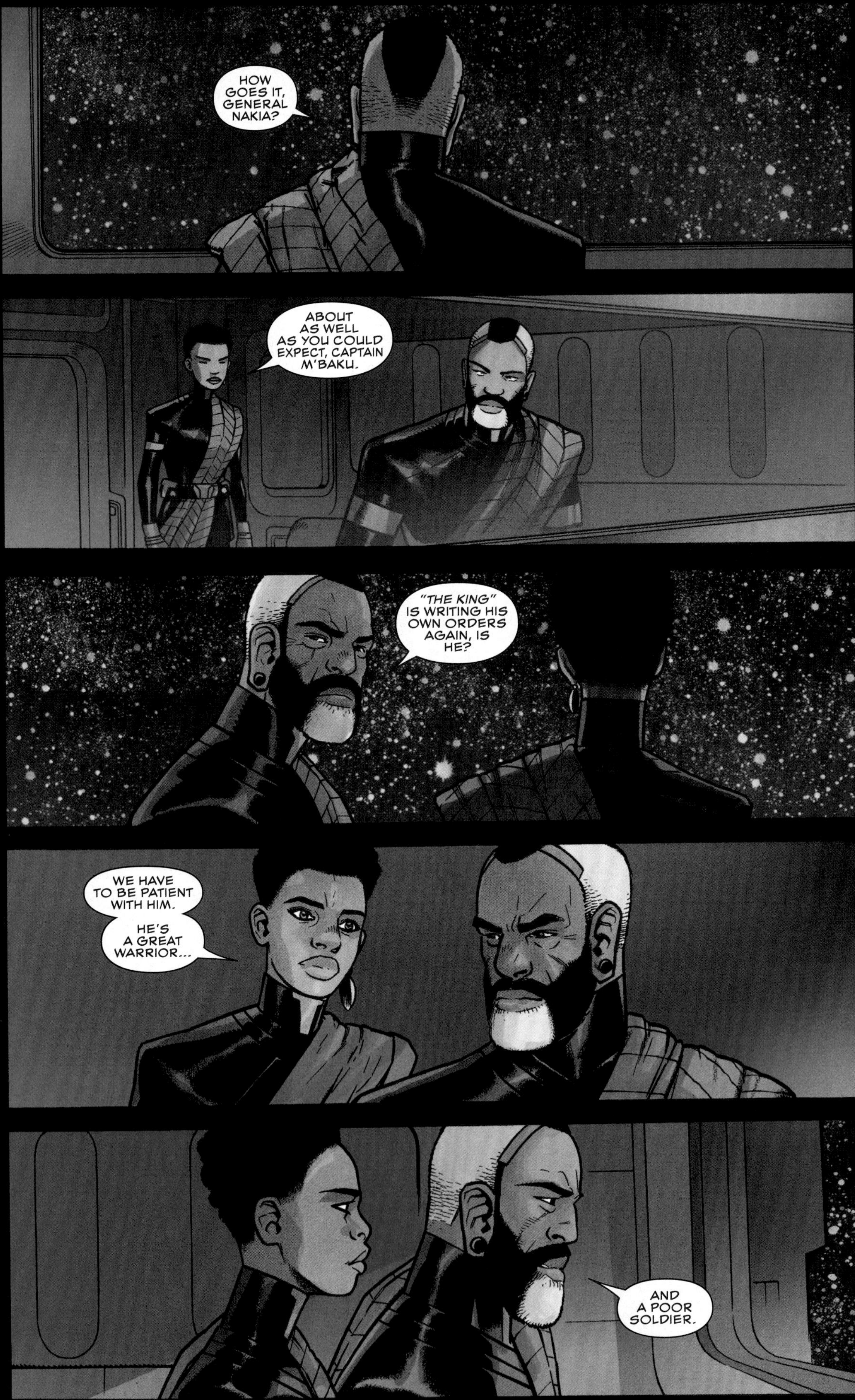
HOW GOES IT, GENERAL NAKIA?
ABOUT AS WELL AS YOU COULD EXPECT, CAPTAIN M'BAKU.
"THE KING" IS WRITING HIS OWN ORDERS AGAIN, IS HE?
WE HAVE TO BE PATIENT WITH HIM.
HE'S A GREAT WARRIOR...
AND A POOR SOLDIER.

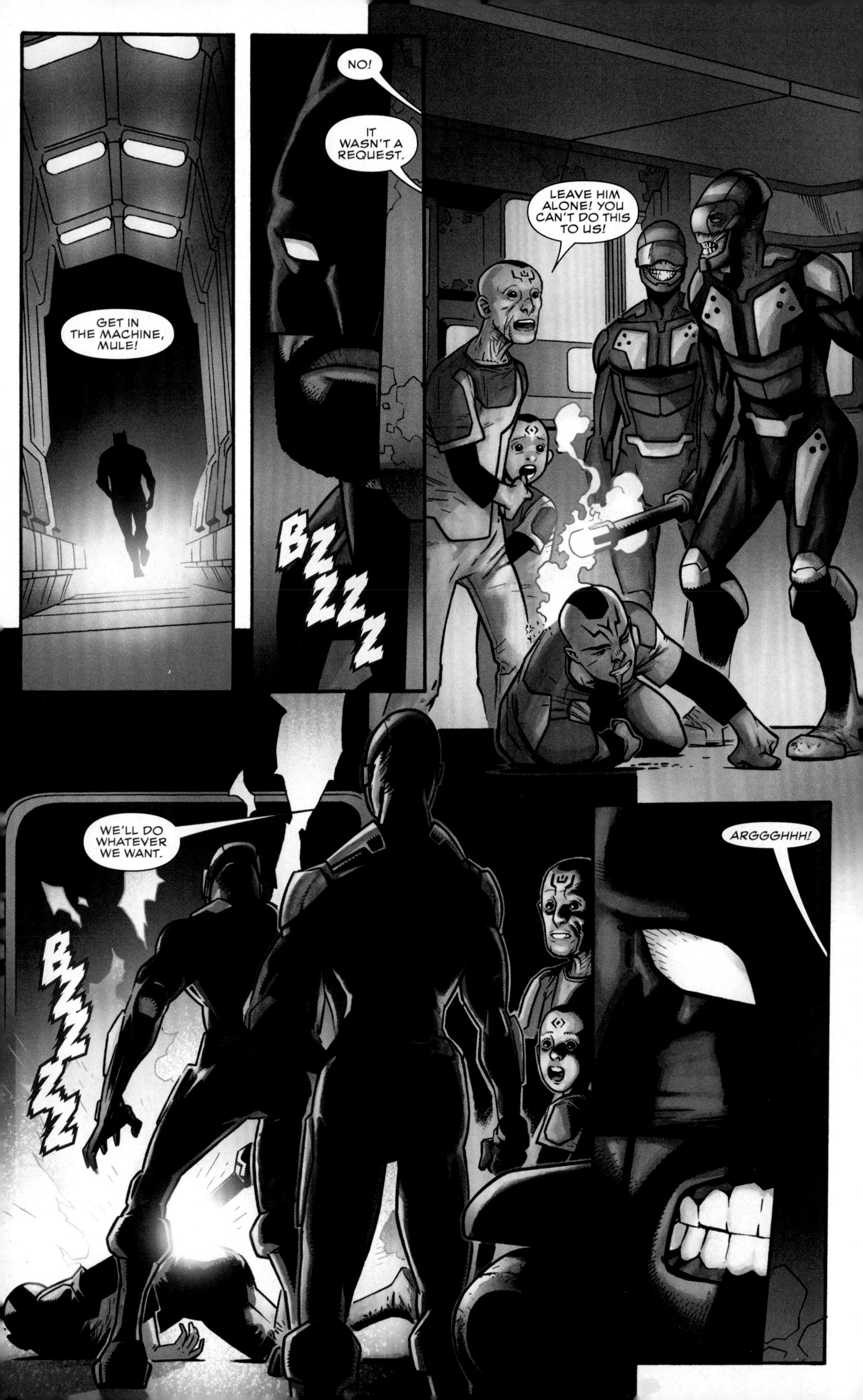
GET IN THE MACHINE, MULE!
NO!
IT WASN'T A REQUEST.
LEAVE HIM ALONE! YOU CAN'T DO THIS TO US!
BZZZZZ
WE'LL DO WHATEVER WE WANT.
BZZZZZ
ARGGGHHH!

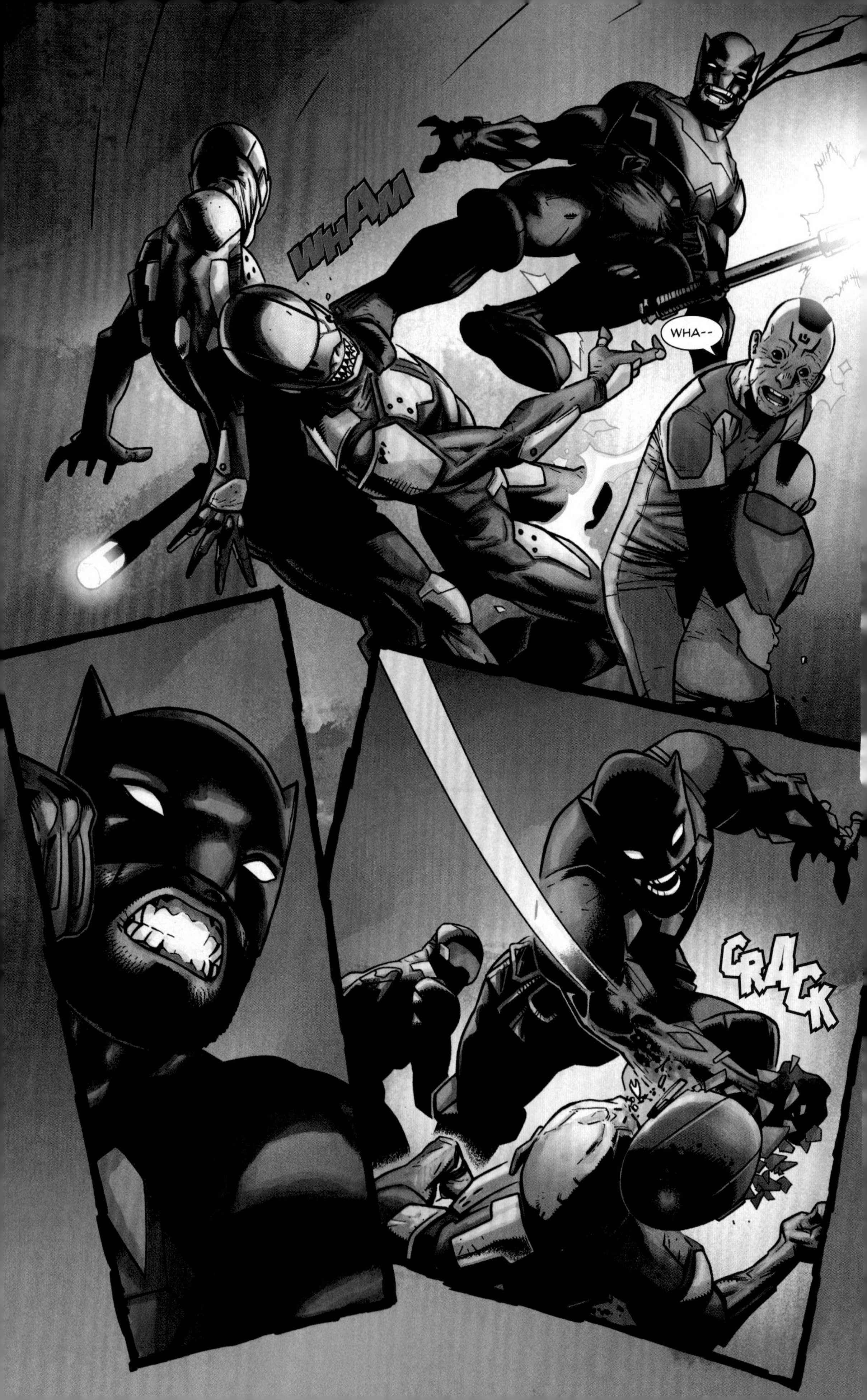
WHAM
WHA--
CRACK

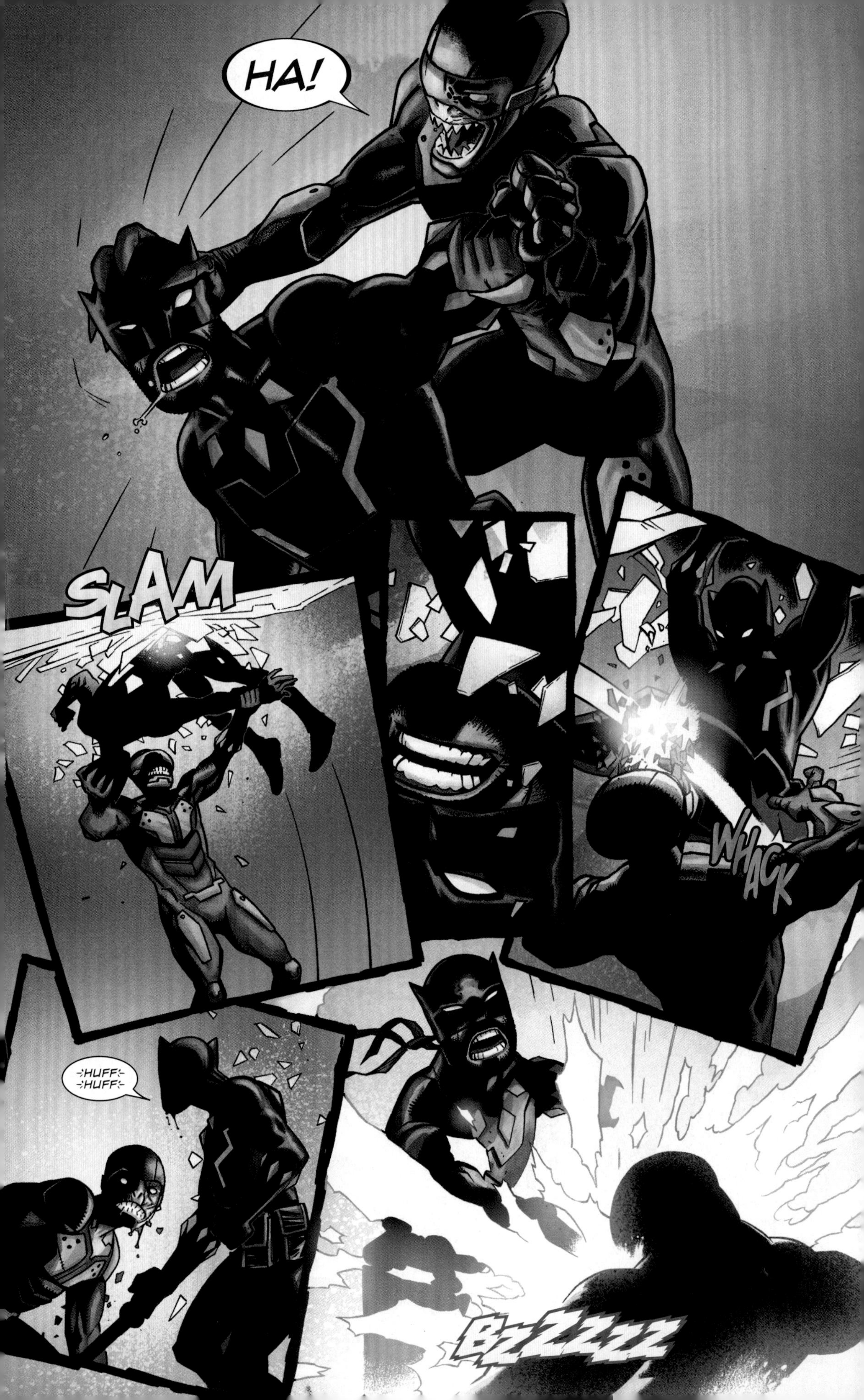
HA!
SLAM
WHACK
HUFF HUFF
BZZZZZ

BY THE LIGHT OF BAST, IT *IS* YOU!

THE *AVENGER!* THE ONE WHO SHALL PUT THE KNIFE WHERE IT BELONGS!

THE *SAVIOR!*

I AM A FIGHTER, BABA, NOT A SAVIOR.

BUT ONE DOES NOT DISQUALIFY THE OTHER, MY SON.

TODAY IT DOES.

GO BACK TO YOUR CELLS. IT WILL BE WORSE IF THEY FIND YOU HERE.

I...I DON'T UNDERSTAND.

YOU HAVE NOT COME TO SAVE US? B-BUT TO ABANDON US?

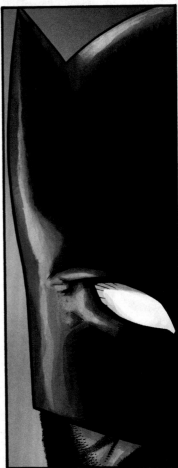

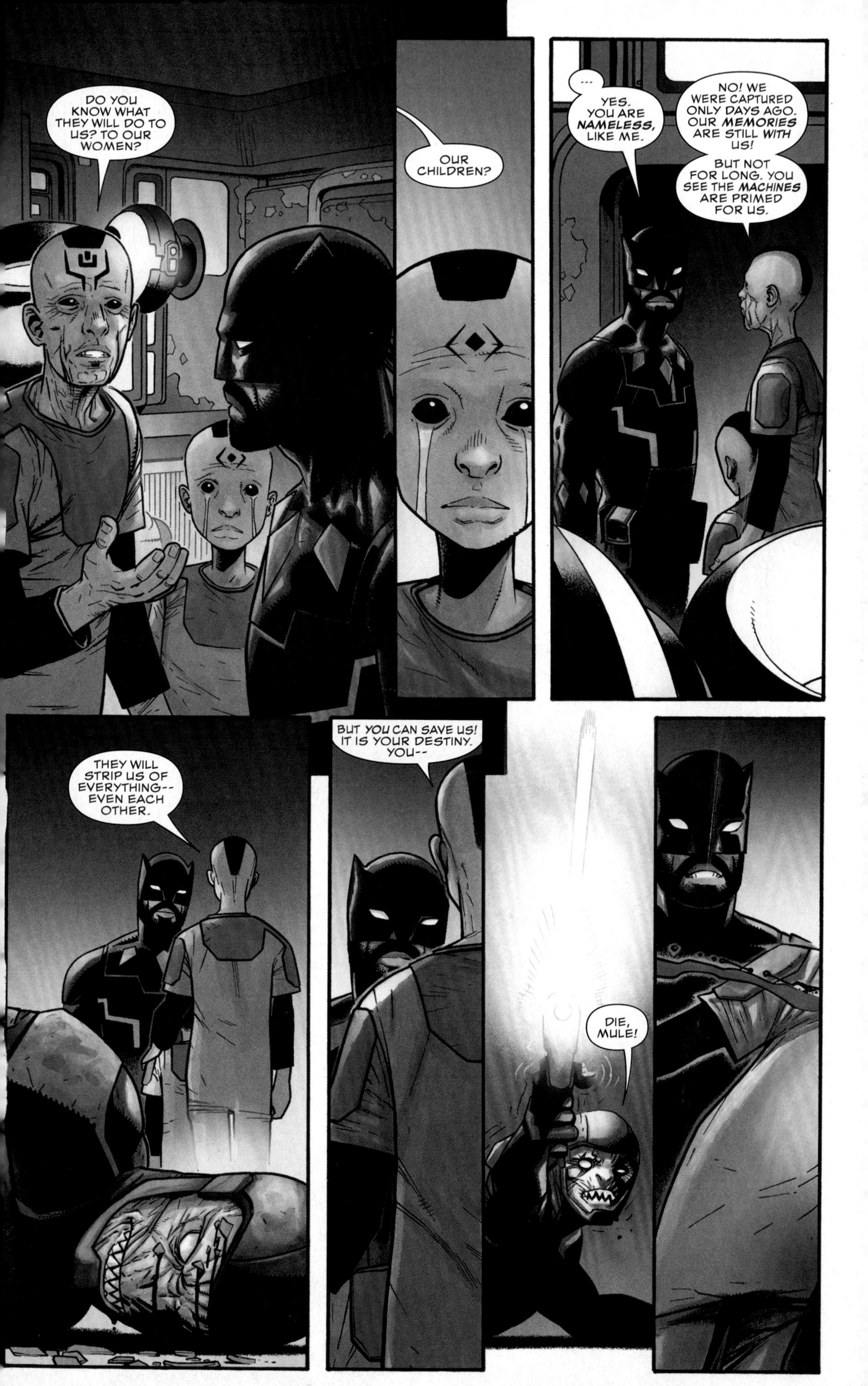
DO YOU KNOW WHAT THEY WILL DO TO US? TO OUR WOMEN?
OUR CHILDREN?
...
YES. YOU ARE NAMELESS, LIKE ME.
NO! WE WERE CAPTURED ONLY DAYS AGO. OUR MEMORIES ARE STILL WITH US!
BUT NOT FOR LONG. YOU SEE THE MACHINES ARE PRIMED FOR US.
THEY WILL STRIP US OF EVERYTHING-- EVEN EACH OTHER.
BUT YOU CAN SAVE US! IT IS YOUR DESTINY. YOU--
DIE, MULE!

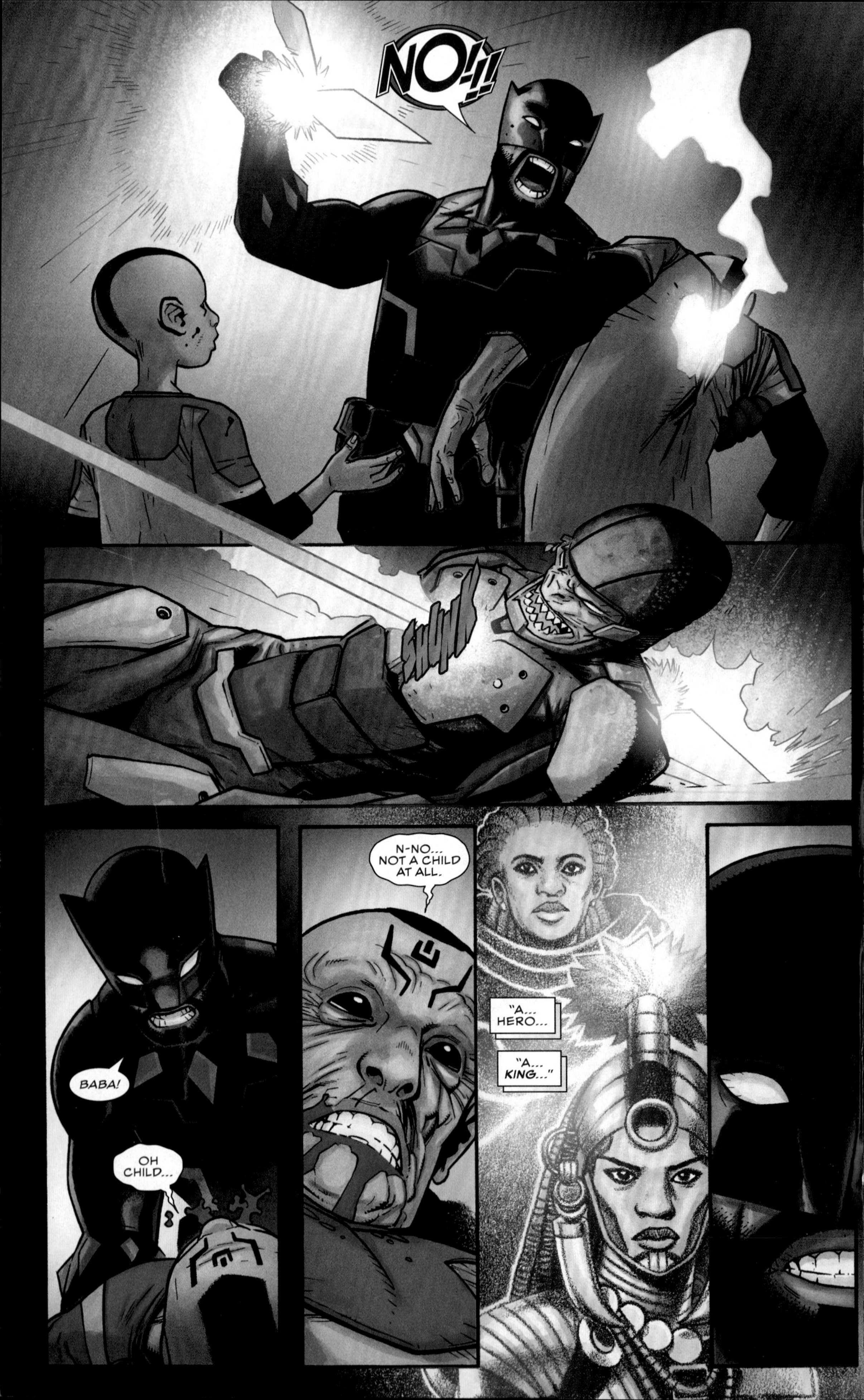
NO-!!!
SHUNK
BABA!
OH CHILD...
N-NO... NOT A CHILD AT ALL.
"A... HERO...
"A... KING..."

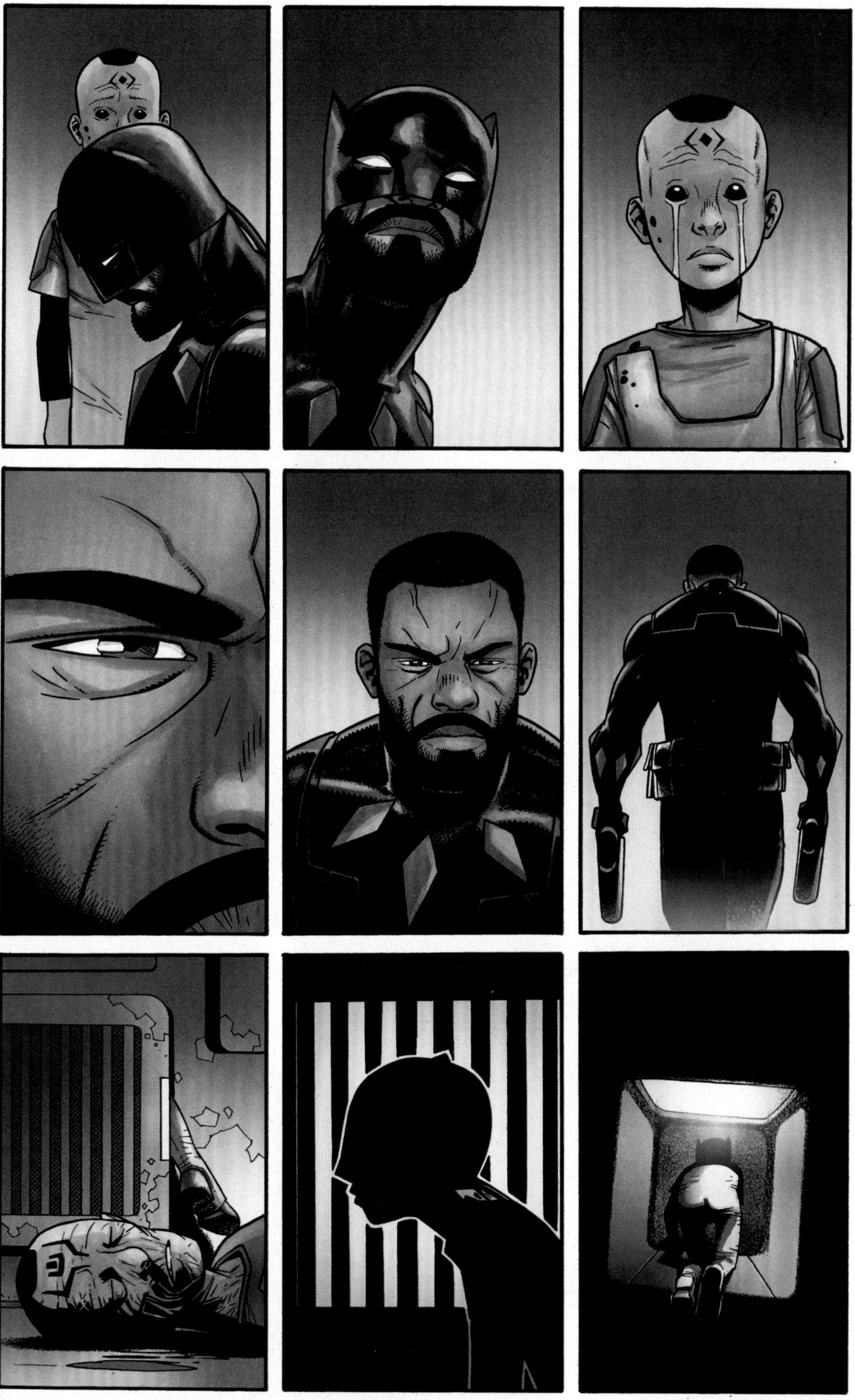

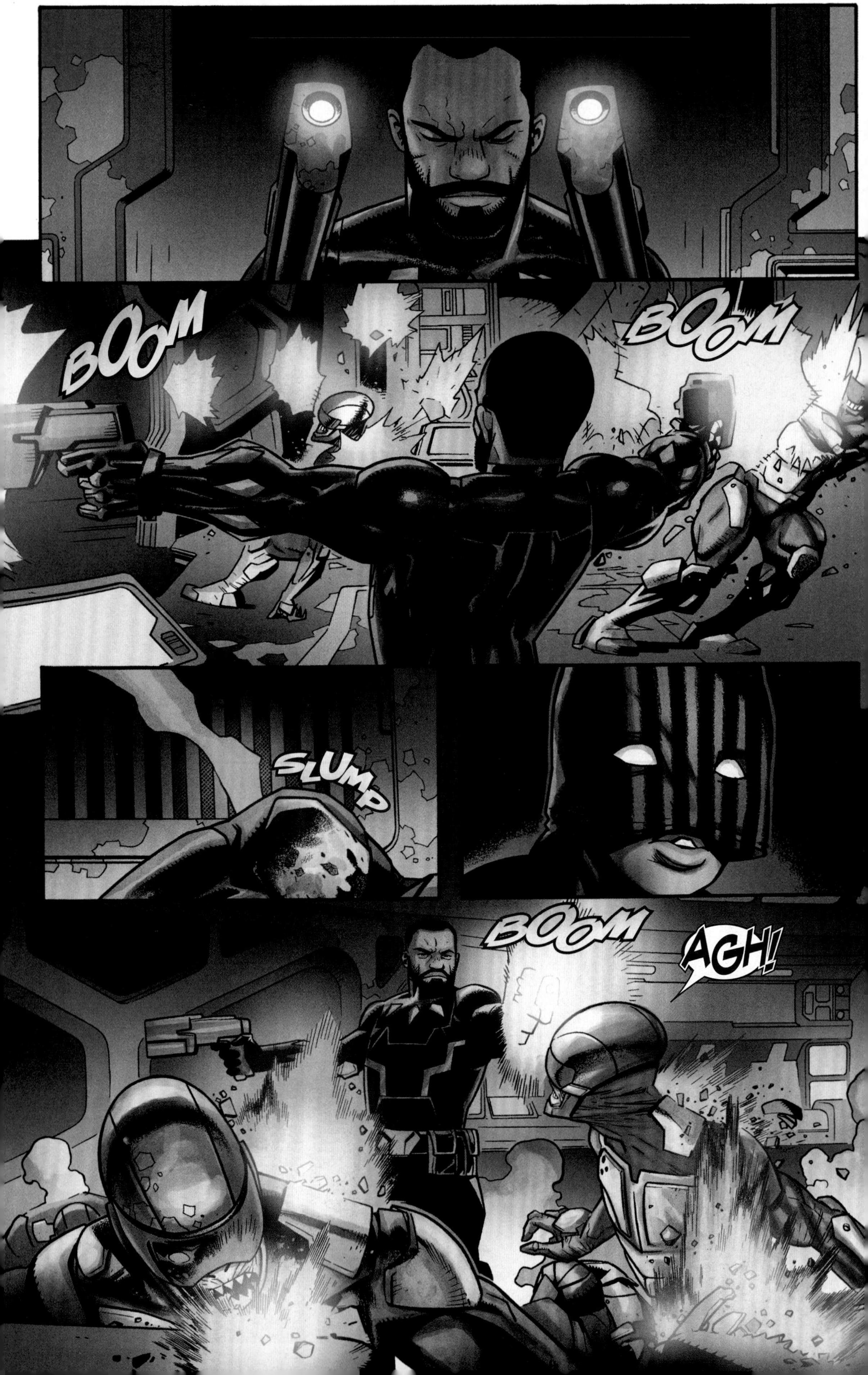
BOOM
BOOOM
SLUMP
BOOM
AGH!

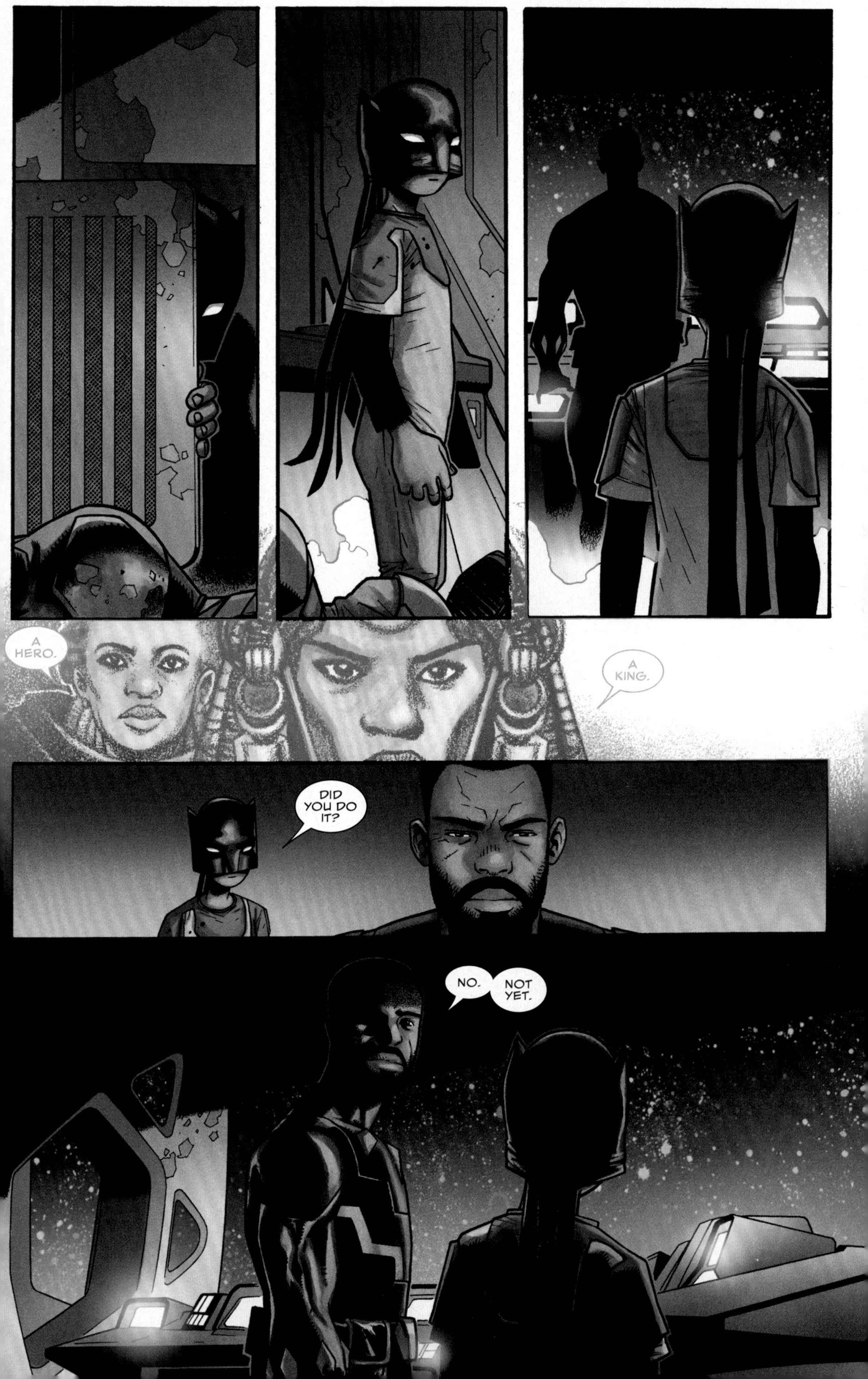
A HERO.
A KING.
DID YOU DO IT?
NO.
NOT YET.

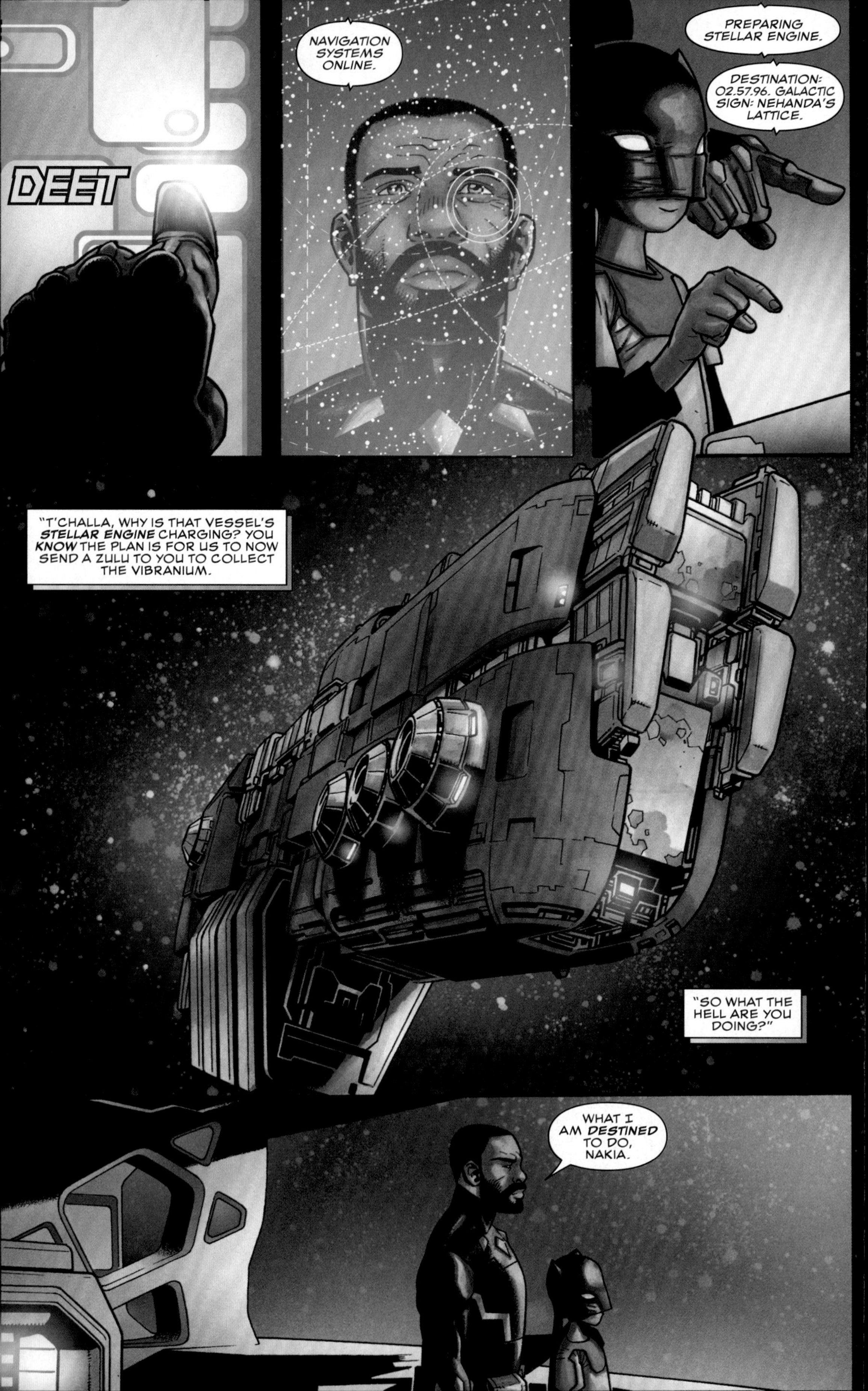
DEET
NAVIGATION SYSTEMS ONLINE.
PREPARING STELLAR ENGINE.
DESTINATION: 02.57.96. GALACTIC SIGN: NEHANDA'S LATTICE.
"T'CHALLA, WHY IS THAT VESSEL'S STELLAR ENGINE CHARGING? YOU KNOW THE PLAN IS FOR US TO NOW SEND A ZULU TO YOU TO COLLECT THE VIBRANIUM.
"SO WHAT THE HELL ARE YOU DOING?"
WHAT I AM DESTINED TO DO, NAKIA.

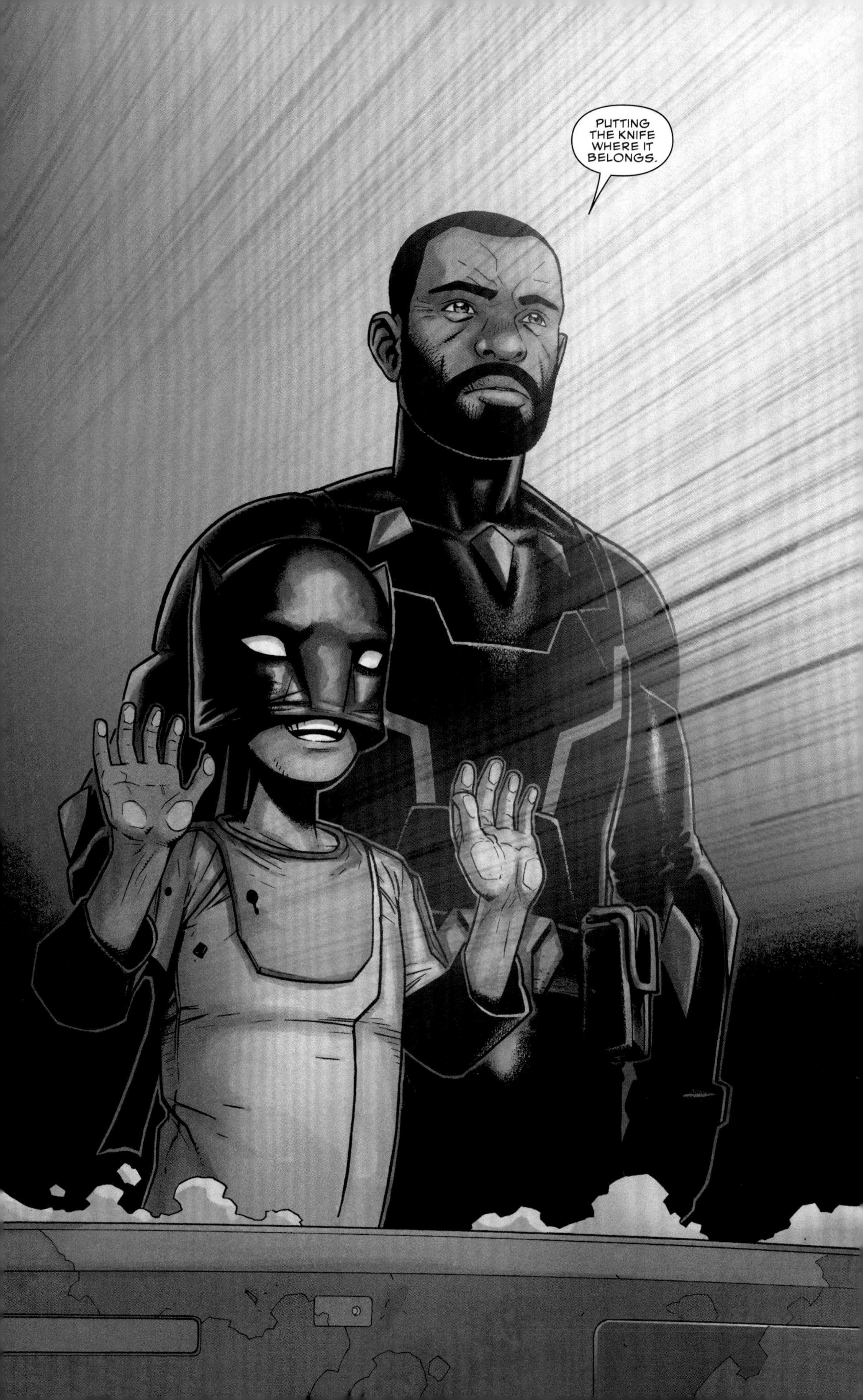
PUTTING THE KNIFE WHERE IT BELONGS.

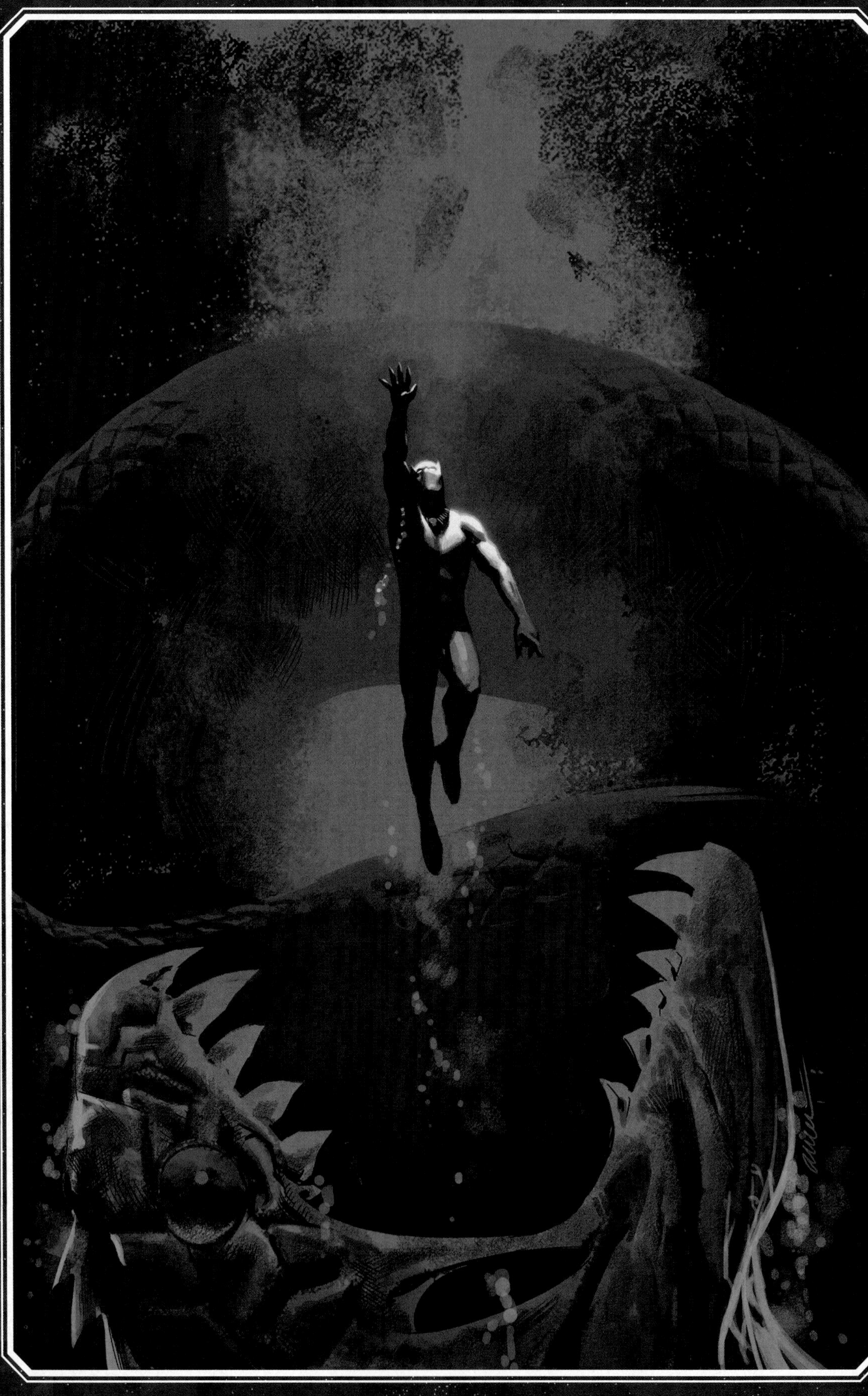

9

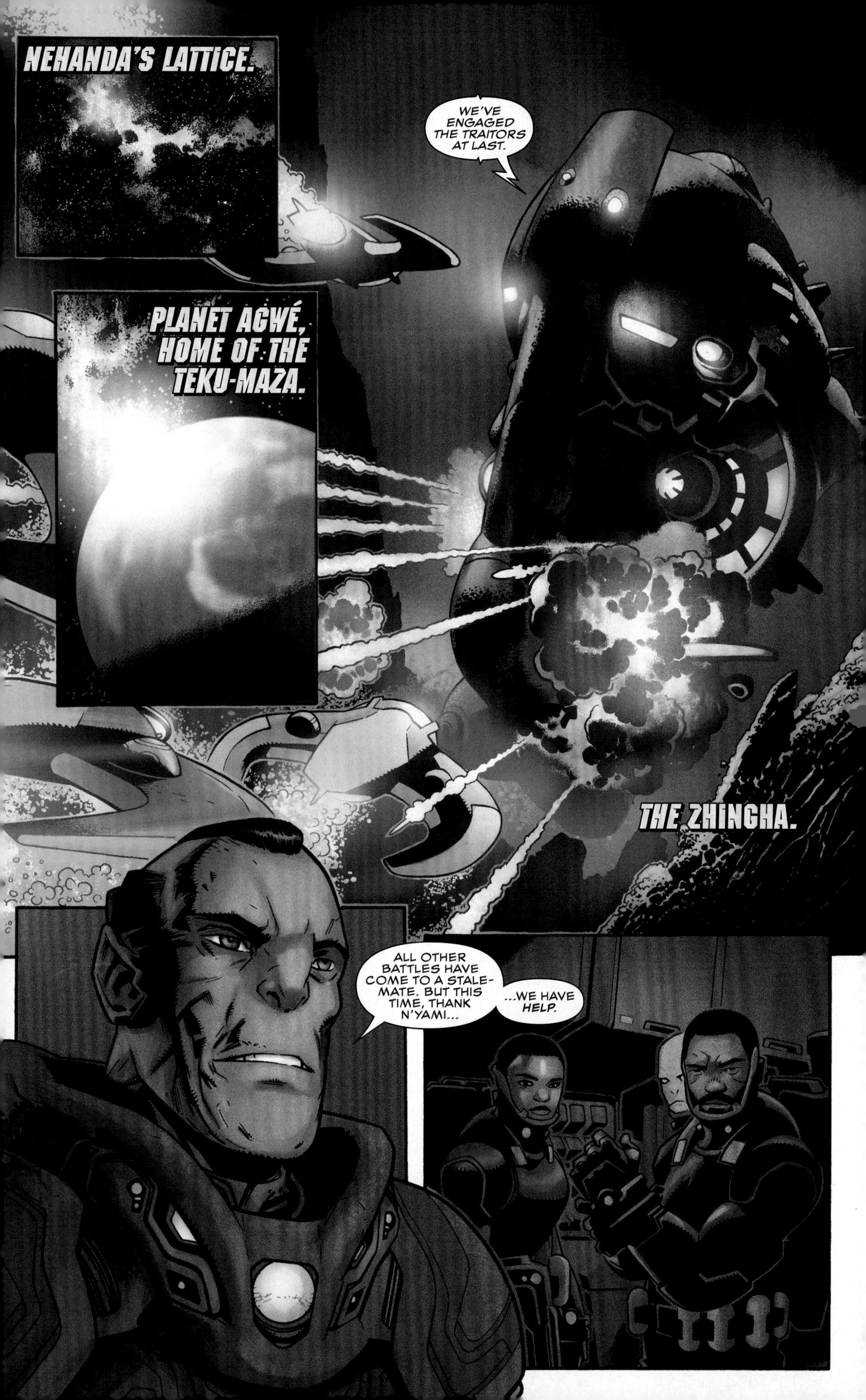

NEHANDA'S LATTICE.
WE'VE ENGAGED THE TRAITORS AT LAST.
PLANET AGWÉ, HOME OF THE TEKU-MAZA.
THE ZHINGHA.
ALL OTHER BATTLES HAVE COME TO A STALE-MATE. BUT THIS TIME, THANK N'YAMI...
...WE HAVE HELP.

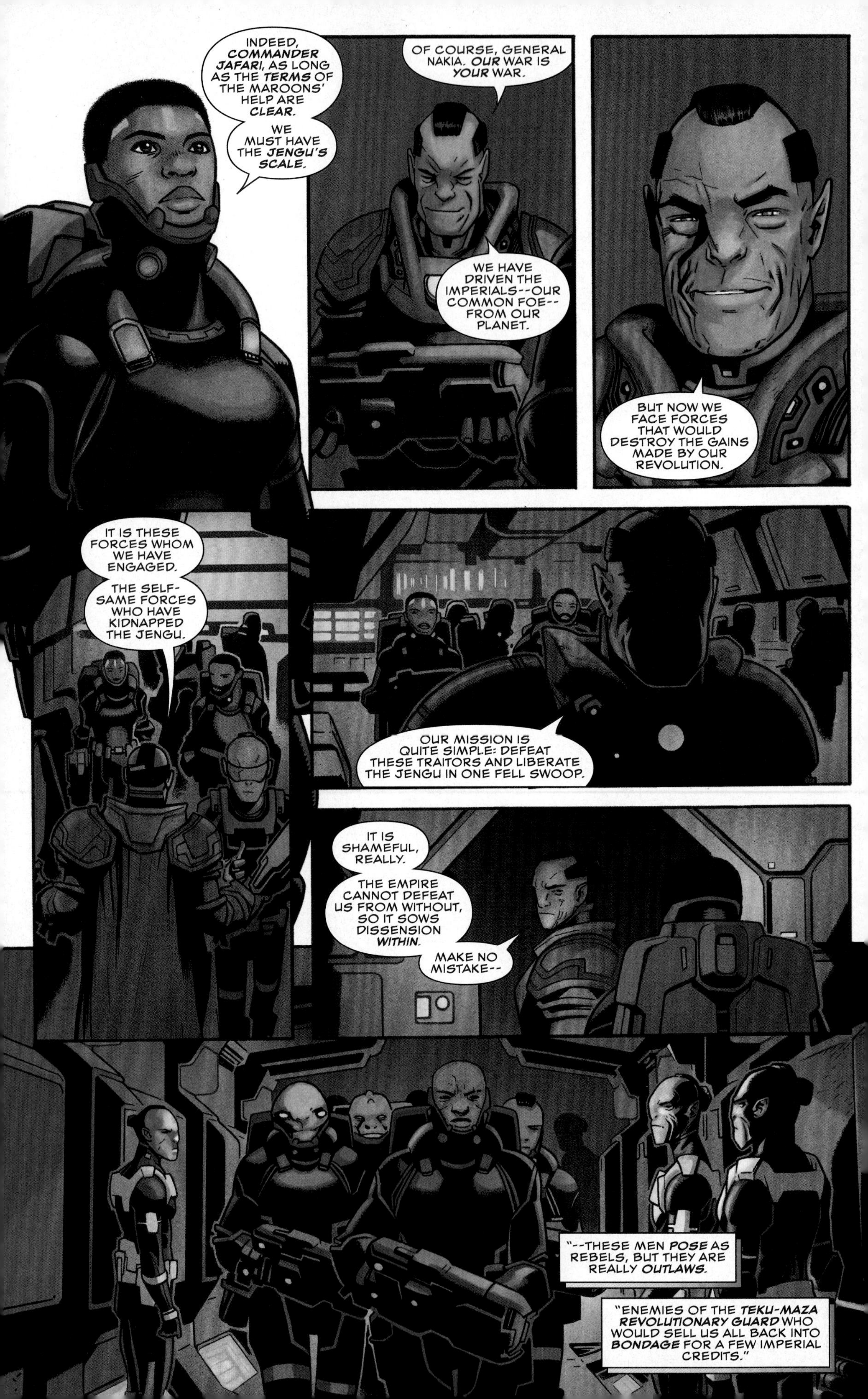
INDEED, COMMANDER JAFARI, AS LONG AS THE TERMS OF THE MAROONS' HELP ARE CLEAR.
WE MUST HAVE THE JENGU'S SCALE.
OF COURSE, GENERAL NAKIA. OUR WAR IS YOUR WAR.
WE HAVE DRIVEN THE IMPERIALS--OUR COMMON FOE--FROM OUR PLANET.
BUT NOW WE FACE FORCES THAT WOULD DESTROY THE GAINS MADE BY OUR REVOLUTION.
IT IS THESE FORCES WHOM WE HAVE ENGAGED.
THE SELF-SAME FORCES WHO HAVE KIDNAPPED THE JENGU.
OUR MISSION IS QUITE SIMPLE: DEFEAT THESE TRAITORS AND LIBERATE THE JENGU IN ONE FELL SWOOP.
IT IS SHAMEFUL, REALLY.
THE EMPIRE CANNOT DEFEAT US FROM WITHOUT, SO IT SOWS DISSENSION WITHIN.
MAKE NO MISTAKE--
"--THESE MEN POSE AS REBELS, BUT THEY ARE REALLY OUTLAWS.
"ENEMIES OF THE TEKU-MAZA REVOLUTIONARY GUARD WHO WOULD SELL US ALL BACK INTO BONDAGE FOR A FEW IMPERIAL CREDITS."

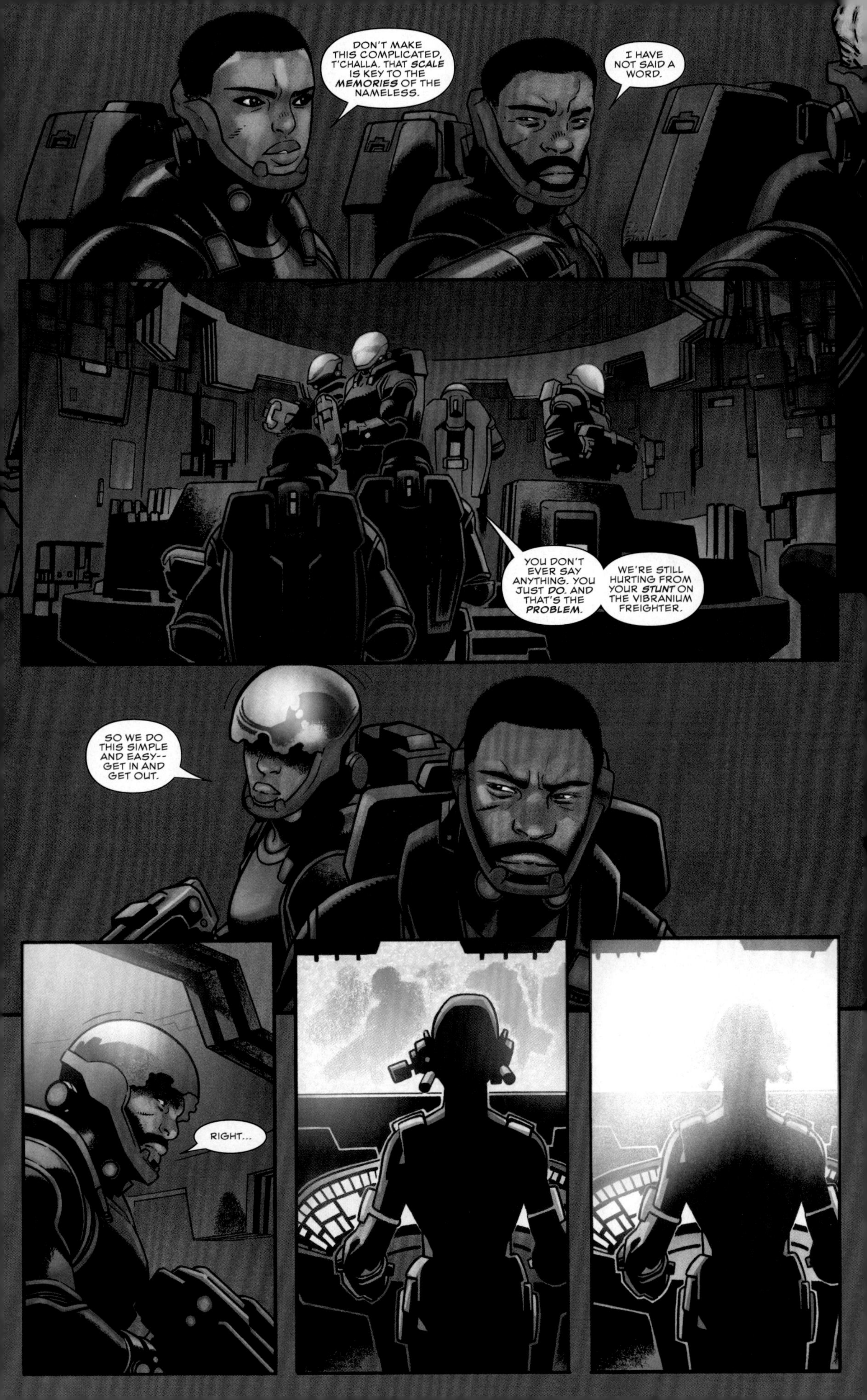
DON'T MAKE THIS COMPLICATED, T'CHALLA. THAT SCALE IS KEY TO THE MEMORIES OF THE NAMELESS.
I HAVE NOT SAID A WORD.
YOU DON'T EVER SAY ANYTHING. YOU JUST DO. AND THAT'S THE PROBLEM.
WE'RE STILL HURTING FROM YOUR STUNT ON THE VIBRANIUM FREIGHTER.
SO WE DO THIS SIMPLE AND EASY-- GET IN AND GET OUT.
RIGHT...

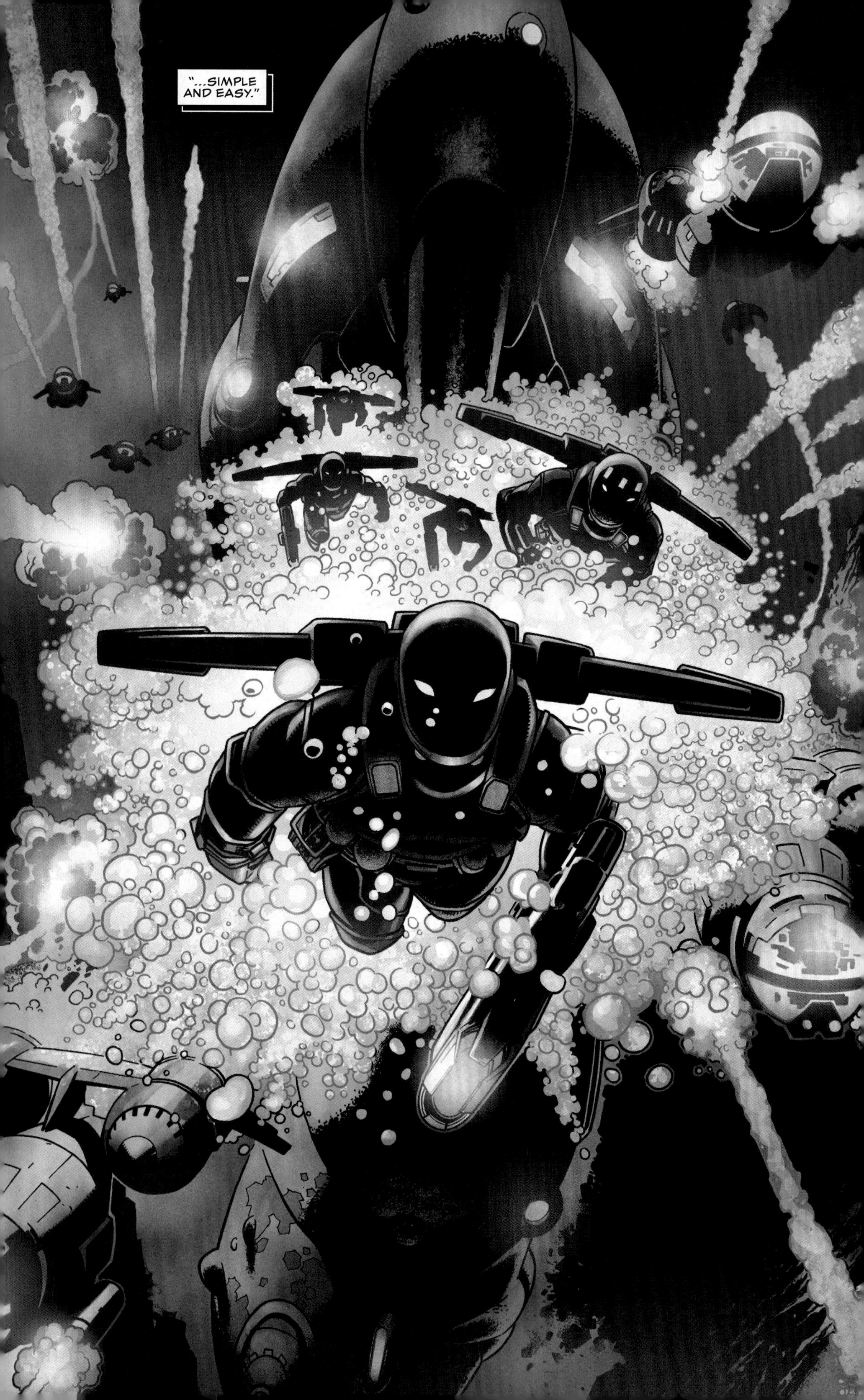
"...SIMPLE AND EASY."

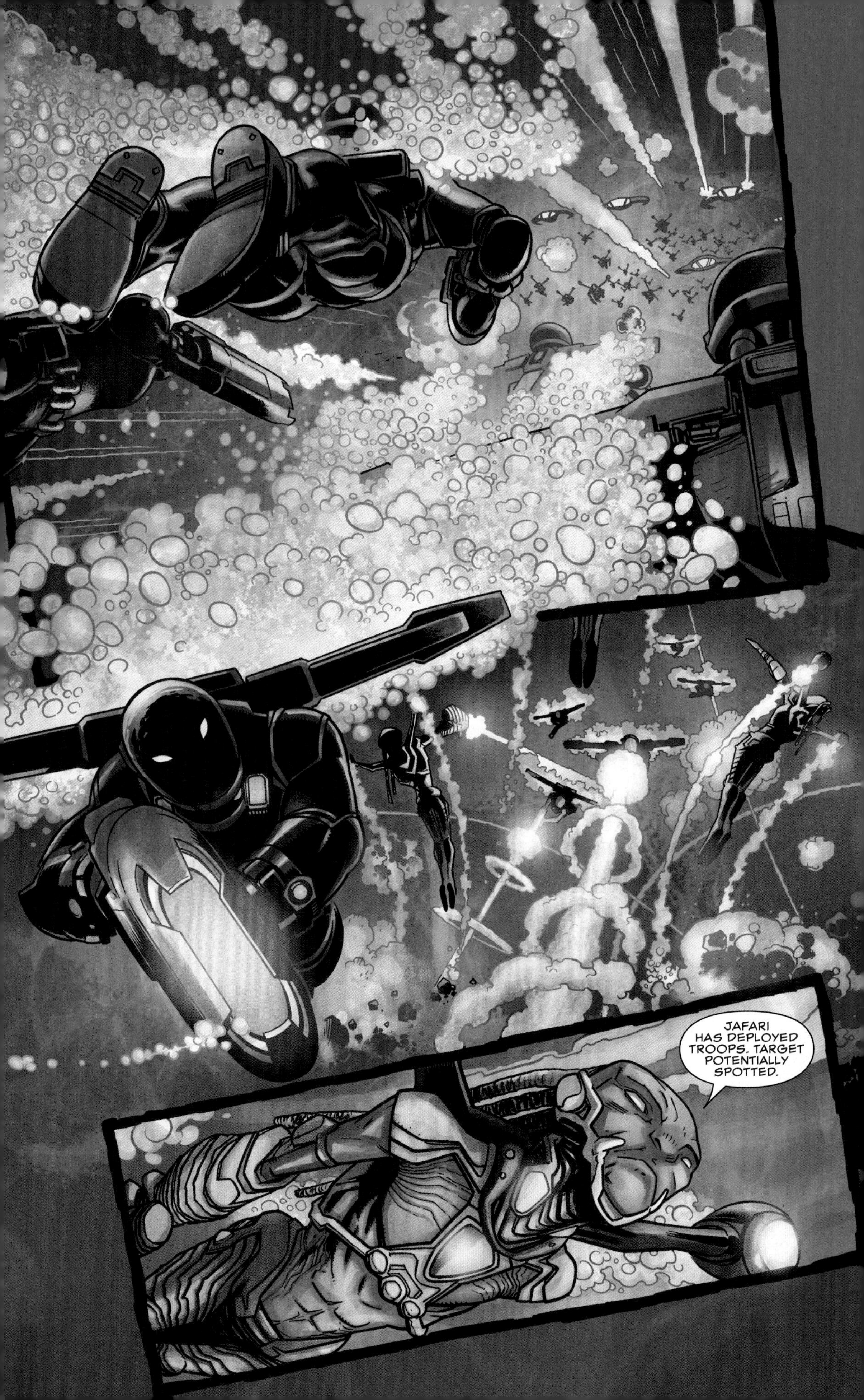
JAFARI HAS DEPLOYED TROOPS. TARGET POTENTIALLY SPOTTED.

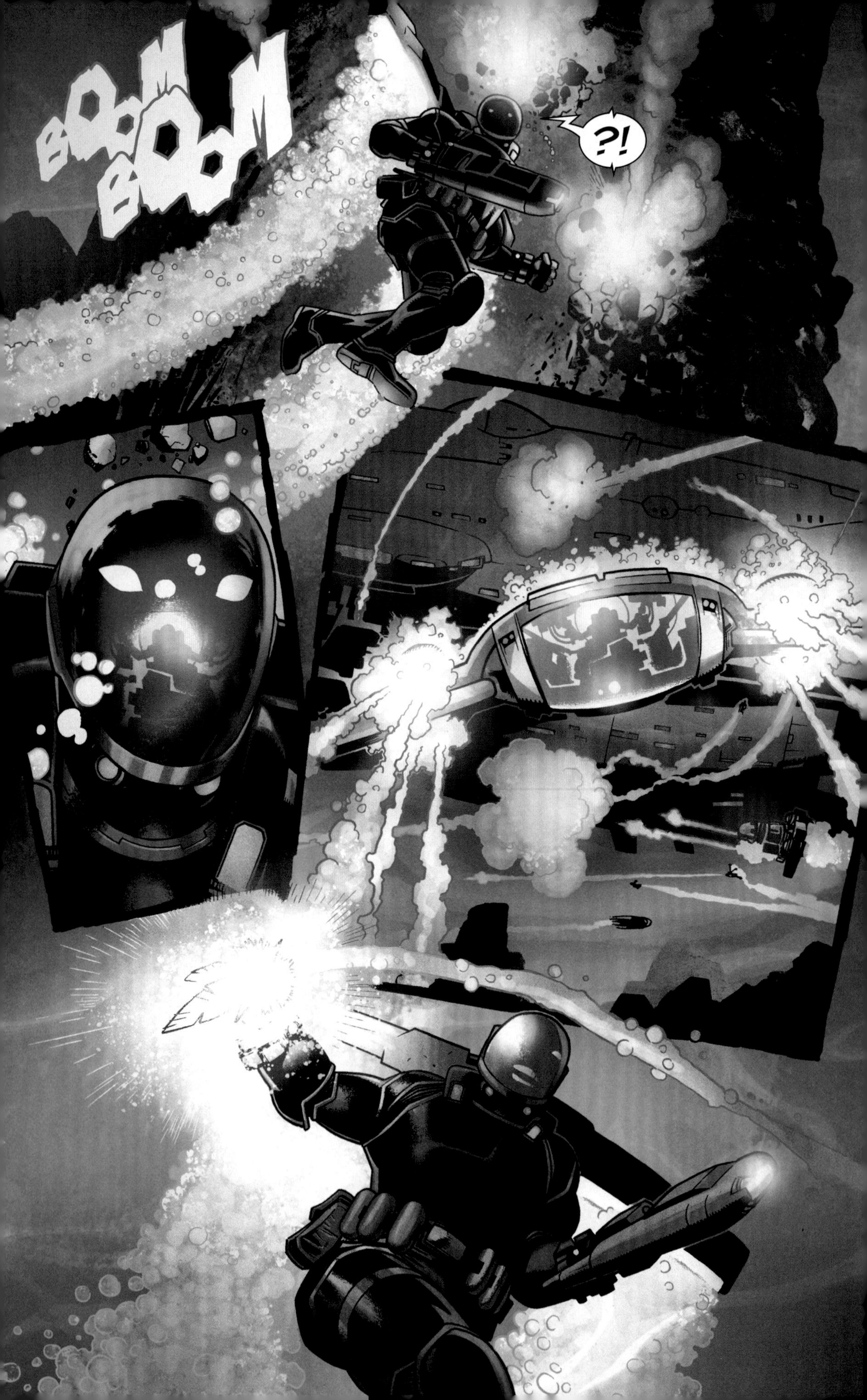
BOOM
BOOM
?!

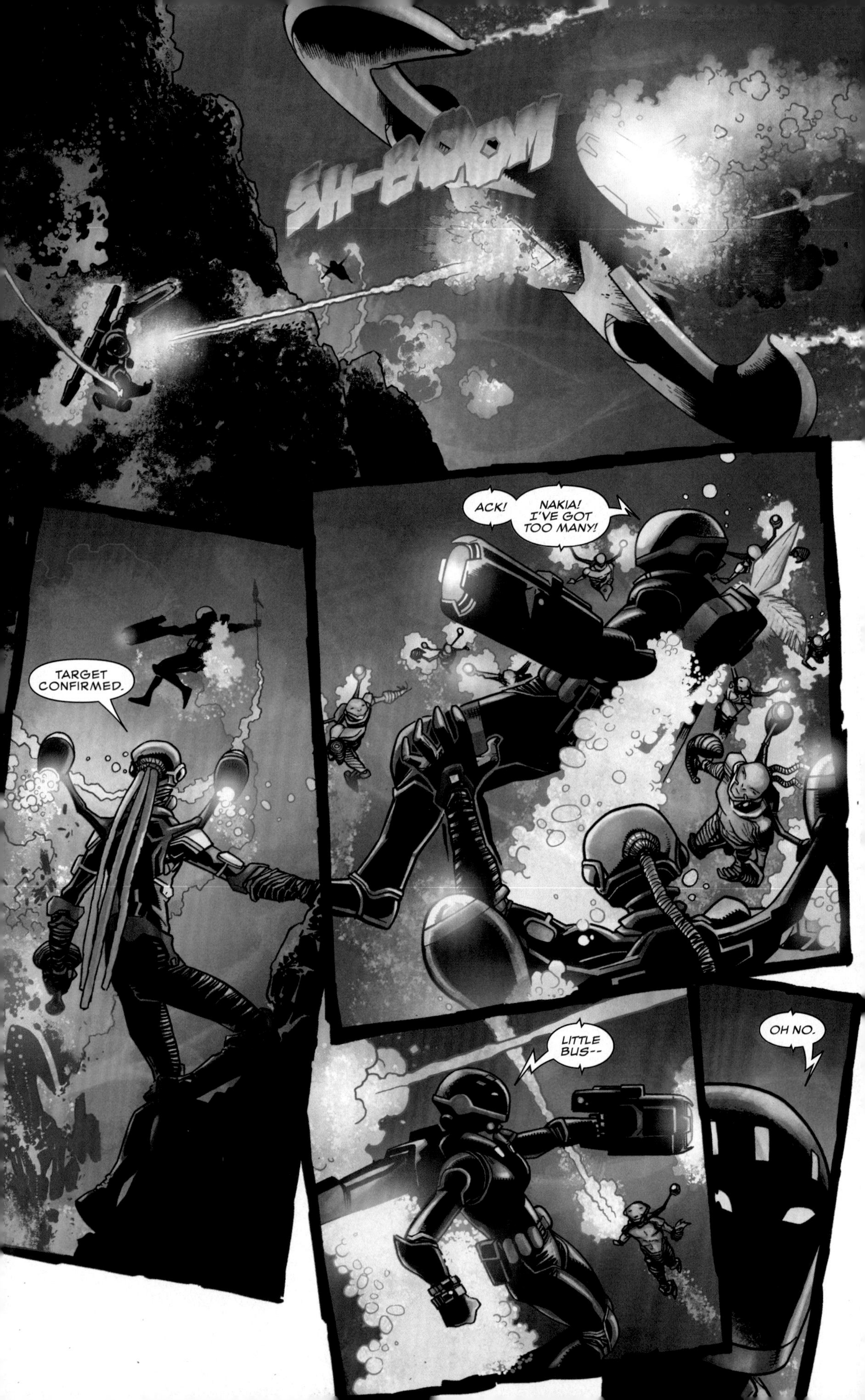
SH-BOOM
TARGET CONFIRMED.
ACK!
NAKIA! I'VE GOT TOO MANY!
LITTLE BUS--
OH NO.

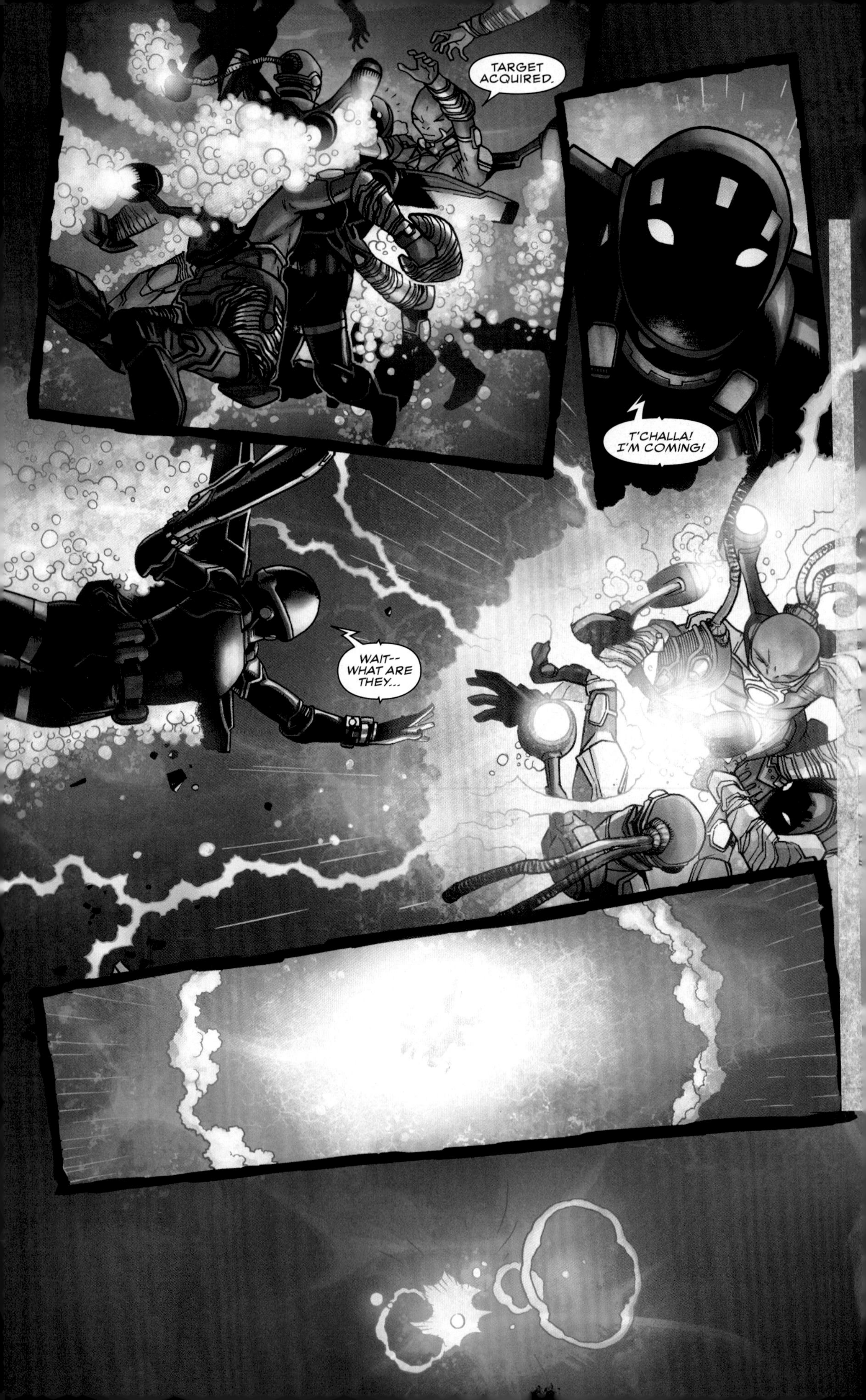
TARGET ACQUIRED.
T'CHALLA! I'M COMING!
WAIT-- WHAT ARE THEY...

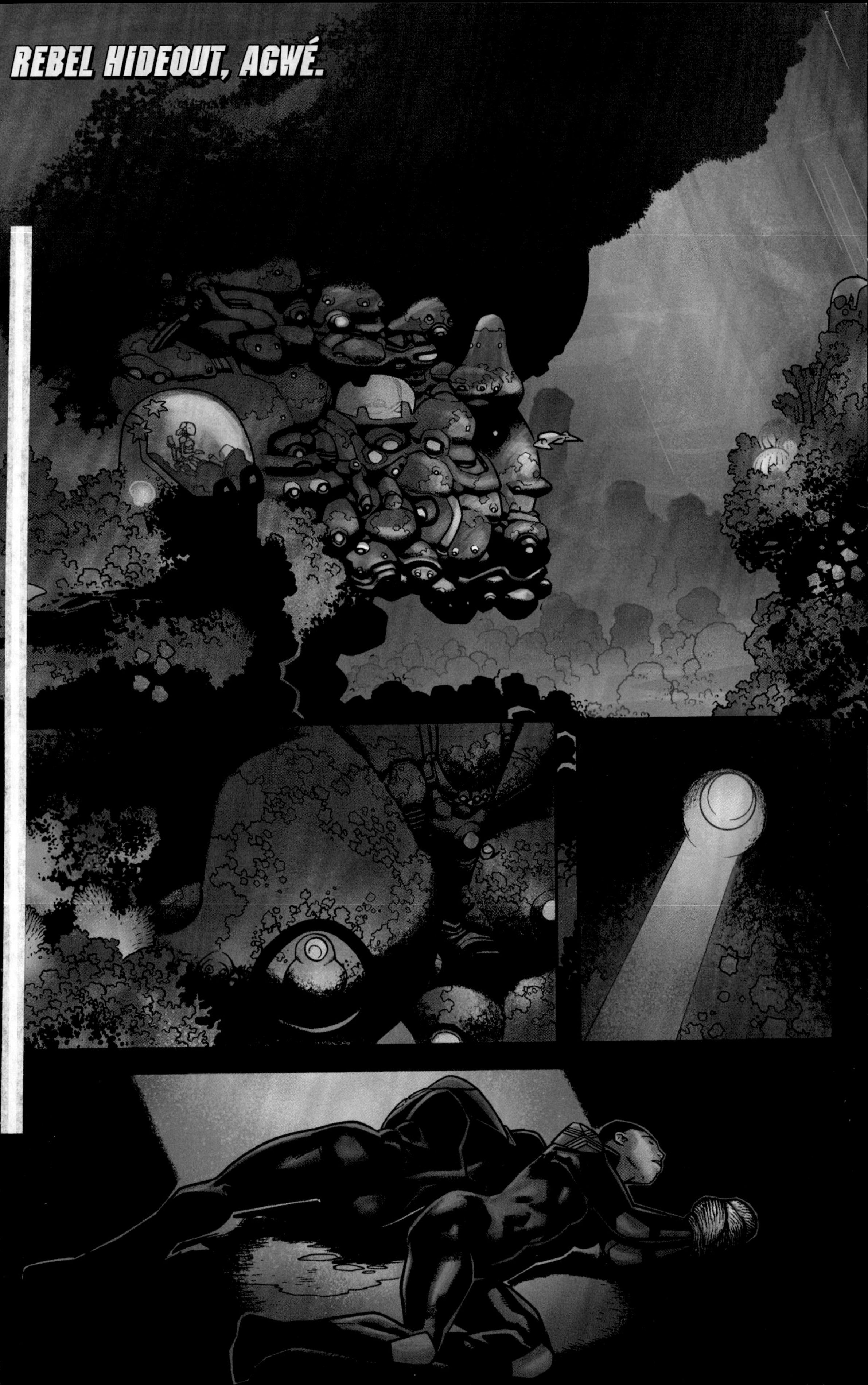
REBEL HIDEOUT, AGWÉ.

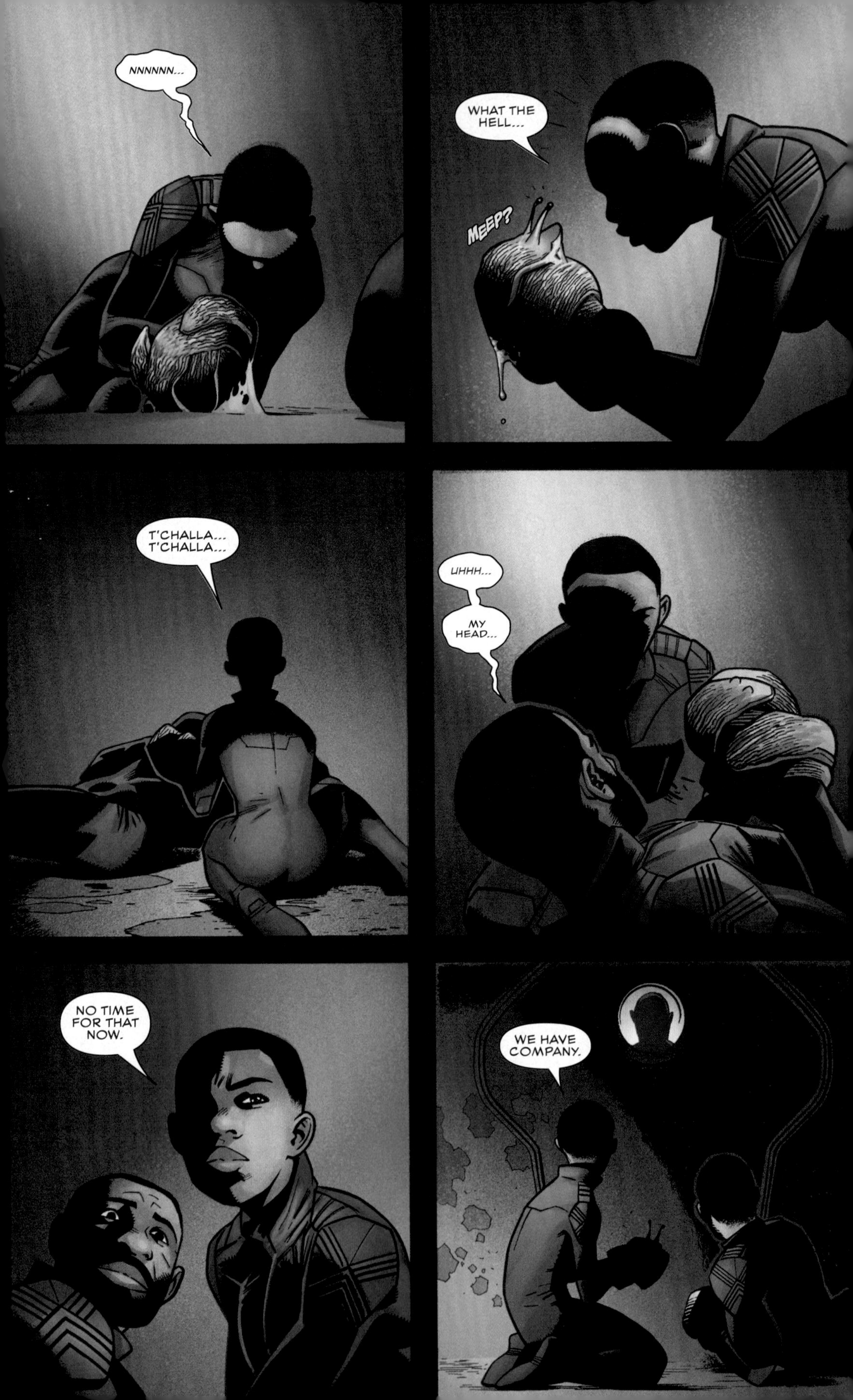
NNNNNN...
WHAT THE HELL...
MEEP?
T'CHALLA... T'CHALLA...
UHHH...
MY HEAD...
NO TIME FOR THAT NOW.
WE HAVE COMPANY.

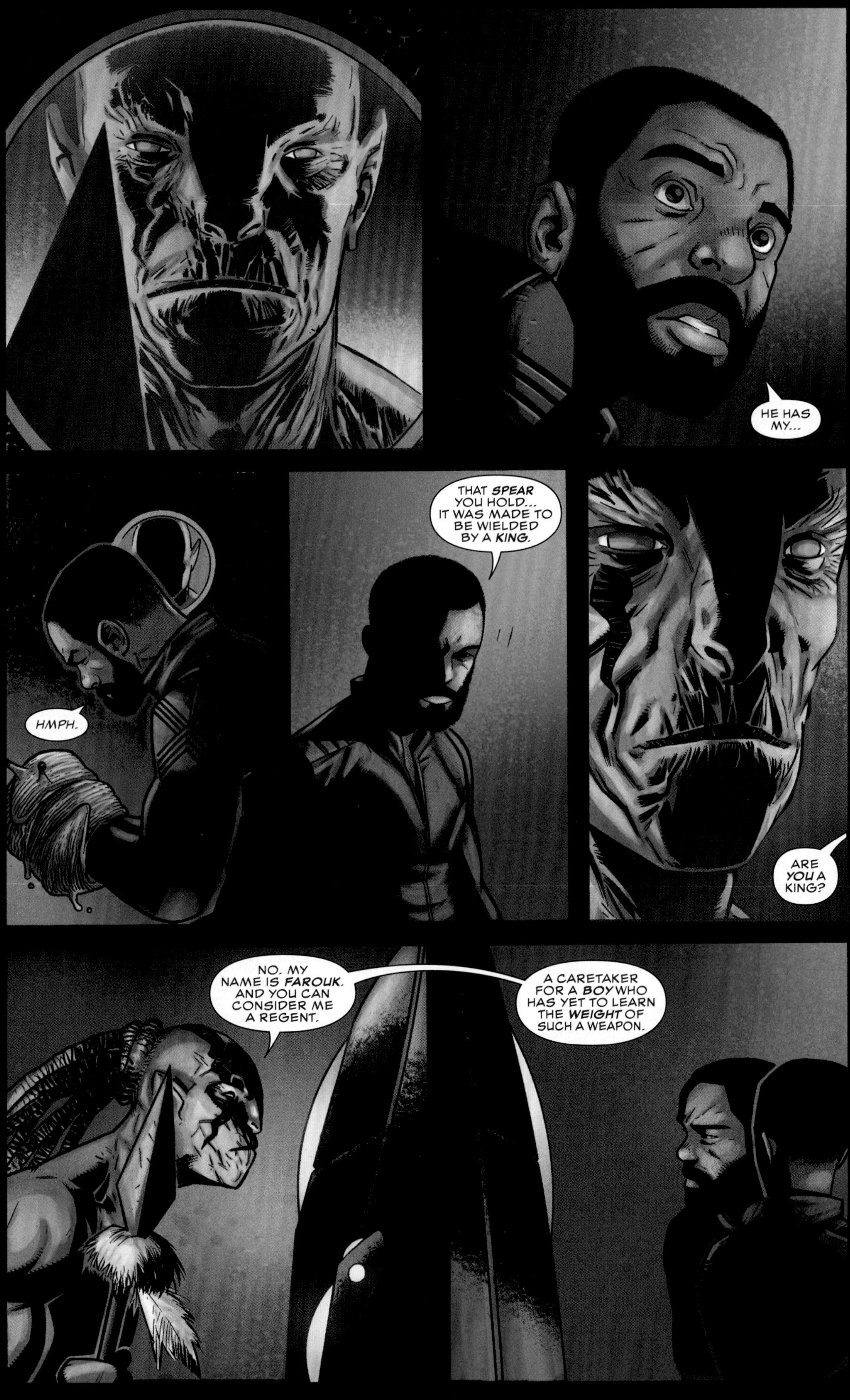
HE HAS MY...
THAT SPEAR YOU HOLD... IT WAS MADE TO BE WIELDED BY A KING.
HMPH.
ARE YOU A KING?
NO. MY NAME IS FAROUK. AND YOU CAN CONSIDER ME A REGENT.
A CARETAKER FOR A BOY WHO HAS YET TO LEARN THE WEIGHT OF SUCH A WEAPON.

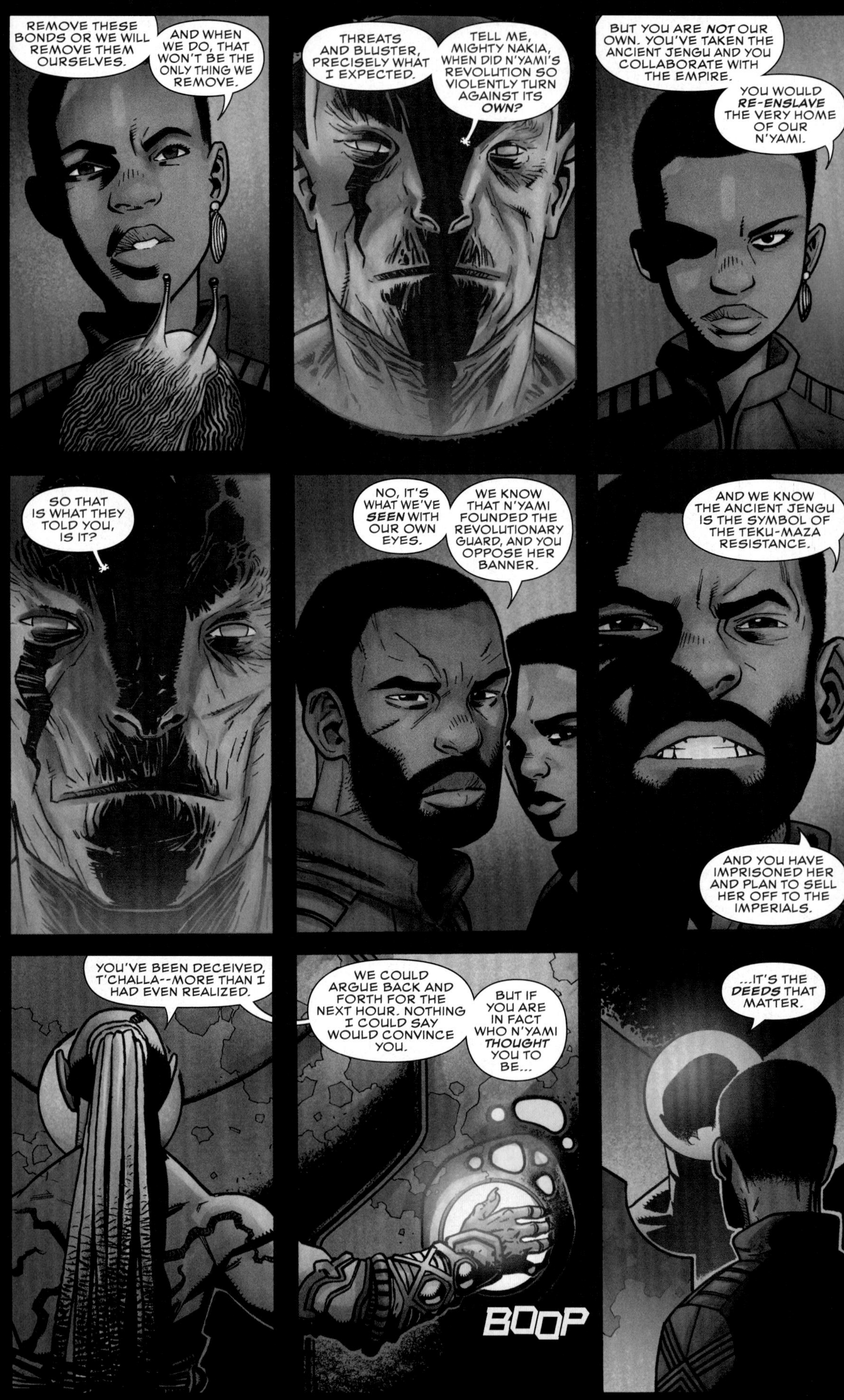
REMOVE THESE BONDS OR WE WILL REMOVE THEM OURSELVES.
AND WHEN WE DO, THAT WON'T BE THE ONLY THING WE REMOVE.
THREATS AND BLUSTER, PRECISELY WHAT I EXPECTED.
TELL ME, MIGHTY NAKIA, WHEN DID N'YAMI'S REVOLUTION SO VIOLENTLY TURN AGAINST ITS OWN?
BUT YOU ARE NOT OUR OWN. YOU'VE TAKEN THE ANCIENT JENGU AND YOU COLLABORATE WITH THE EMPIRE.
YOU WOULD RE-ENSLAVE THE VERY HOME OF OUR N'YAMI.
SO THAT IS WHAT THEY TOLD YOU, IS IT?
NO, IT'S WHAT WE'VE SEEN WITH OUR OWN EYES.
WE KNOW THAT N'YAMI FOUNDED THE REVOLUTIONARY GUARD, AND YOU OPPOSE HER BANNER.
AND WE KNOW THE ANCIENT JENGU IS THE SYMBOL OF THE TEKU-MAZA RESISTANCE.
AND YOU HAVE IMPRISONED HER AND PLAN TO SELL HER OFF TO THE IMPERIALS.
YOU'VE BEEN DECEIVED, T'CHALLA--MORE THAN I HAD EVEN REALIZED.
WE COULD ARGUE BACK AND FORTH FOR THE NEXT HOUR. NOTHING I COULD SAY WOULD CONVINCE YOU.
BUT IF YOU ARE IN FACT WHO N'YAMI THOUGHT YOU TO BE...
BOOP
...IT'S THE DEEDS THAT MATTER.

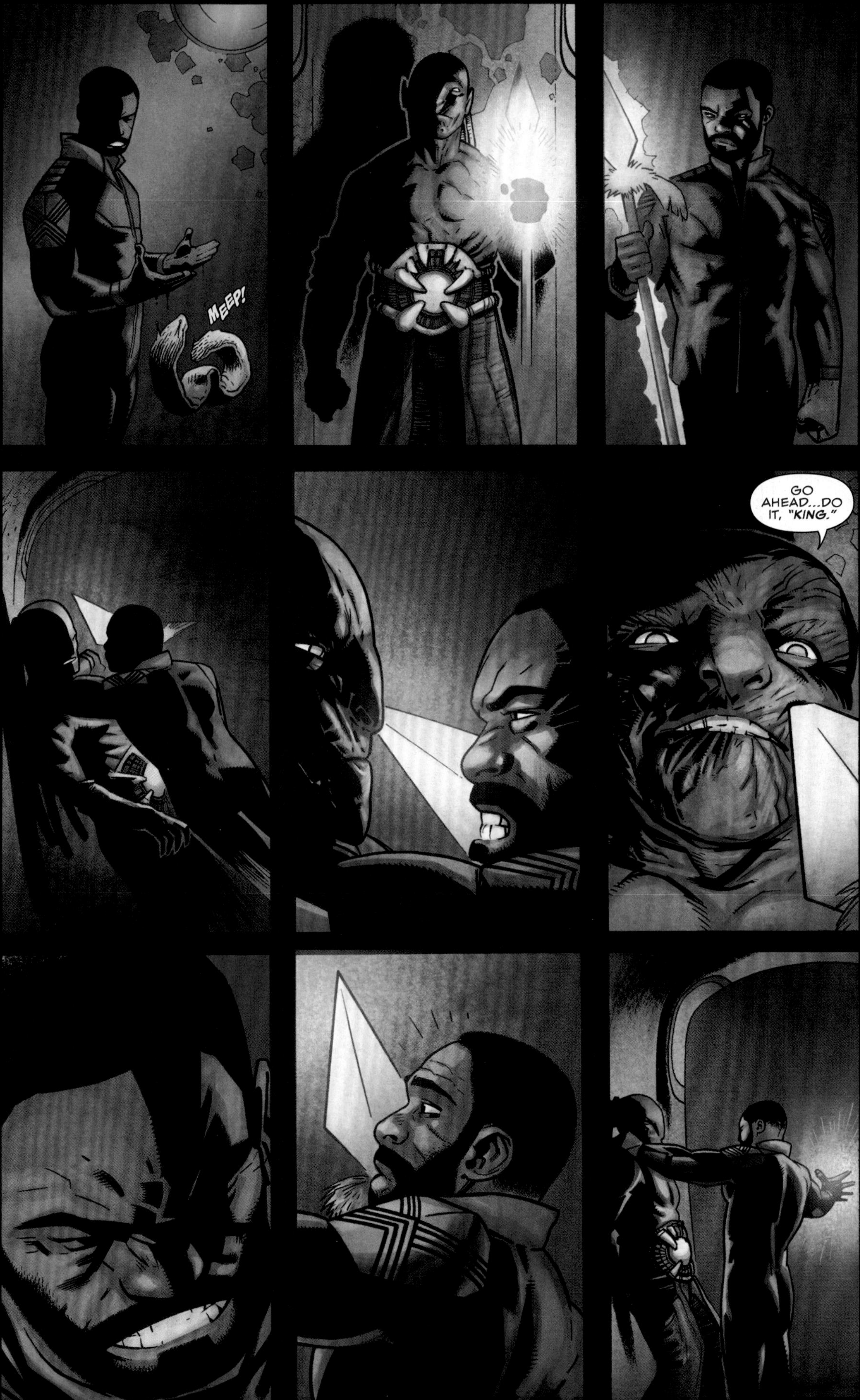
MEEP!
GO AHEAD...DO IT, "KING."

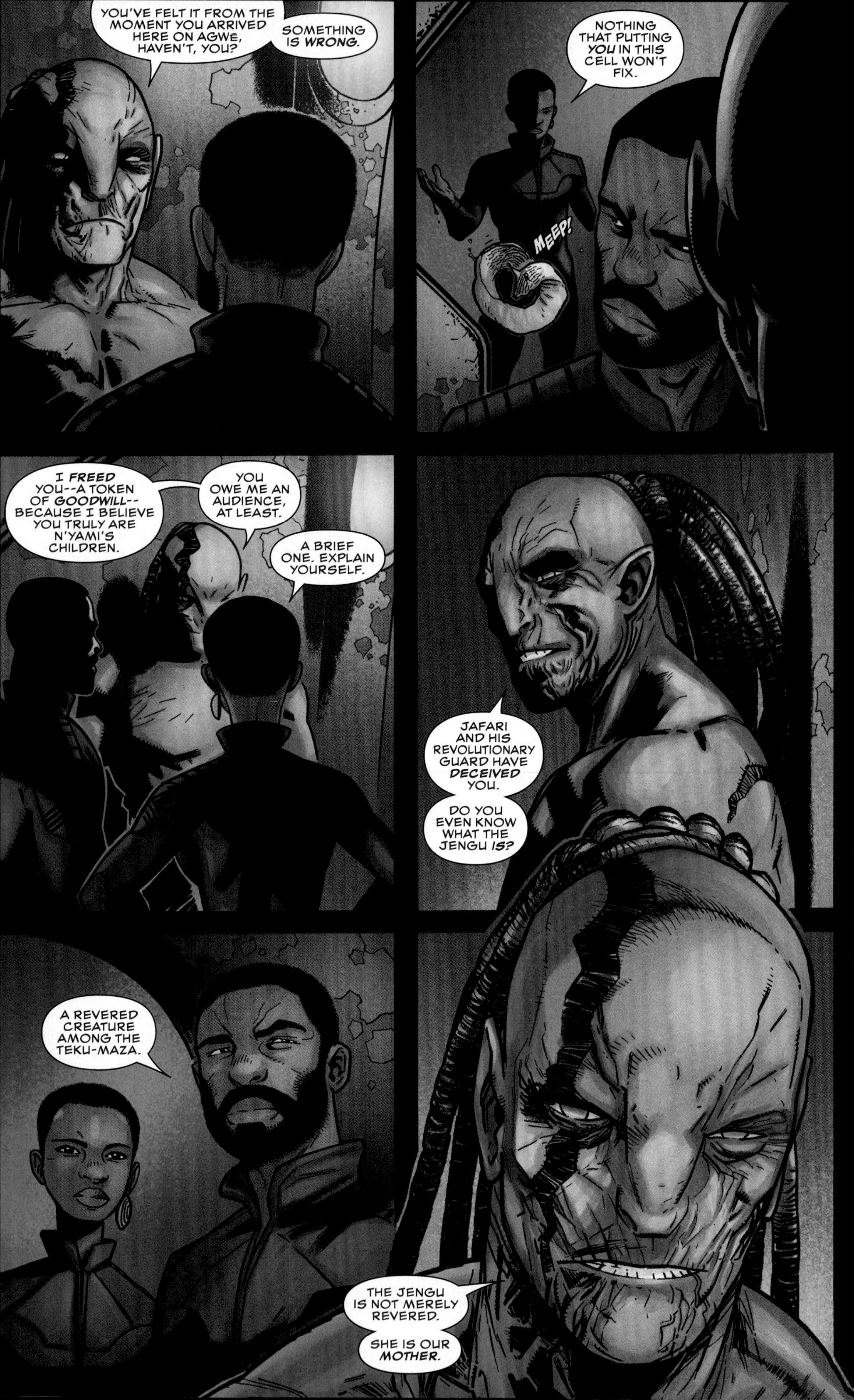

YOU'VE FELT IT FROM THE MOMENT YOU ARRIVED HERE ON AGWE, HAVEN'T, YOU?
SOMETHING IS WRONG.
NOTHING THAT PUTTING YOU IN THIS CELL WON'T FIX.
MEEP!
I FREED YOU--A TOKEN OF GOODWILL--BECAUSE I BELIEVE YOU TRULY ARE N'YAMI'S CHILDREN.
YOU OWE ME AN AUDIENCE, AT LEAST.
A BRIEF ONE. EXPLAIN YOURSELF.
JAFARI AND HIS REVOLUTIONARY GUARD HAVE DECEIVED YOU.
DO YOU EVEN KNOW WHAT THE JENGU IS?
A REVERED CREATURE AMONG THE TEKU-MAZA.
THE JENGU IS NOT MERELY REVERED.
SHE IS OUR MOTHER.

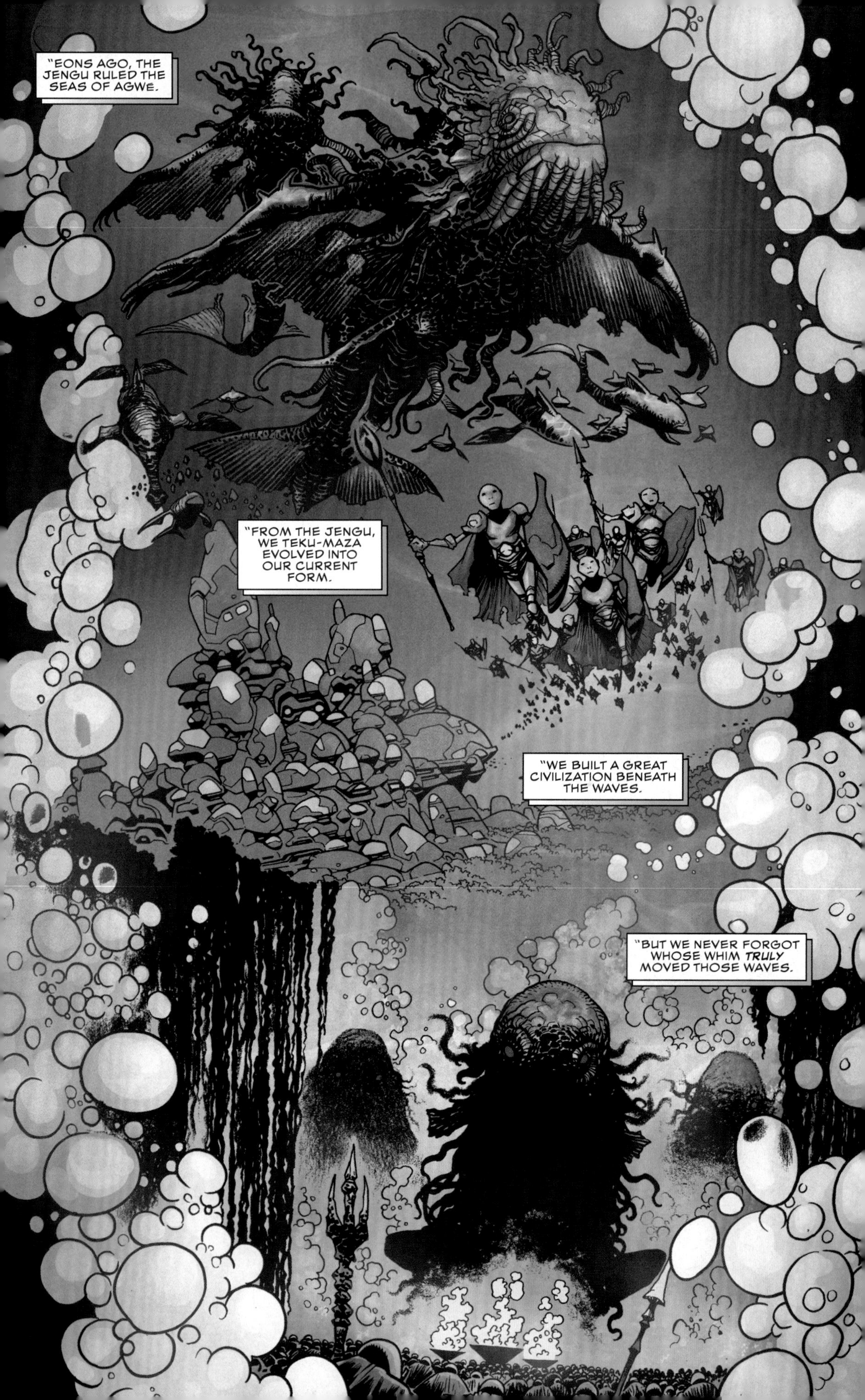
"EONS AGO, THE JENGU RULED THE SEAS OF AGWE.
"FROM THE JENGU, WE TEKU-MAZA EVOLVED INTO OUR CURRENT FORM.
"WE BUILT A GREAT CIVILIZATION BENEATH THE WAVES.
"BUT WE NEVER FORGOT WHOSE WHIM TRULY MOVED THOSE WAVES.

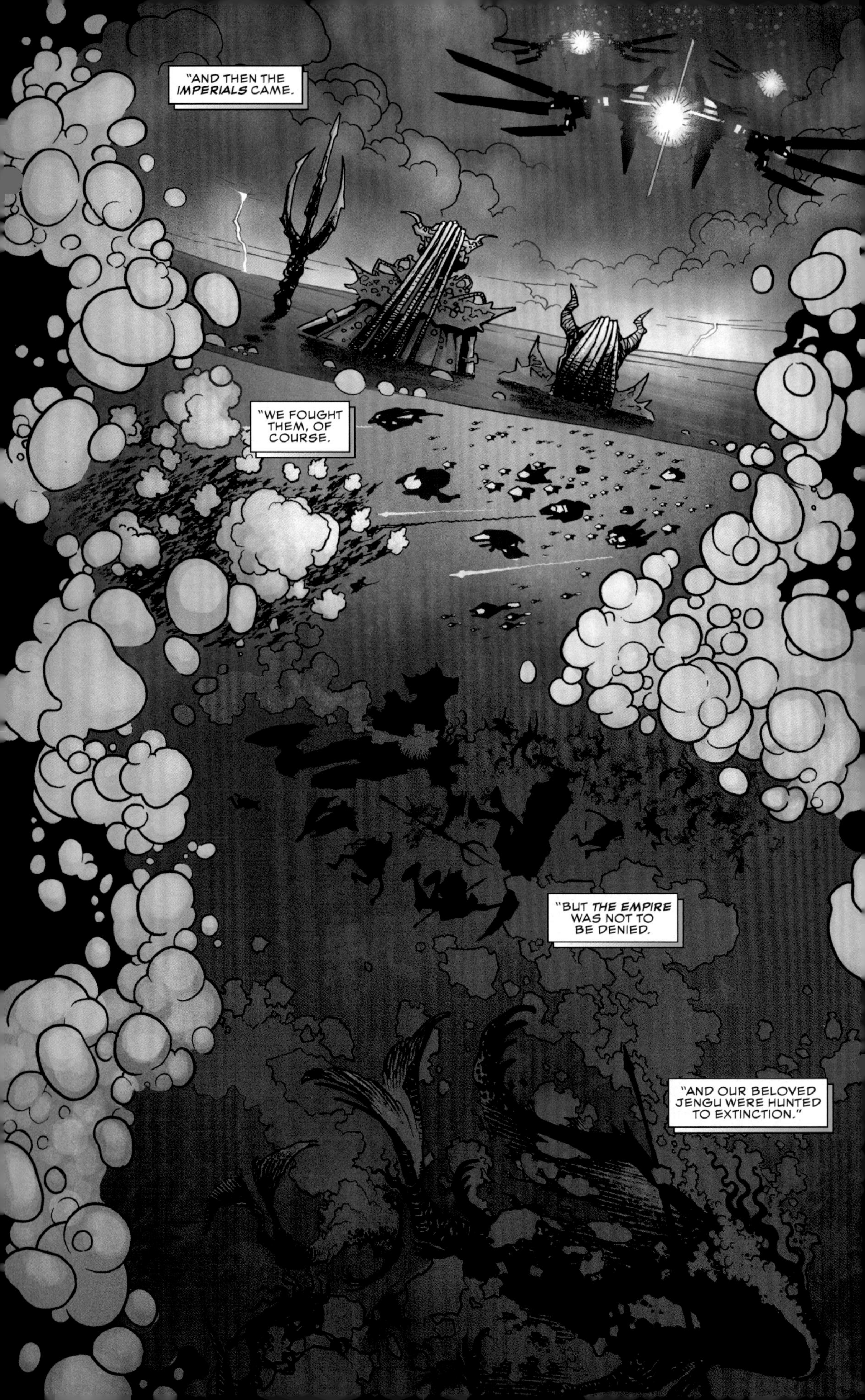
"AND THEN THE IMPERIALS CAME.
"WE FOUGHT THEM, OF COURSE.
"BUT THE EMPIRE WAS NOT TO BE DENIED.
"AND OUR BELOVED JENGU WERE HUNTED TO EXTINCTION."

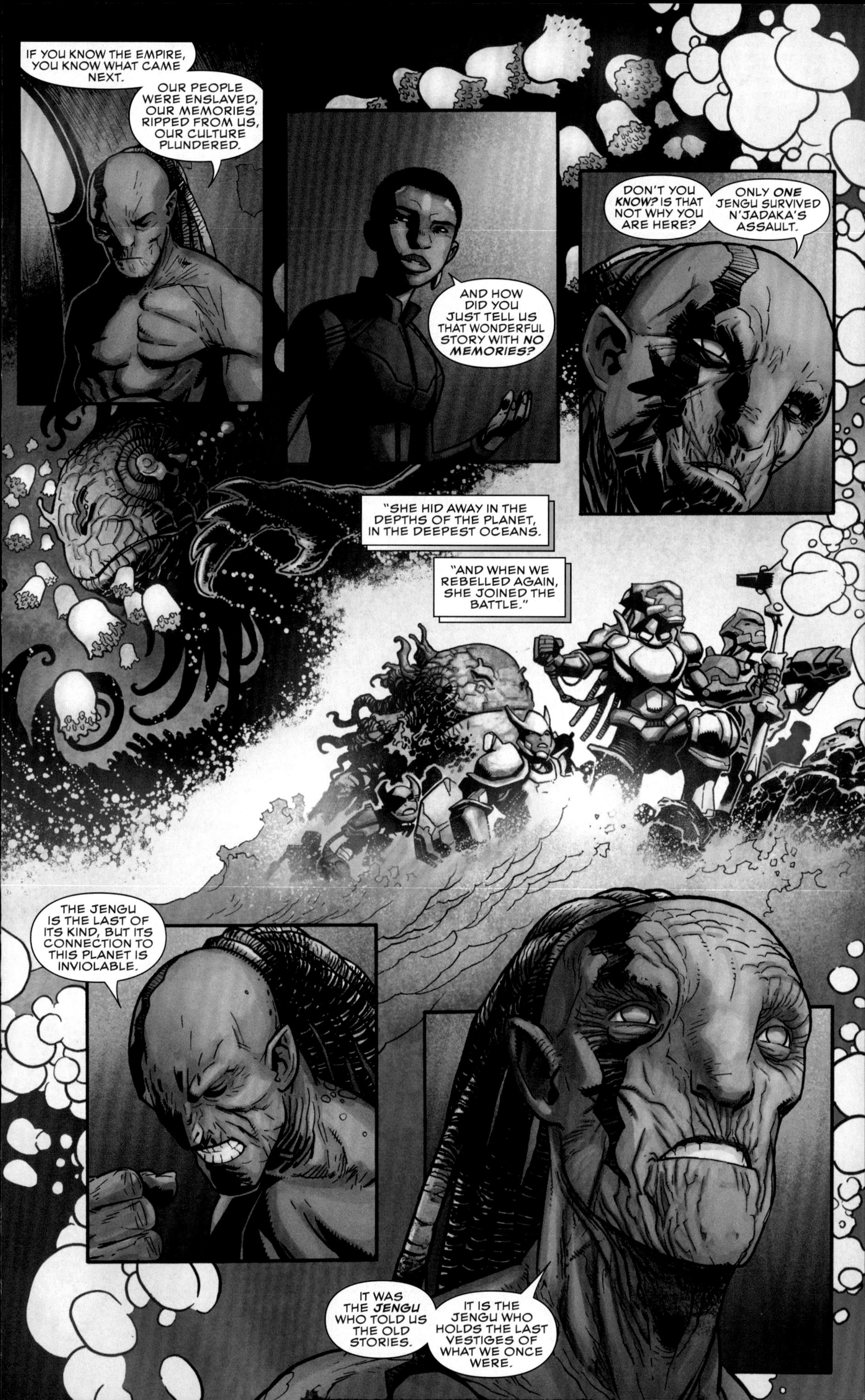
IF YOU KNOW THE EMPIRE, YOU KNOW WHAT CAME NEXT.
OUR PEOPLE WERE ENSLAVED, OUR MEMORIES RIPPED FROM US, OUR CULTURE PLUNDERED.
AND HOW DID YOU JUST TELL US THAT WONDERFUL STORY WITH NO MEMORIES?
DON'T YOU KNOW? IS THAT NOT WHY YOU ARE HERE?
ONLY ONE JENGU SURVIVED N'JADAKA'S ASSAULT.
"SHE HID AWAY IN THE DEPTHS OF THE PLANET, IN THE DEEPEST OCEANS.
"AND WHEN WE REBELLED AGAIN, SHE JOINED THE BATTLE."
THE JENGU IS THE LAST OF ITS KIND, BUT ITS CONNECTION TO THIS PLANET IS INVIOLABLE.
IT WAS THE JENGU WHO TOLD US THE OLD STORIES.
IT IS THE JENGU WHO HOLDS THE LAST VESTIGES OF WHAT WE ONCE WERE.

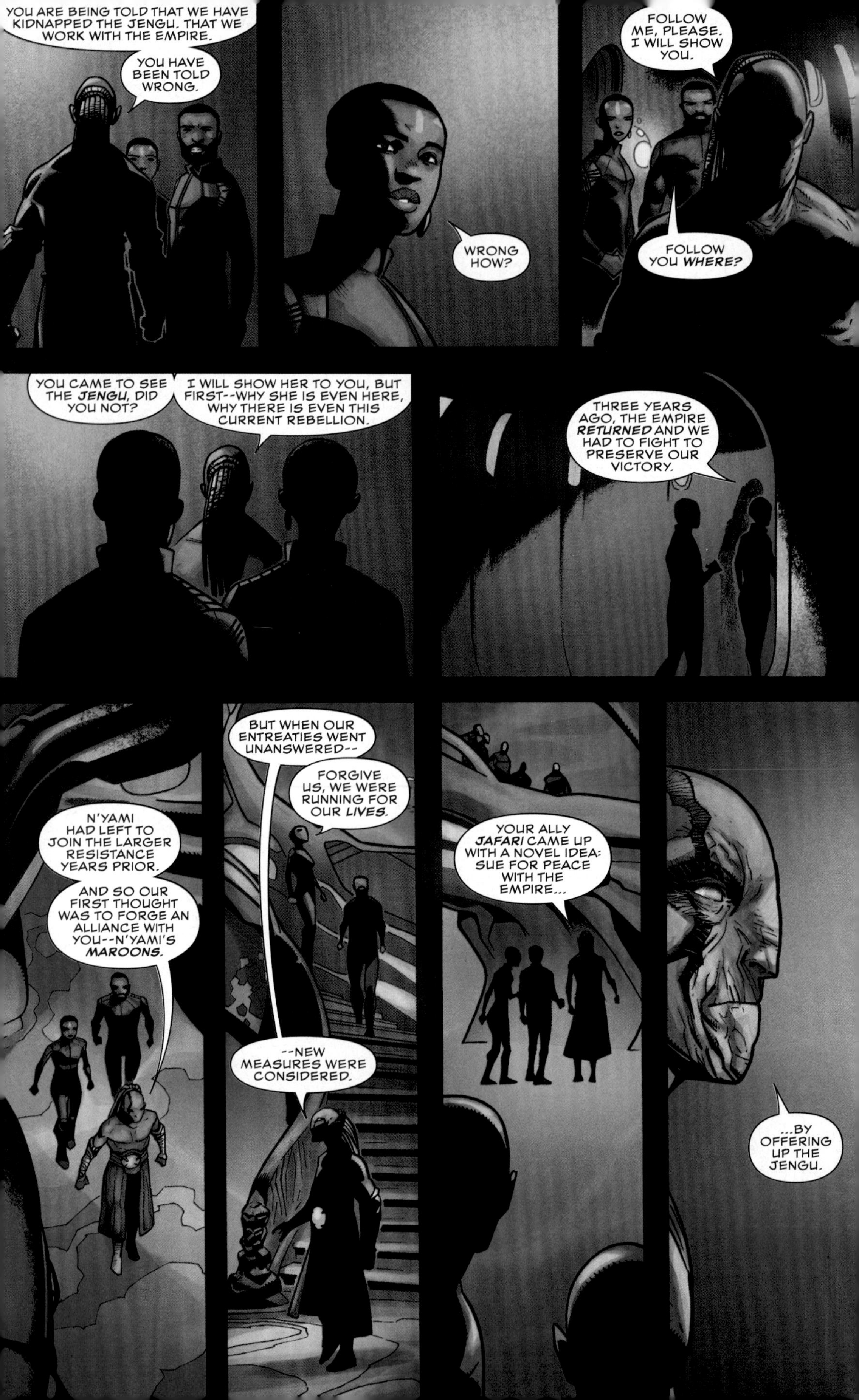
YOU ARE BEING TOLD THAT WE HAVE KIDNAPPED THE JENGU. THAT WE WORK WITH THE EMPIRE.
YOU HAVE BEEN TOLD WRONG.
WRONG HOW?
FOLLOW ME, PLEASE. I WILL SHOW YOU.
FOLLOW YOU *WHERE?*
YOU CAME TO SEE THE *JENGU*, DID YOU NOT?
I WILL SHOW HER TO YOU, BUT FIRST--WHY SHE IS EVEN HERE, WHY THERE IS EVEN THIS CURRENT REBELLION.
THREE YEARS AGO, THE EMPIRE *RETURNED* AND WE HAD TO FIGHT TO PRESERVE OUR VICTORY.
N'YAMI HAD LEFT TO JOIN THE LARGER RESISTANCE YEARS PRIOR.
AND SO OUR FIRST THOUGHT WAS TO FORGE AN ALLIANCE WITH YOU--N'YAMI'S *MAROONS.*
BUT WHEN OUR ENTREATIES WENT UNANSWERED--
FORGIVE US, WE WERE RUNNING FOR OUR *LIVES.*
--NEW MEASURES WERE CONSIDERED.
YOUR ALLY *JAFARI* CAME UP WITH A NOVEL IDEA: SUE FOR PEACE WITH THE EMPIRE...
...BY OFFERING UP THE JENGU.

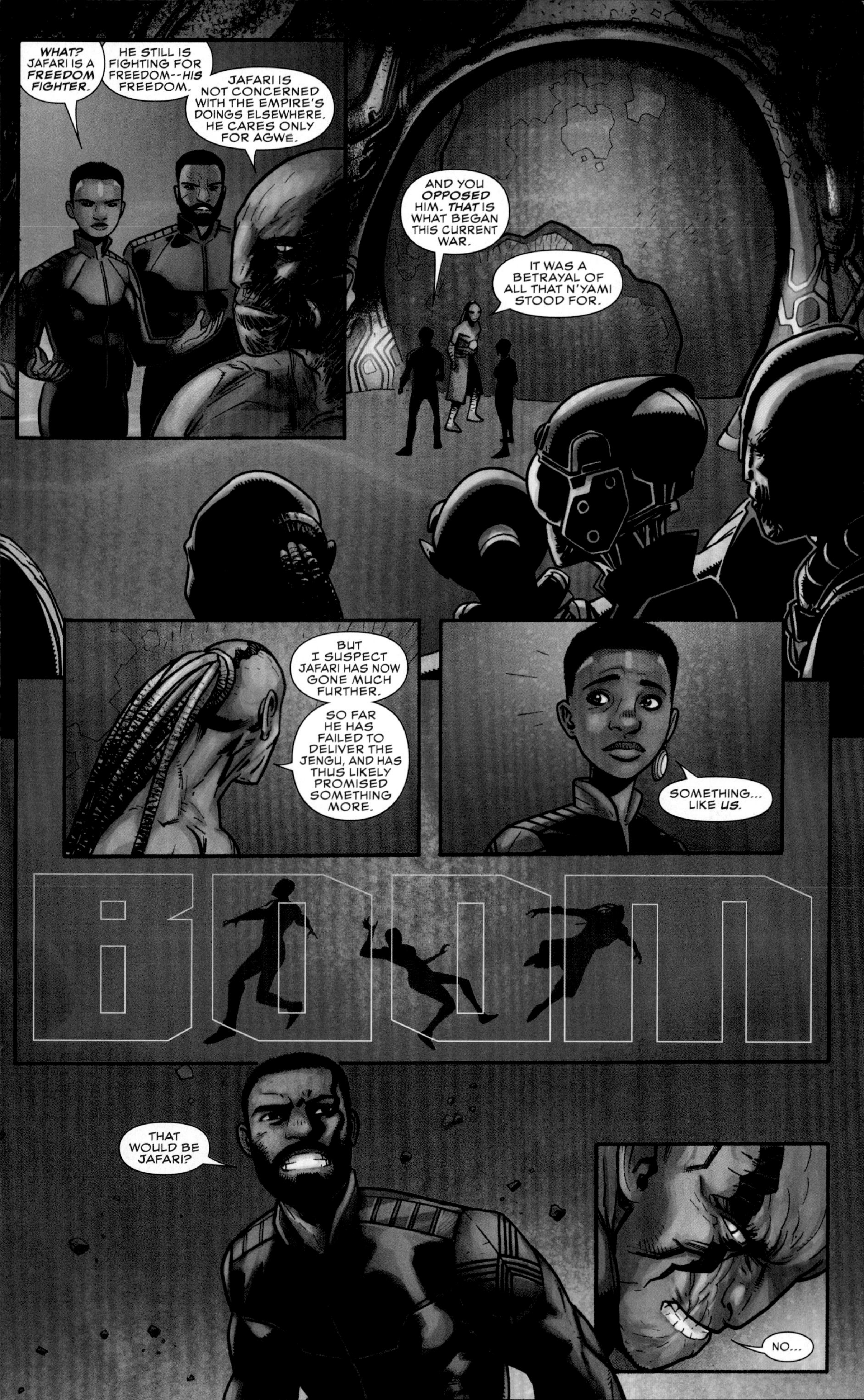
WHAT? JAFARI IS A FREEDOM FIGHTER.
HE STILL IS FIGHTING FOR FREEDOM--HIS FREEDOM.
JAFARI IS NOT CONCERNED WITH THE EMPIRE'S DOINGS ELSEWHERE. HE CARES ONLY FOR AGWE.
AND YOU OPPOSED HIM. THAT IS WHAT BEGAN THIS CURRENT WAR.
IT WAS A BETRAYAL OF ALL THAT N'YAMI STOOD FOR.
BUT I SUSPECT JAFARI HAS NOW GONE MUCH FURTHER.
SO FAR HE HAS FAILED TO DELIVER THE JENGU, AND HAS THUS LIKELY PROMISED SOMETHING MORE.
SOMETHING... LIKE US.
BOOM
THAT WOULD BE JAFARI?
NO...

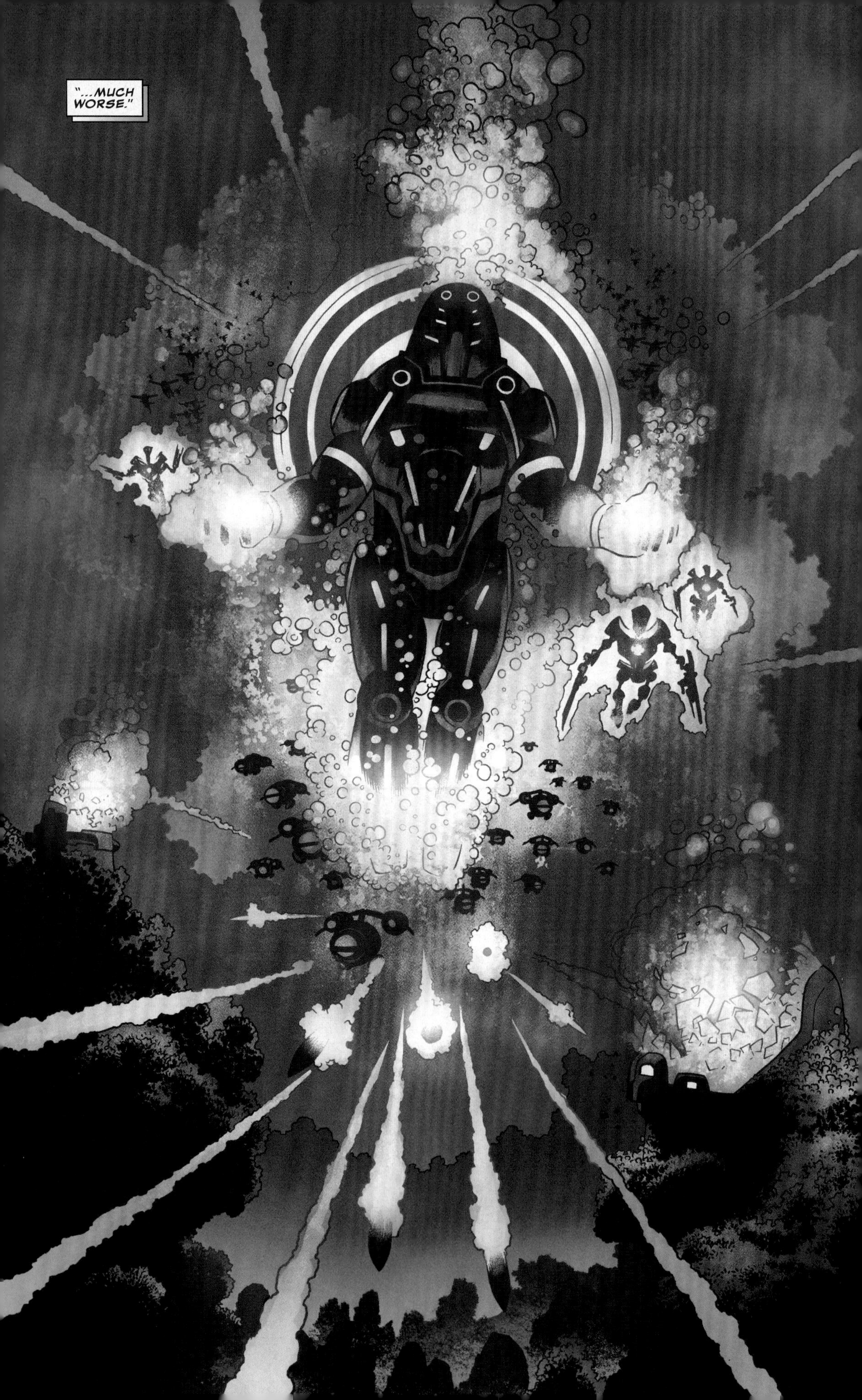
"...MUCH
WORSE."

THE INTERGALACTIC EMPIRE OF WAKANDA

OCCUPYING THE FAR REACHES OF THE UNIVERSE, THE INTERGALACTIC EMPIRE OF WAKANDA IS A SPRAWLING IMPERIUM MADE UP OF FIVE STAR CLUSTERS.

THE EARLY WAKANDAN SETTLERS OF THE BENHAZIN SYSTEM WERE INITIALLY PEACEFUL, PREFERRING TO REMAIN AMONG THEIR OWN, AS WAS THE WAY OF THEIR FOREFATHERS. BUT A SERIES OF ATTEMPTED INVASIONS CONVINCED THE SETTLERS THAT SELF-DEFENSE WOULD NOT BE ENOUGH FOR THIS BARBARIC PORTION OF SPACE--PREVENTIVE STRIKES MUST BE MADE. THEN, AFTER THE WAKANDANS MASTERED THE TECHNOLOGY OF DEEP-SPACE PASSAGE, THOSE PREVENTIVE STRIKES BECAME PREVENTIVE OCCUPATION AND FINALLY PREVENTIVE CONQUEST.

ARMED WITH SUPERIOR TECHNOLOGY AND A TYPICAL WAKANDAN FEROCITY IN BATTLE, THE CONQUERORS QUICKLY BECAME MASTERS OF THEIR CORNER OF THE UNIVERSE--AND THERE IS NO REASON TO BELIEVE THEY WILL SIMPLY SETTLE FOR THAT CORNER.

THIS ISSUE TAKES PLACE ON AGWÉ, A JOVIAN PLANET WHOSE MASS CONSISTS MOSTLY OF LIQUID AND IS HOME OF THE AMPHIBIOUS TEKU-MAZA. ONE OF THE EARLIEST PEOPLES TO BE INCORPORATED INTO THE WAKANDAN EMPIRE, THE TEKU-MAZA WERE ORIGINALLY AQUATIC, BUT AFTER CERTAIN GENETIC MODIFICATIONS, THEY BECAME AMPHIBIOUS.

FALLEN MAROON COMMANDER N'YAMI WAS A TEKU-MAZA. N'YAMI WAS BORN OFF-WORLD-- AWAY FROM AGWÉ--AND HAD HER MEMORIES STRIPPED BY THE EMPIRE. THOUGH SHE NEVER RECOVERED HER OWN MEMORIES, SHE BELIEVED THE KEY TO THE PROCESS LAY ON AGWÉ. AFTER JOINING THE MAROONS, N'YAMI EVENTUALLY RETURNED TO HER ANCESTRAL HOME, WHERE SHE FOUNDED AND LED THE REVOLUTIONARY GUARD IN A SUCCESSFUL STRUGGLE THAT LIBERATED THE PLANET. SHE THEN REJOINED THE MAIN BRANCH OF THE MAROONS AND ROSE IN THE RANKS TO BECOME COMMANDER--UNTIL SHE WAS KILLED BY THE MANIFOLD WHEN THE EMPIRE DISCOVERED THE MAROONS' MAIN BASE AND DESTROYED IT, SETTING THE REBELLION BACK YEARS.

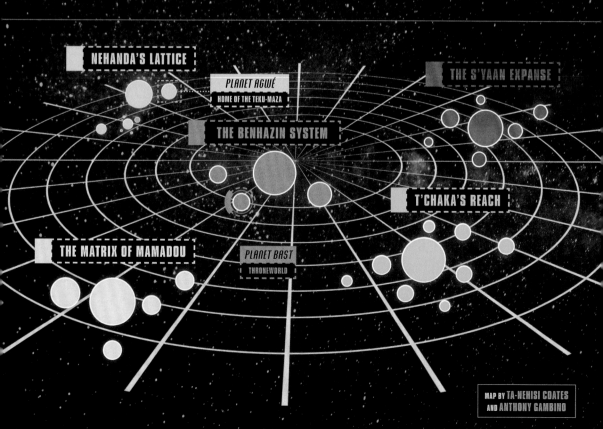

NEHANDA'S LATTICE

PLANET AGWÉ
HOME OF THE TEKU-MAZA

THE S'YAAN EXPANSE

THE BENHAZIN SYSTEM

T'CHAKA'S REACH

THE MATRIX OF MAMADOU

PLANET BAST
THRONEWORLD

MAP BY TA-NEHISI COATES AND ANTHONY GAMBINO

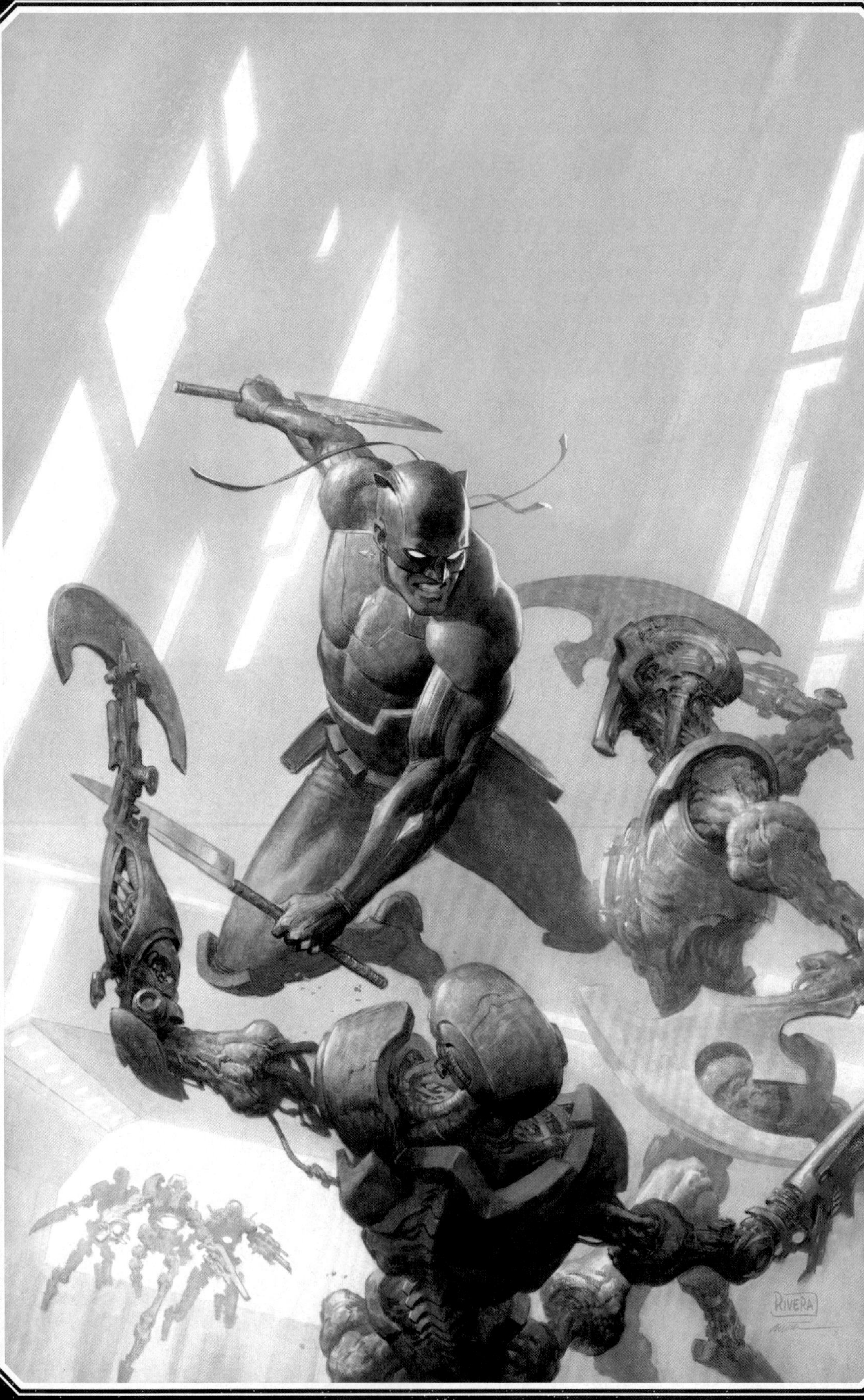
RIVERA

10

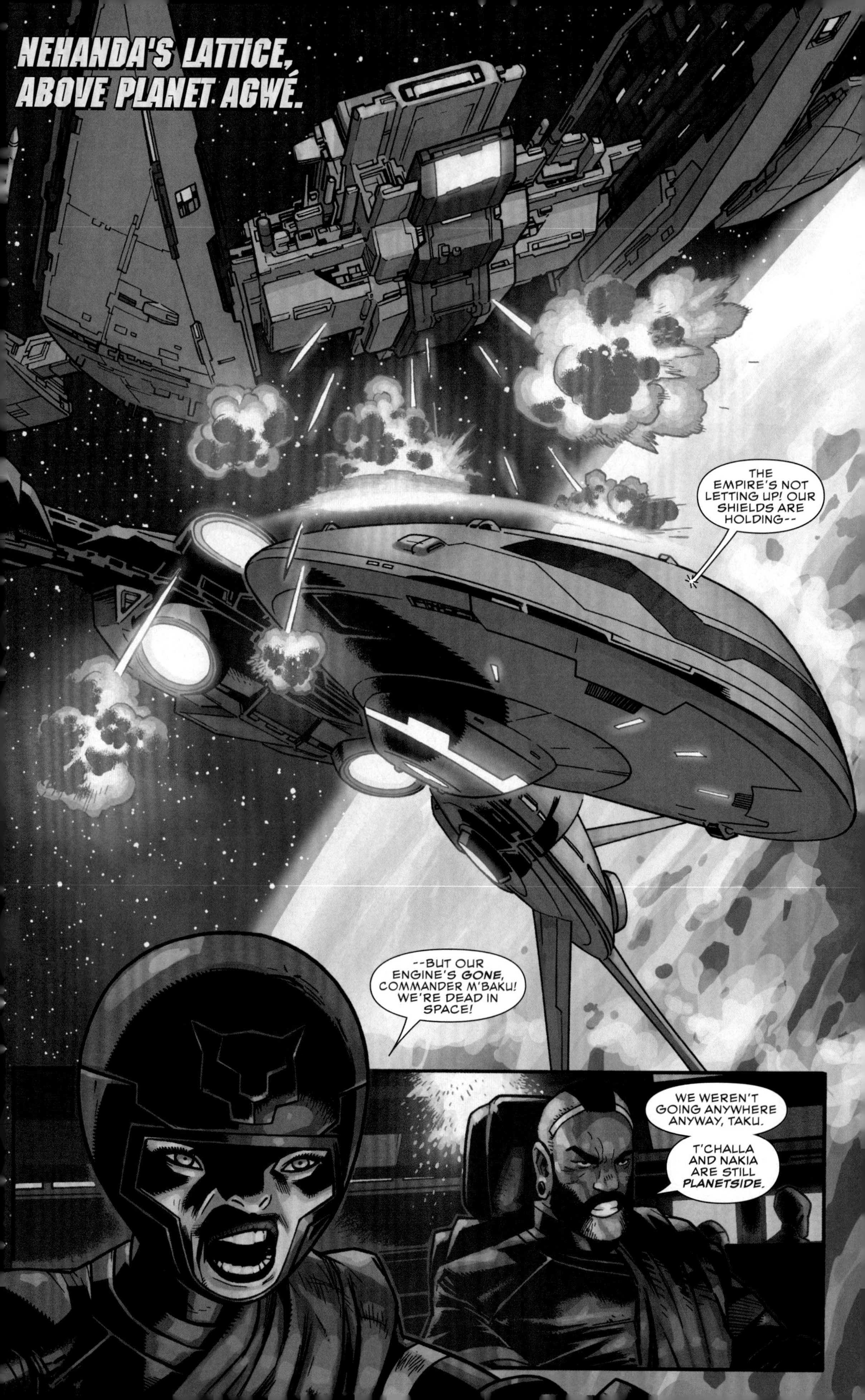
NEHANDA'S LATTICE, ABOVE PLANET AGWÉ.
THE EMPIRE'S NOT LETTING UP! OUR SHIELDS ARE HOLDING--
--BUT OUR ENGINE'S GONE, COMMANDER M'BAKU! WE'RE DEAD IN SPACE!
WE WEREN'T GOING ANYWHERE ANYWAY, TAKU.
T'CHALLA AND NAKIA ARE STILL PLANETSIDE.

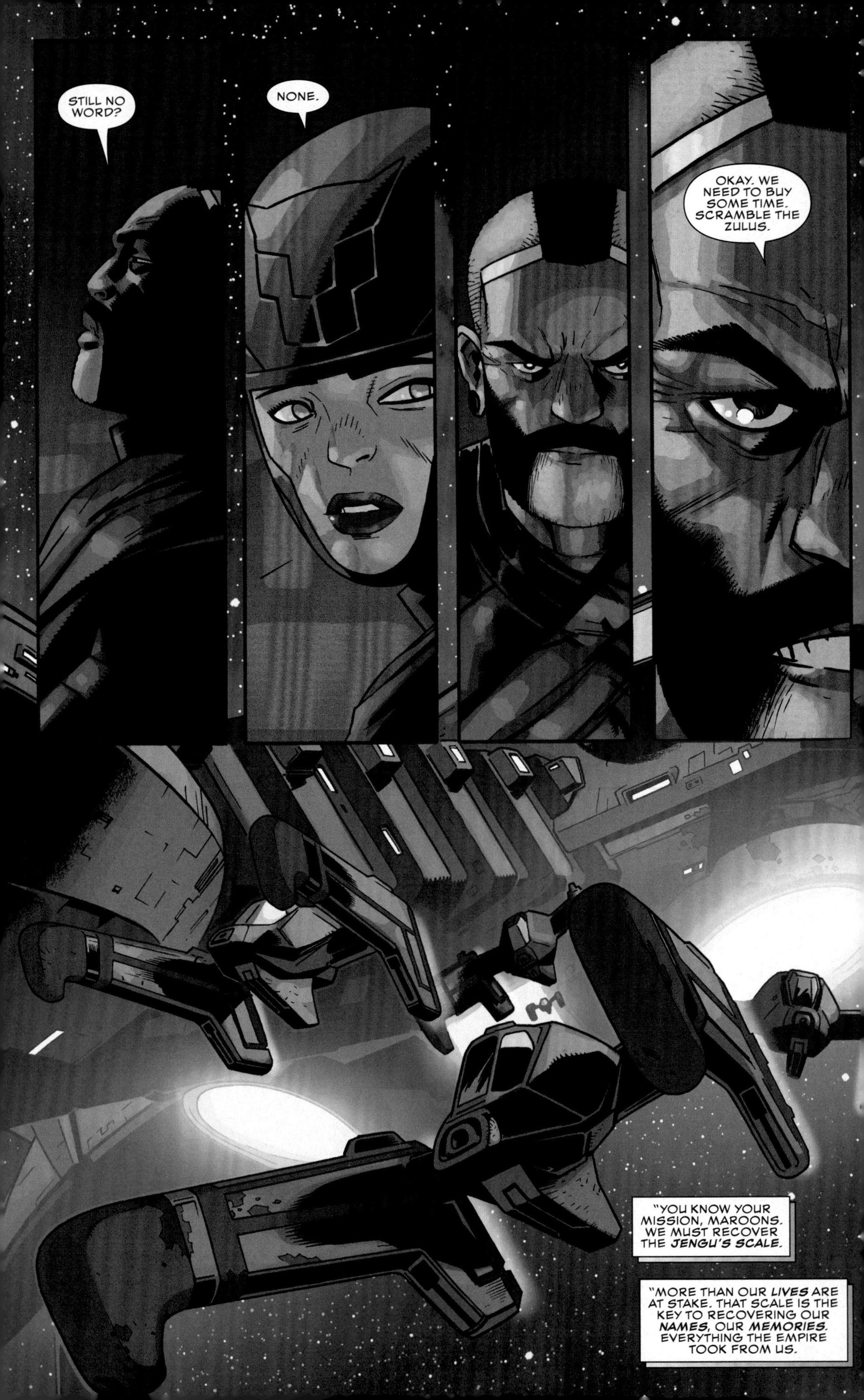
STILL NO WORD?
NONE.
OKAY. WE NEED TO BUY SOME TIME. SCRAMBLE THE ZULUS.
"YOU KNOW YOUR MISSION, MAROONS. WE MUST RECOVER THE JENGU'S SCALE.
"MORE THAN OUR LIVES ARE AT STAKE. THAT SCALE IS THE KEY TO RECOVERING OUR NAMES, OUR MEMORIES. EVERYTHING THE EMPIRE TOOK FROM US.

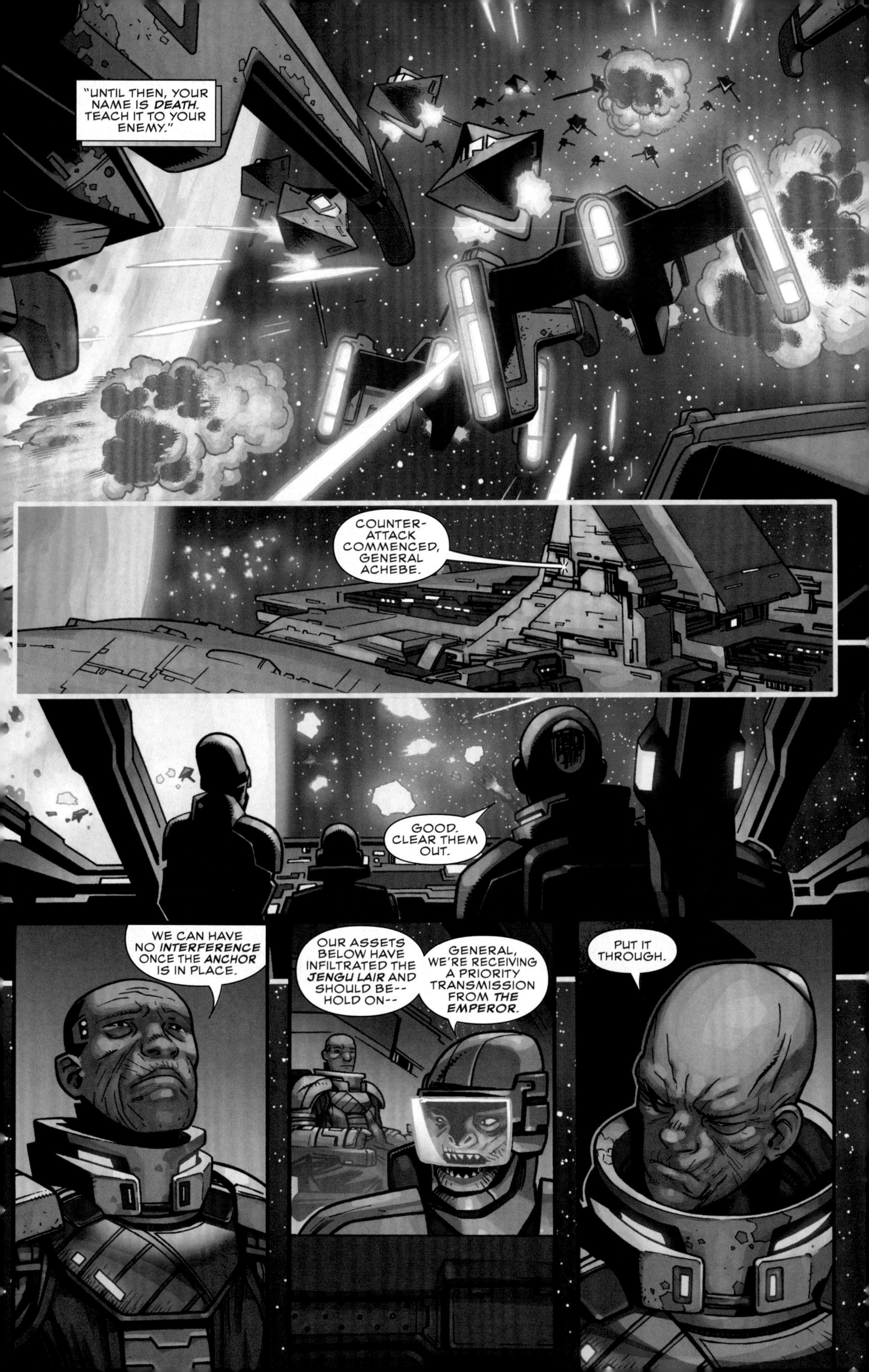
"UNTIL THEN, YOUR NAME IS *DEATH*. TEACH IT TO YOUR ENEMY."
COUNTER-ATTACK COMMENCED, GENERAL ACHEBE.
GOOD. CLEAR THEM OUT.
WE CAN HAVE NO *INTERFERENCE* ONCE THE *ANCHOR* IS IN PLACE.
OUR ASSETS BELOW HAVE INFILTRATED THE *JENGU LAIR* AND SHOULD BE-- HOLD ON--
GENERAL, WE'RE RECEIVING A PRIORITY TRANSMISSION FROM *THE EMPEROR*.
PUT IT THROUGH.

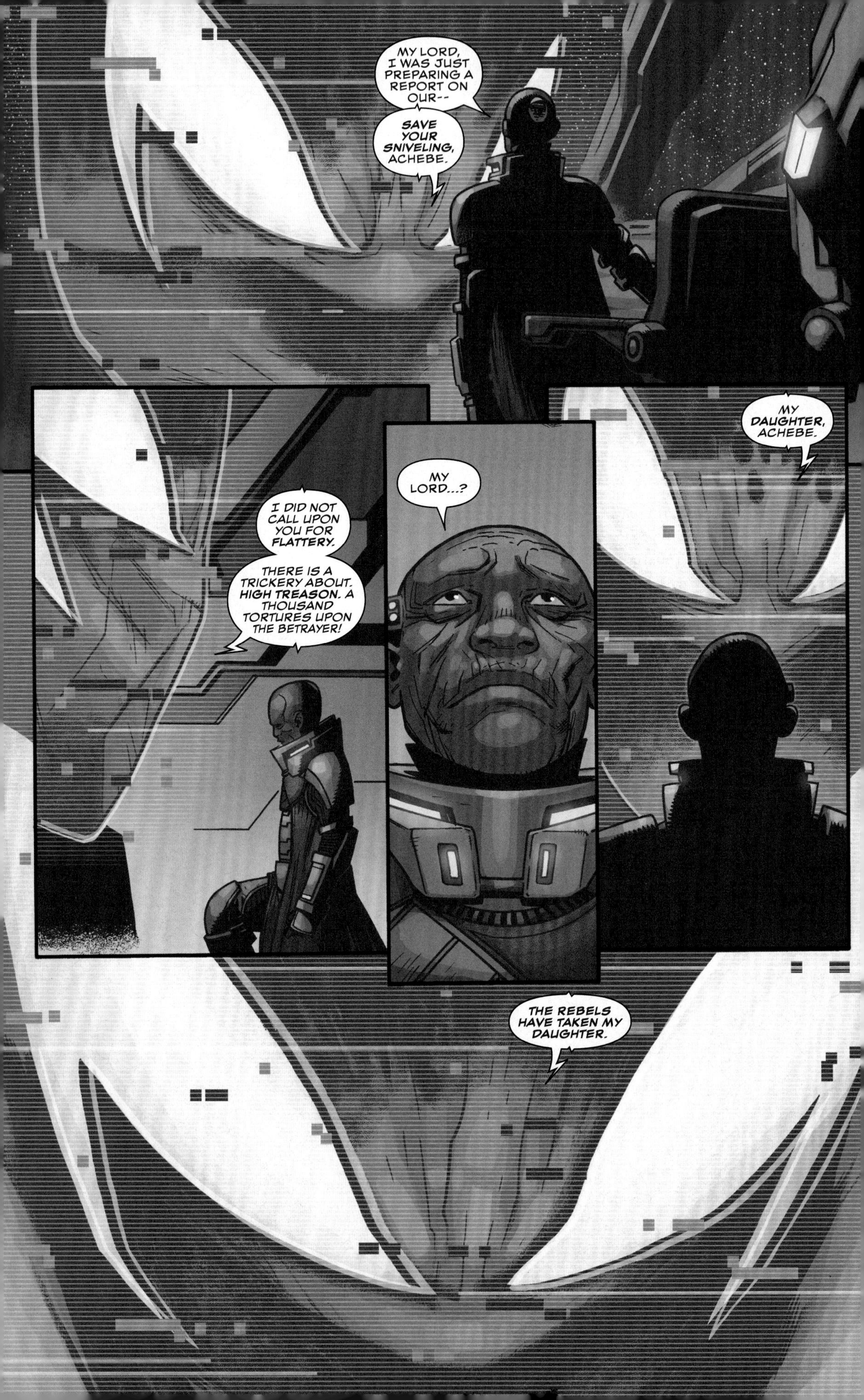
MY LORD, I WAS JUST PREPARING A REPORT ON OUR--
SAVE YOUR SNIVELING, ACHEBE.
I DID NOT CALL UPON YOU FOR FLATTERY.
THERE IS A TRICKERY ABOUT. HIGH TREASON. A THOUSAND TORTURES UPON THE BETRAYER!
MY LORD...?
MY DAUGHTER, ACHEBE.
THE REBELS HAVE TAKEN MY DAUGHTER.

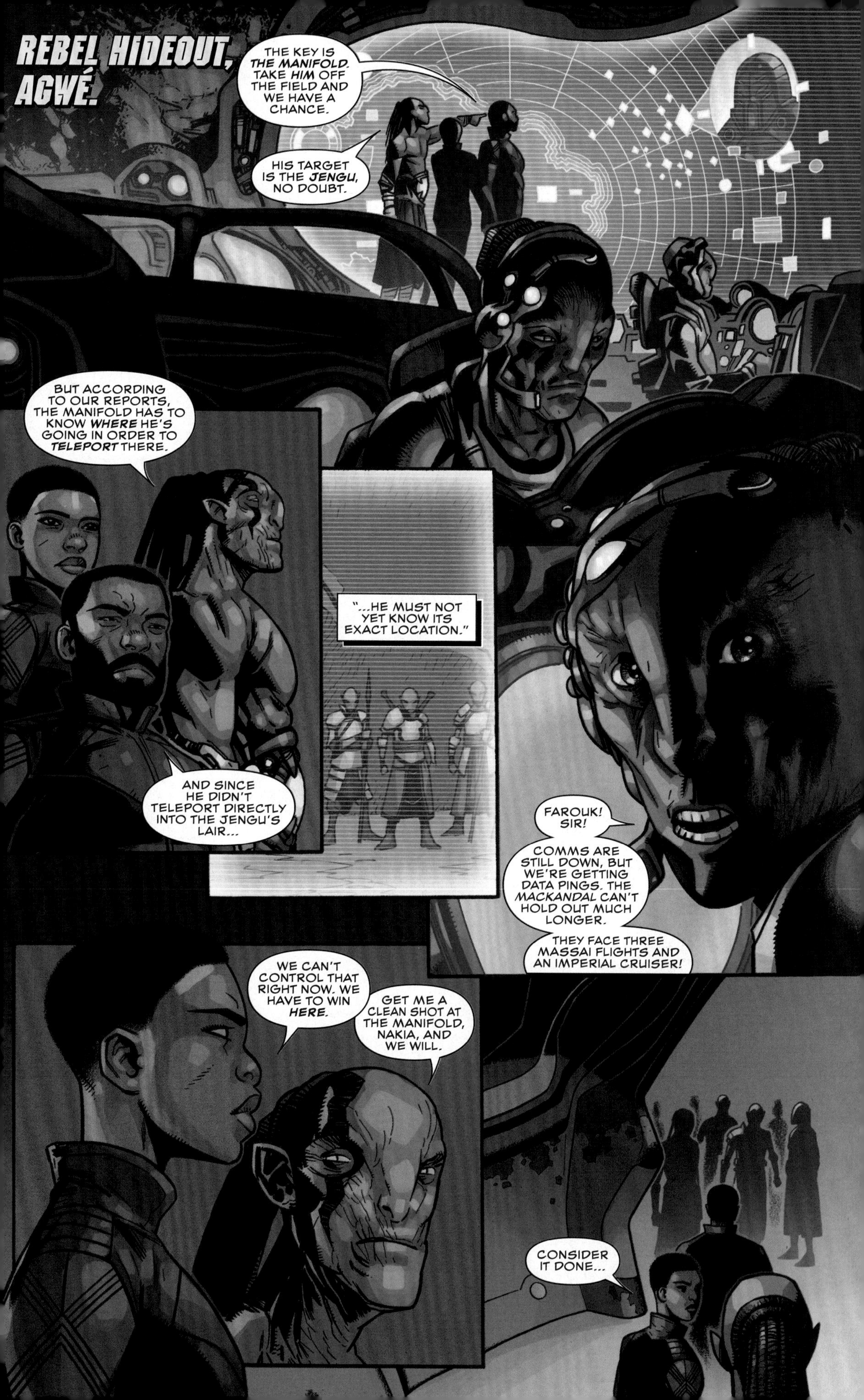
REBEL HIDEOUT, AGWÉ.
THE KEY IS THE MANIFOLD. TAKE HIM OFF THE FIELD AND WE HAVE A CHANCE.
HIS TARGET IS THE JENGU, NO DOUBT.
BUT ACCORDING TO OUR REPORTS, THE MANIFOLD HAS TO KNOW WHERE HE'S GOING IN ORDER TO TELEPORT THERE.
AND SINCE HE DIDN'T TELEPORT DIRECTLY INTO THE JENGU'S LAIR...
"...HE MUST NOT YET KNOW ITS EXACT LOCATION."
FAROUK! SIR!
COMMS ARE STILL DOWN, BUT WE'RE GETTING DATA PINGS. THE MACKANDAL CAN'T HOLD OUT MUCH LONGER.
THEY FACE THREE MASSAI FLIGHTS AND AN IMPERIAL CRUISER!
WE CAN'T CONTROL THAT RIGHT NOW. WE HAVE TO WIN HERE.
GET ME A CLEAN SHOT AT THE MANIFOLD, NAKIA, AND WE WILL.
CONSIDER IT DONE...

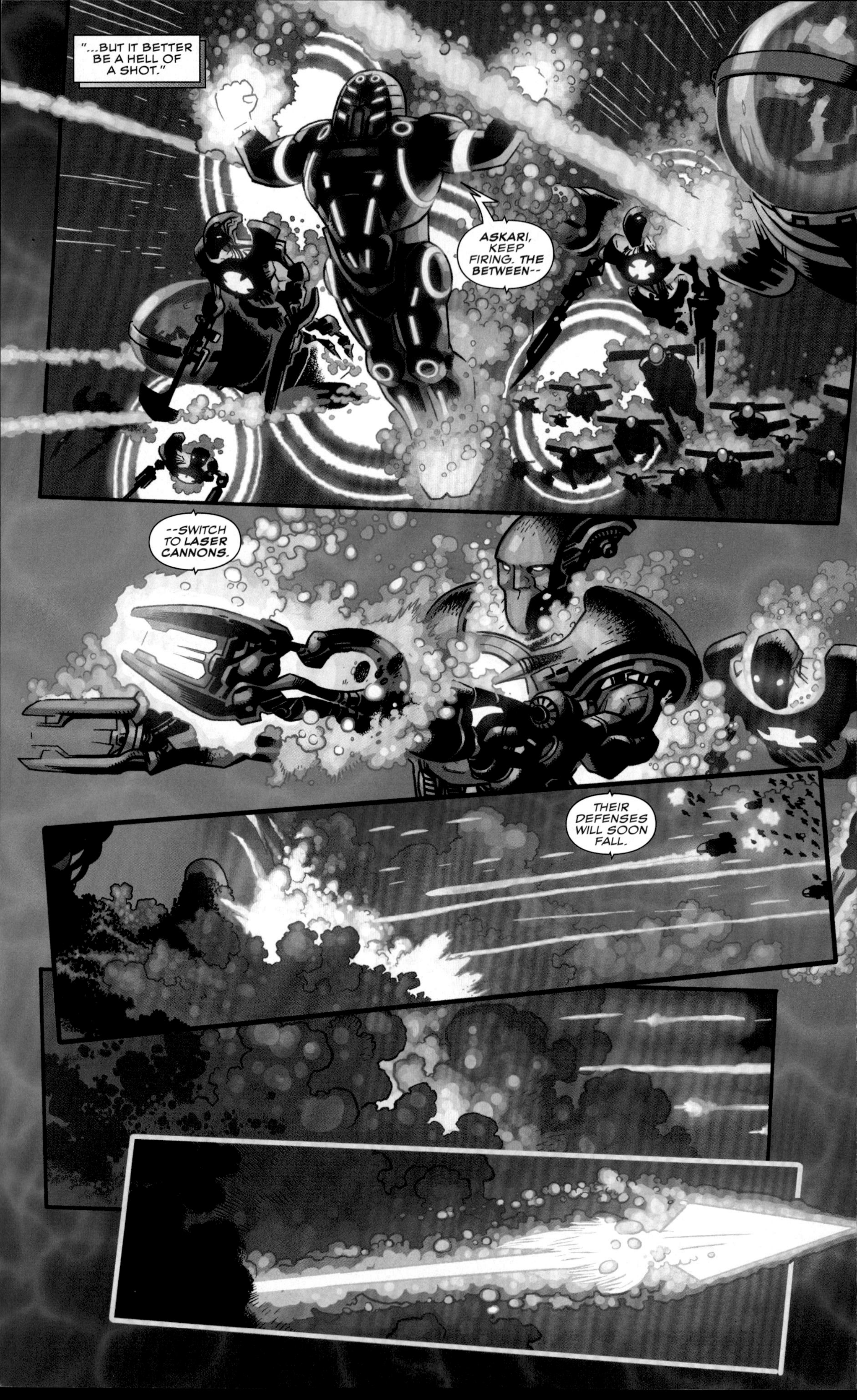
"...BUT IT BETTER BE A HELL OF A SHOT."
ASKARI, KEEP FIRING. THE BETWEEN--
--SWITCH TO LASER CANNONS.
THEIR DEFENSES WILL SOON FALL.

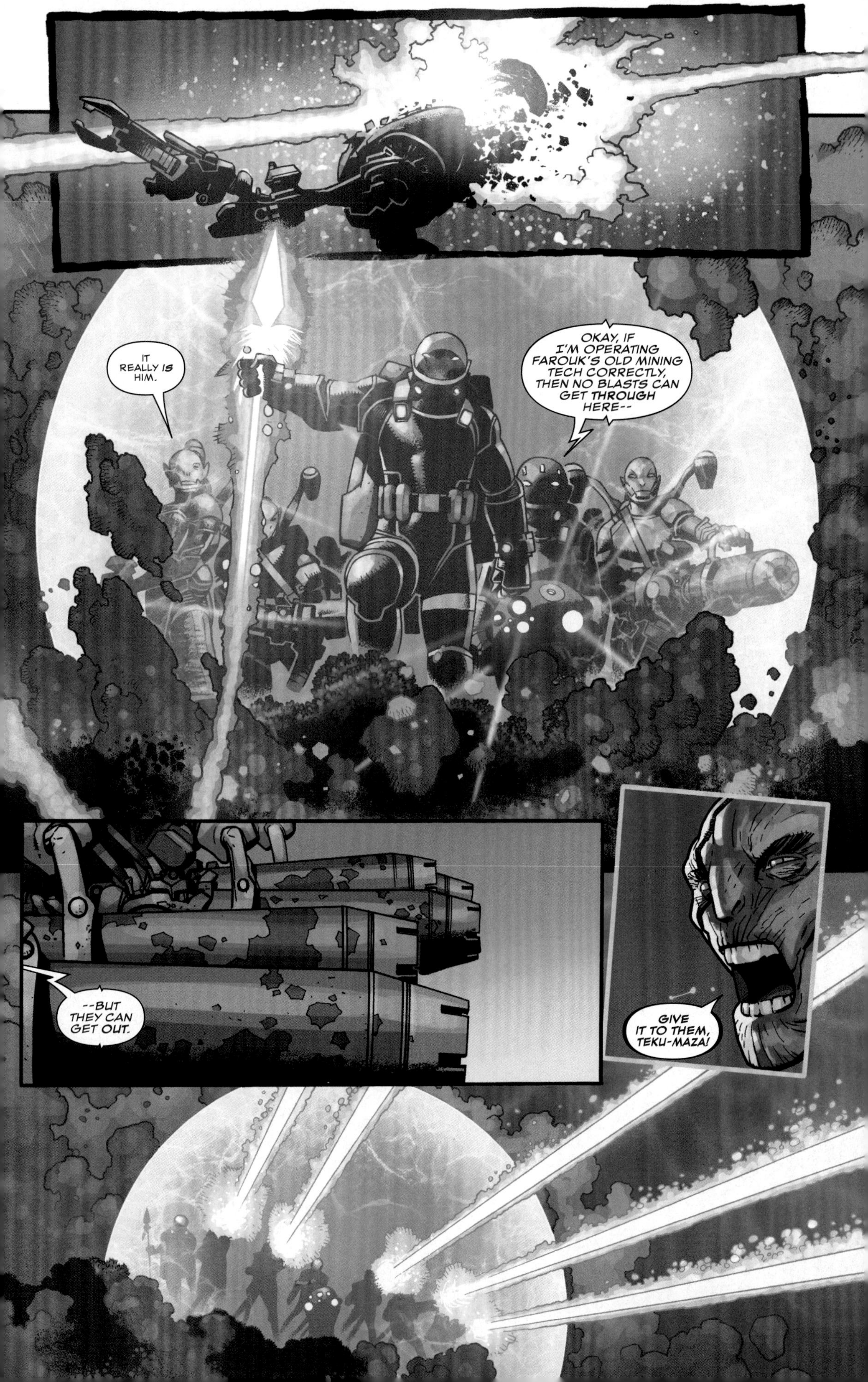
IT REALLY IS HIM.
OKAY, IF I'M OPERATING FAROUK'S OLD MINING TECH CORRECTLY, THEN NO BLASTS CAN GET THROUGH HERE--
--BUT THEY CAN GET OUT.
GIVE IT TO THEM, TEKU-MAZA!

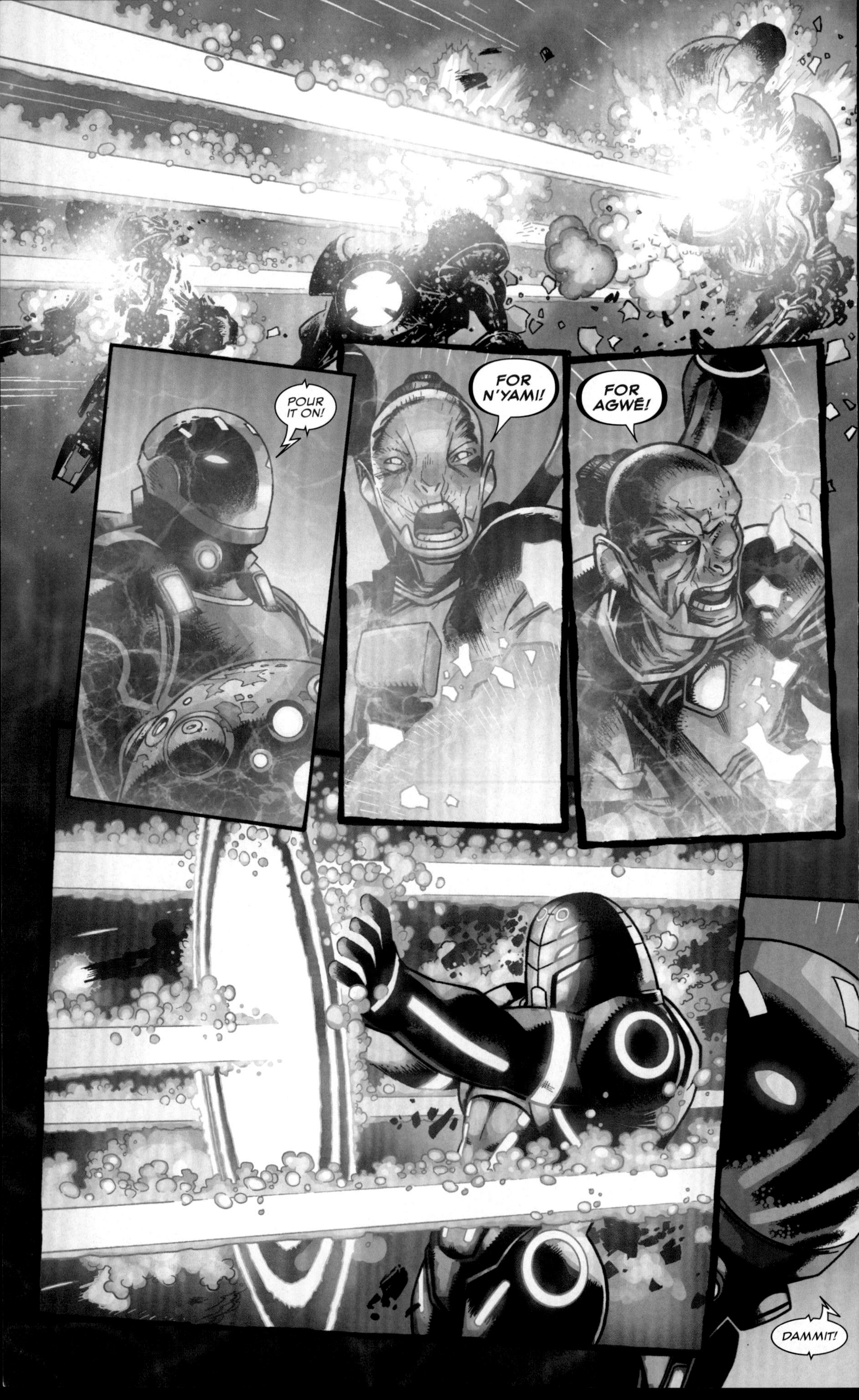

POUR IT ON!
FOR N'YAMI!
FOR AGWÉ!
DAMMIT!

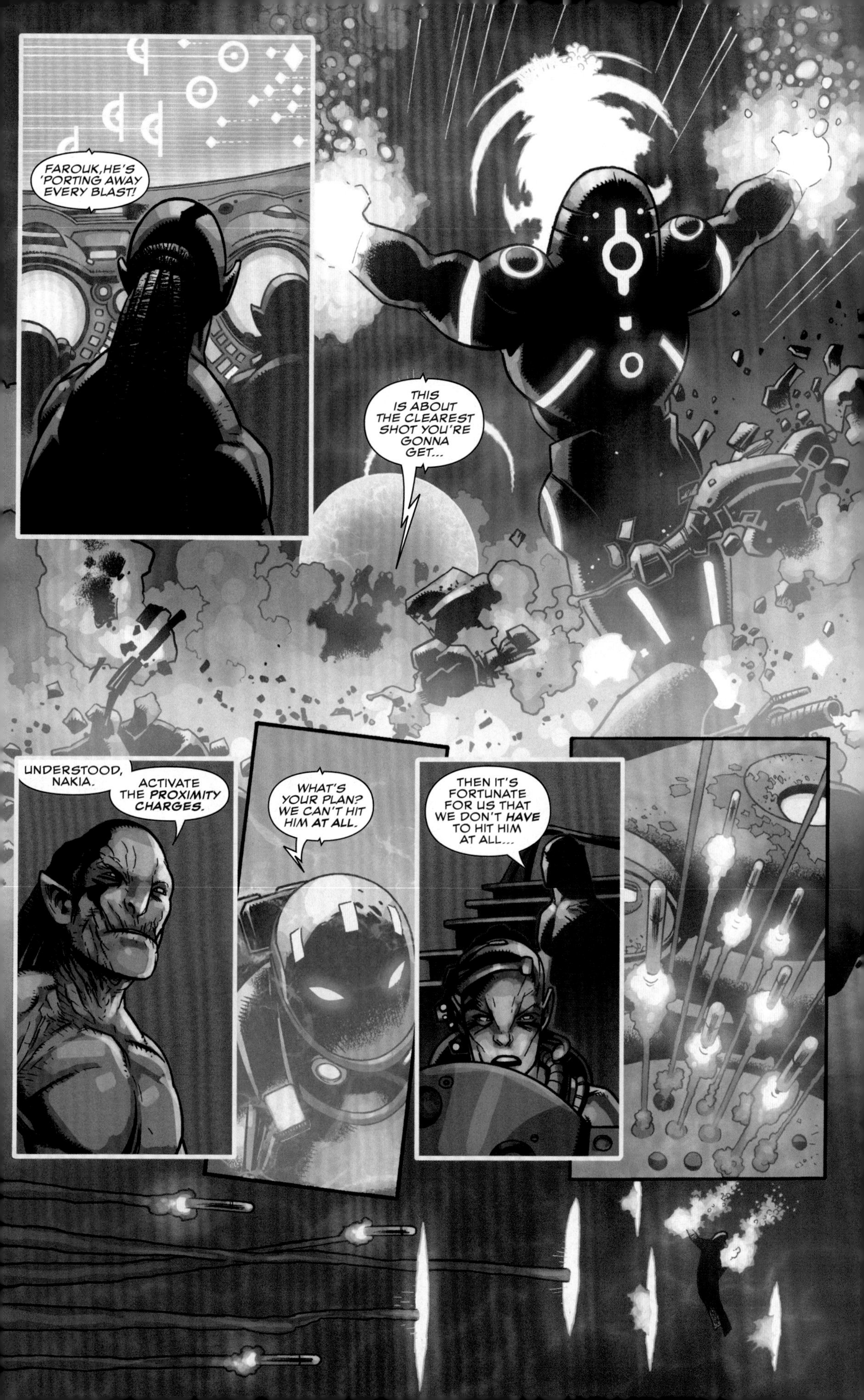
FAROUK, HE'S 'PORTING AWAY EVERY BLAST!
THIS IS ABOUT THE CLEAREST SHOT YOU'RE GONNA GET...
UNDERSTOOD, NAKIA.
ACTIVATE THE PROXIMITY CHARGES.
WHAT'S YOUR PLAN? WE CAN'T HIT HIM AT ALL.
THEN IT'S FORTUNATE FOR US THAT WE DON'T HAVE TO HIT HIM AT ALL...

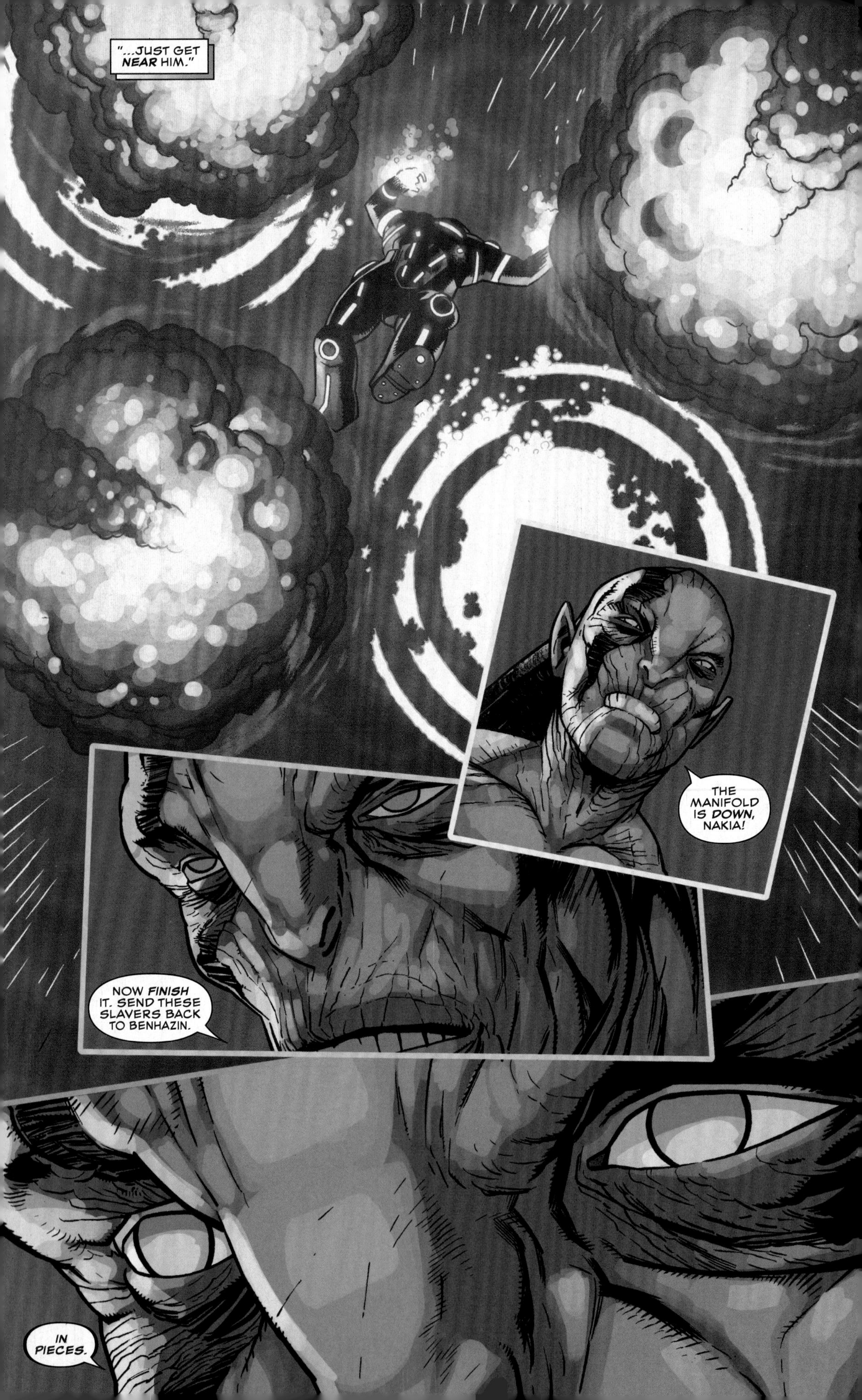
"...JUST GET NEAR HIM."
THE MANIFOLD IS DOWN, NAKIA!
NOW FINISH IT. SEND THESE SLAVERS BACK TO BENHAZIN.
IN PIECES.

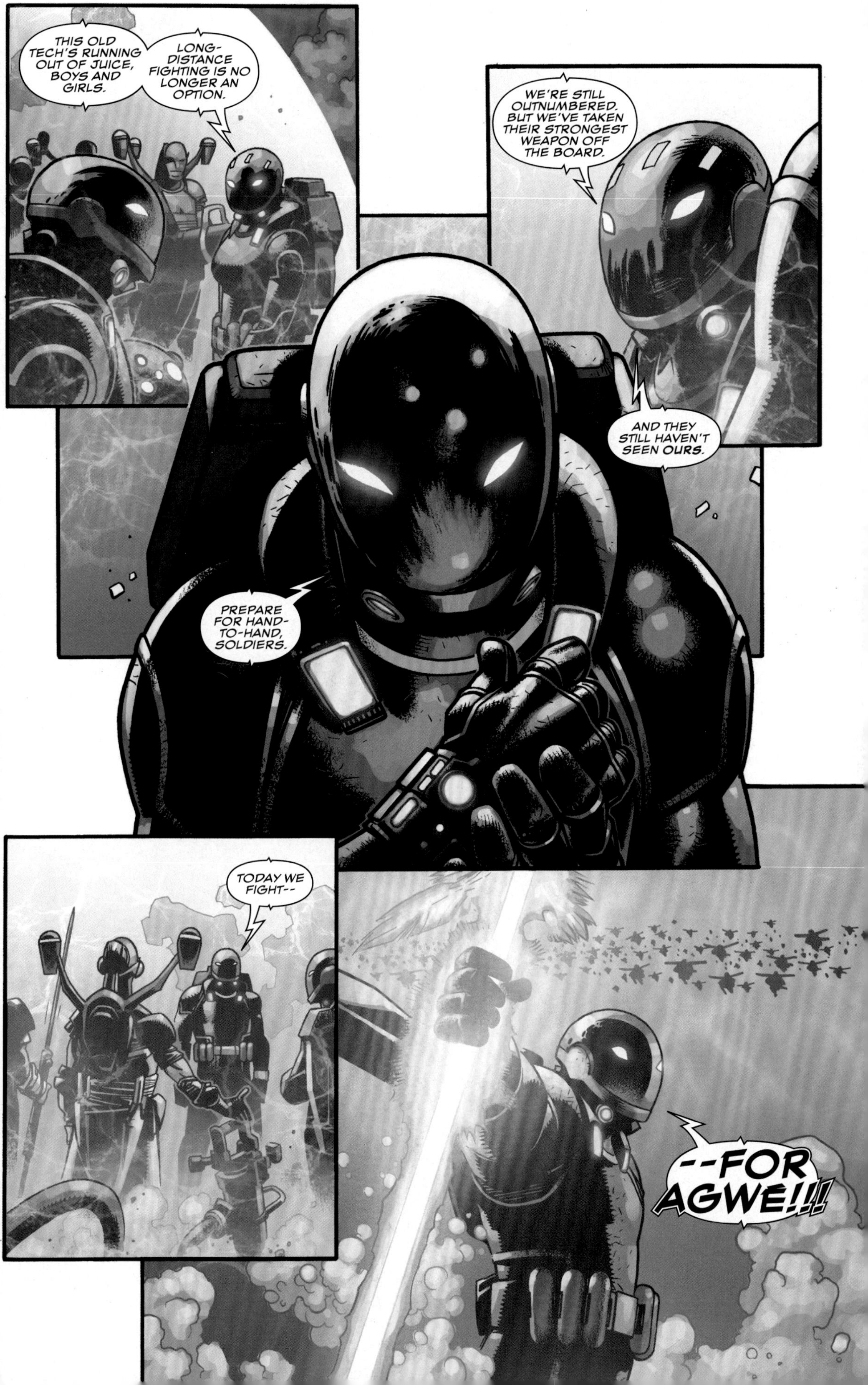
THIS OLD TECH'S RUNNING OUT OF JUICE, BOYS AND GIRLS.
LONG-DISTANCE FIGHTING IS NO LONGER AN OPTION.
WE'RE STILL OUTNUMBERED. BUT WE'VE TAKEN THEIR STRONGEST WEAPON OFF THE BOARD.
AND THEY STILL HAVEN'T SEEN OURS.
PREPARE FOR HAND-TO-HAND, SOLDIERS.
TODAY WE FIGHT--
--FOR AGWE!!!

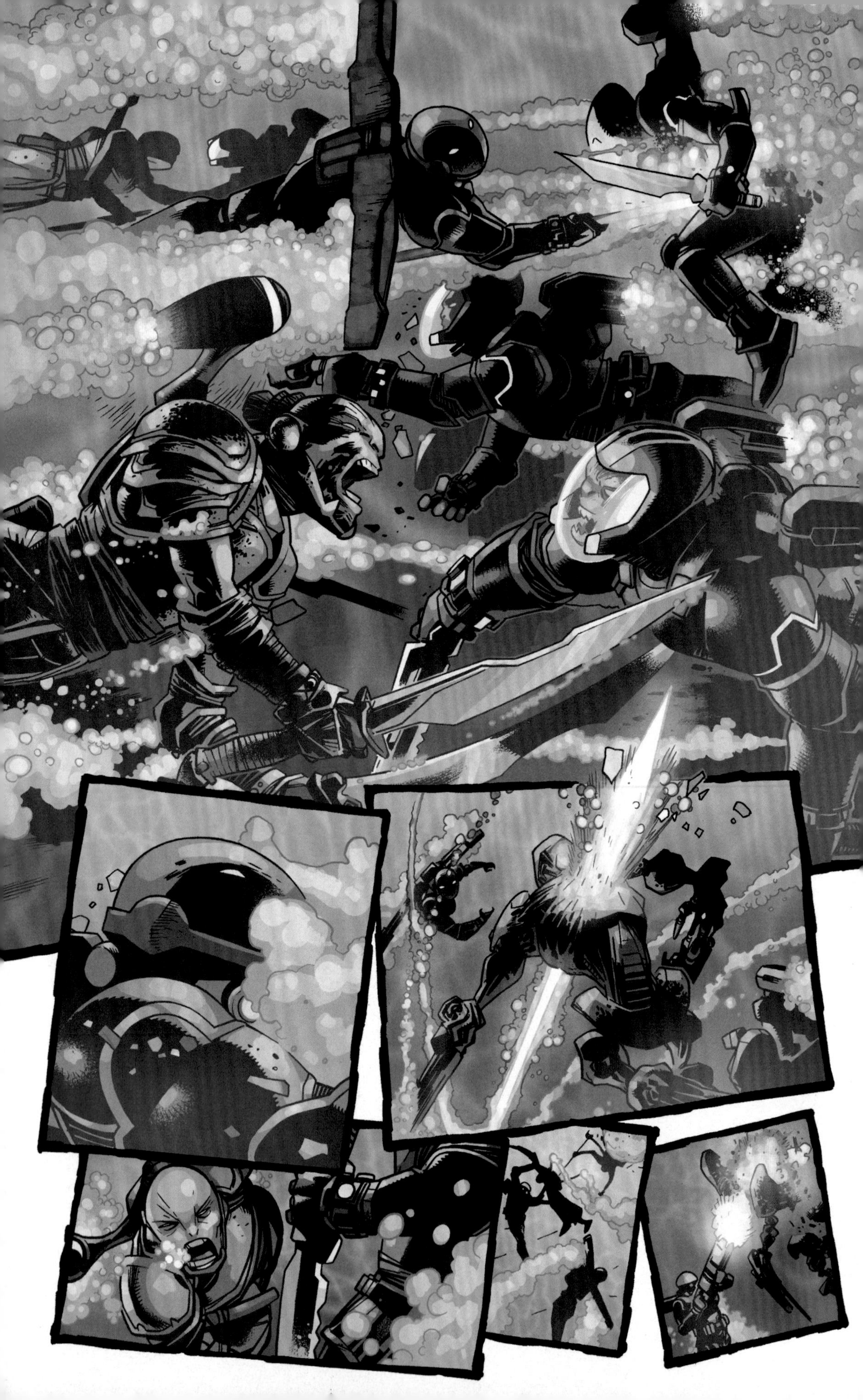

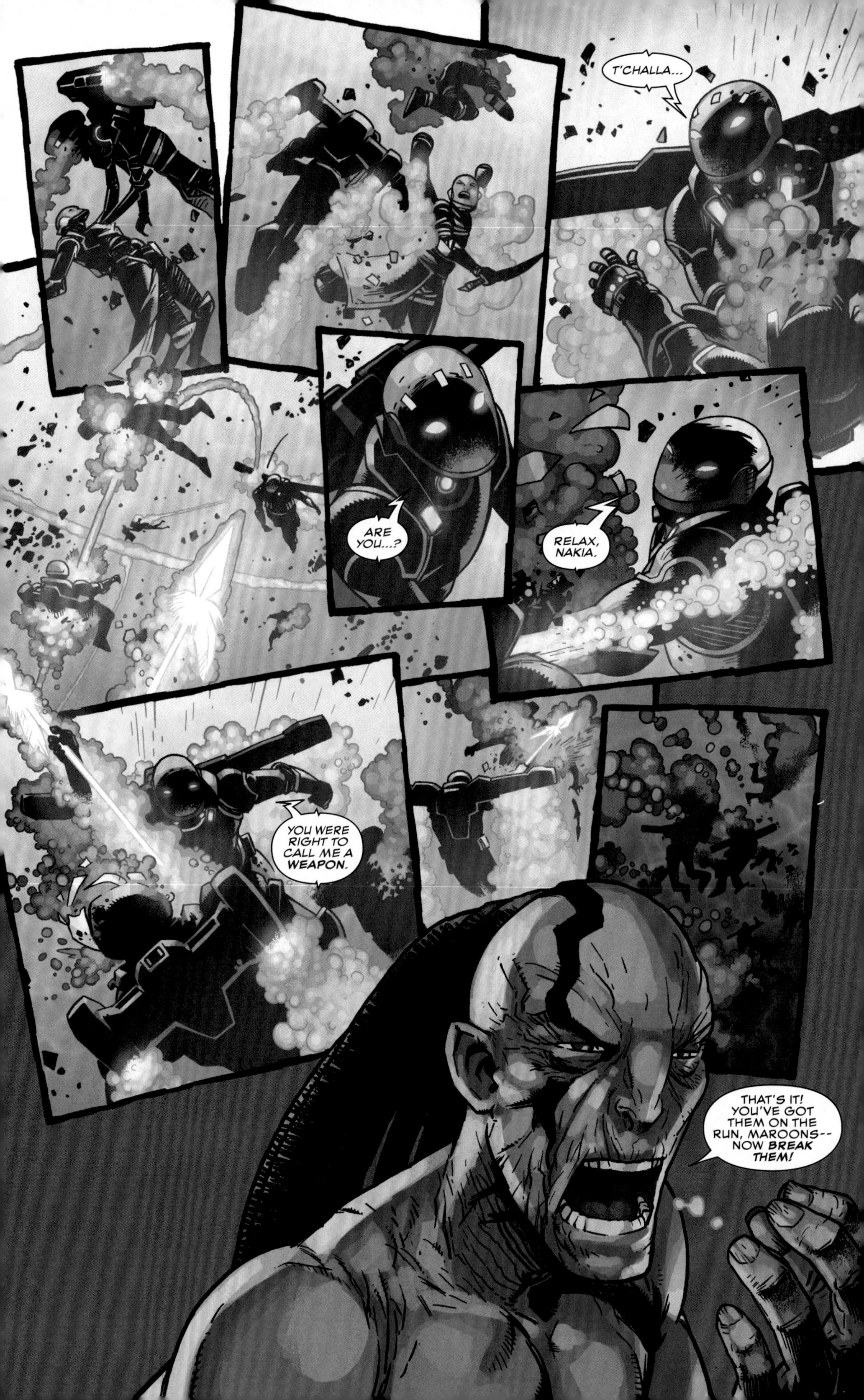
T'CHALLA...
ARE YOU...?
RELAX, NAKIA.
YOU WERE RIGHT TO CALL ME A **WEAPON**.
THAT'S IT! YOU'VE GOT THEM ON THE RUN, MAROONS-- NOW **BREAK THEM!**

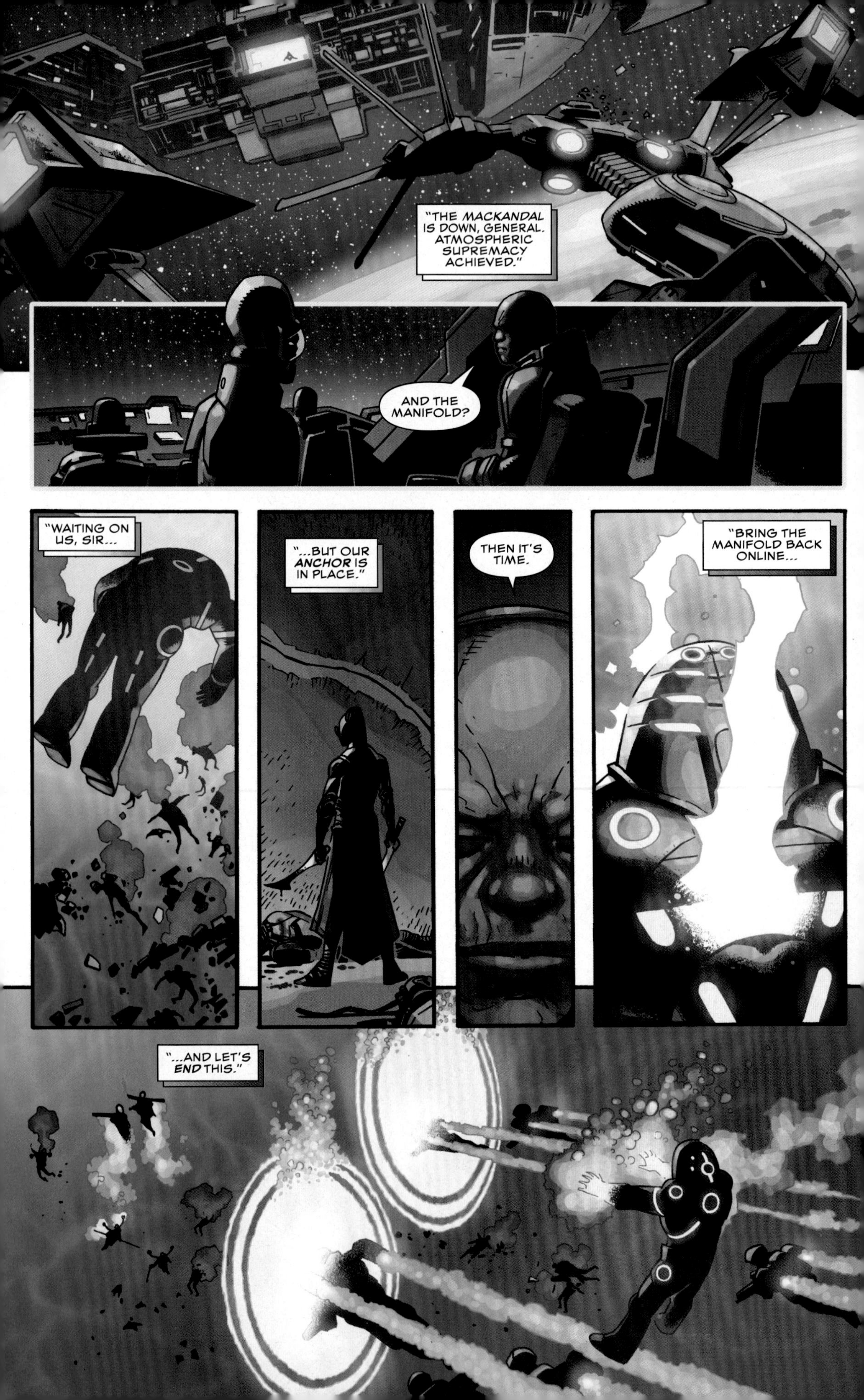
"THE MACKANDAL IS DOWN, GENERAL. ATMOSPHERIC SUPREMACY ACHIEVED."
AND THE MANIFOLD?
"WAITING ON US, SIR...
"...BUT OUR ANCHOR IS IN PLACE."
THEN IT'S TIME.
"BRING THE MANIFOLD BACK ONLINE...
"...AND LET'S END THIS."

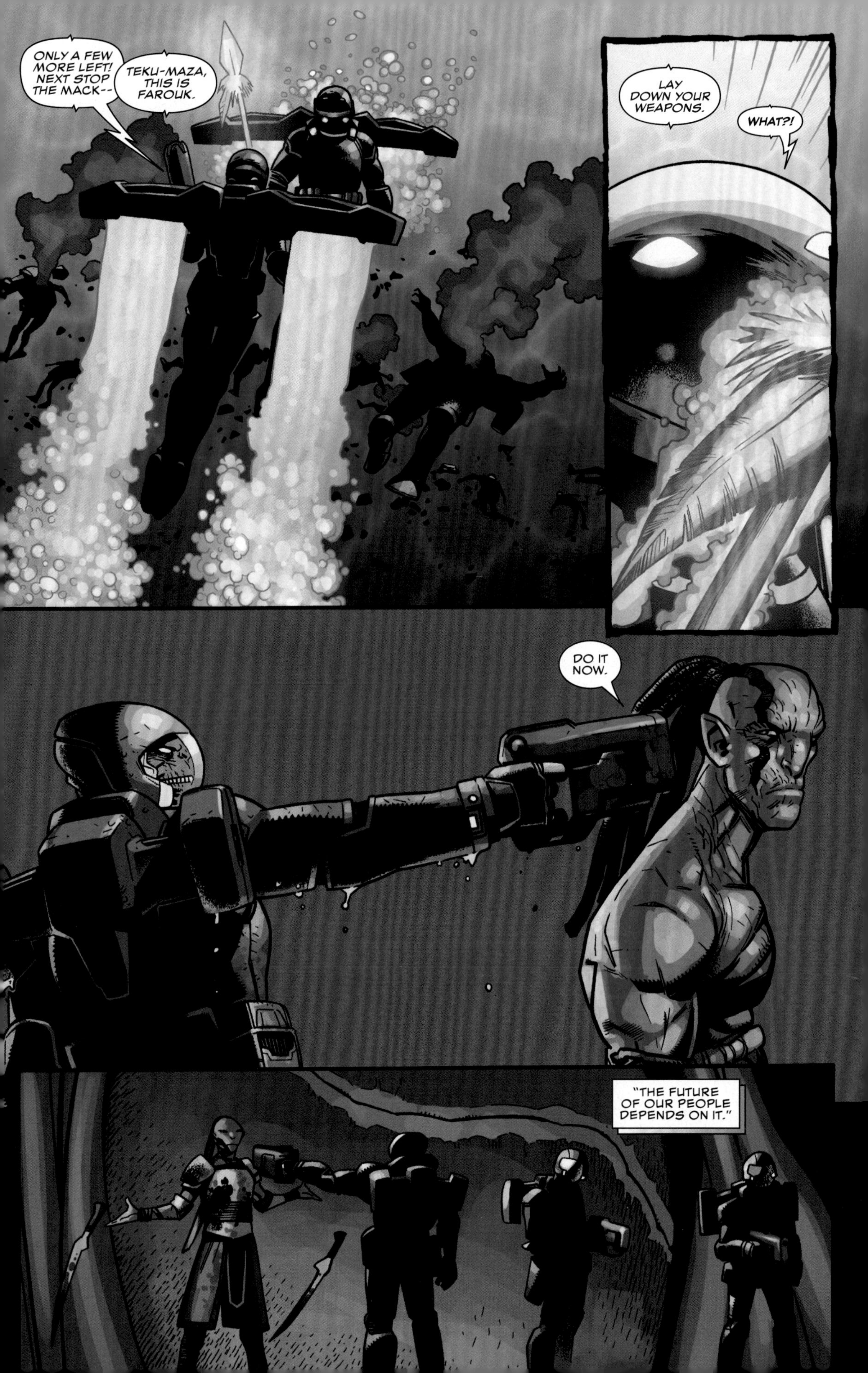
ONLY A FEW MORE LEFT! NEXT STOP THE MACK--
TEKU-MAZA, THIS IS FAROUK.
LAY DOWN YOUR WEAPONS.
WHAT?!
DO IT NOW.
"THE FUTURE OF OUR PEOPLE DEPENDS ON IT."

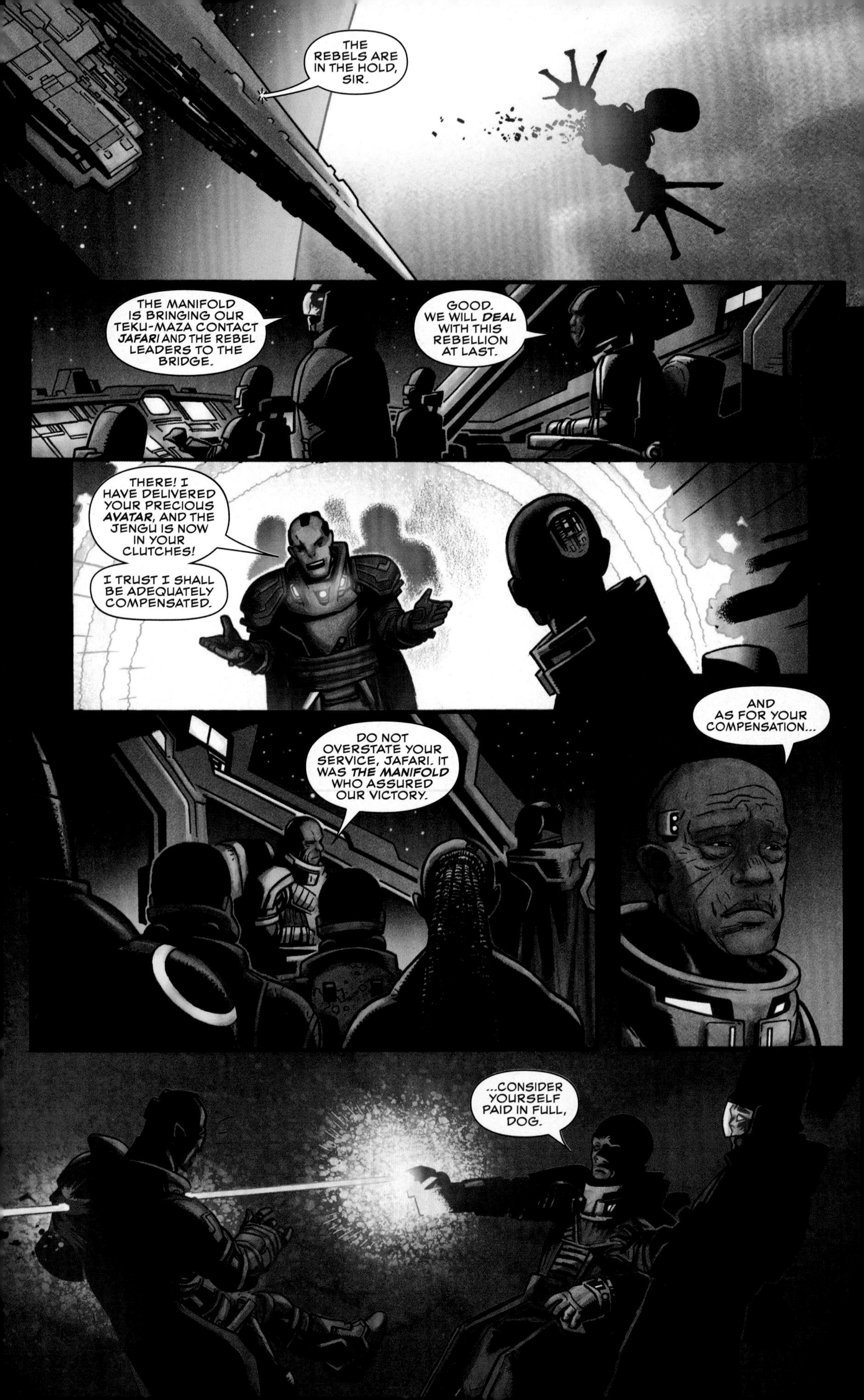
THE REBELS ARE IN THE HOLD, SIR.
THE MANIFOLD IS BRINGING OUR TEKU-MAZA CONTACT JAFARI AND THE REBEL LEADERS TO THE BRIDGE.
GOOD. WE WILL DEAL WITH THIS REBELLION AT LAST.
THERE! I HAVE DELIVERED YOUR PRECIOUS AVATAR, AND THE JENGU IS NOW IN YOUR CLUTCHES!
I TRUST I SHALL BE ADEQUATELY COMPENSATED.
DO NOT OVERSTATE YOUR SERVICE, JAFARI. IT WAS THE MANIFOLD WHO ASSURED OUR VICTORY.
AND AS FOR YOUR COMPENSATION...
...CONSIDER YOURSELF PAID IN FULL, DOG.

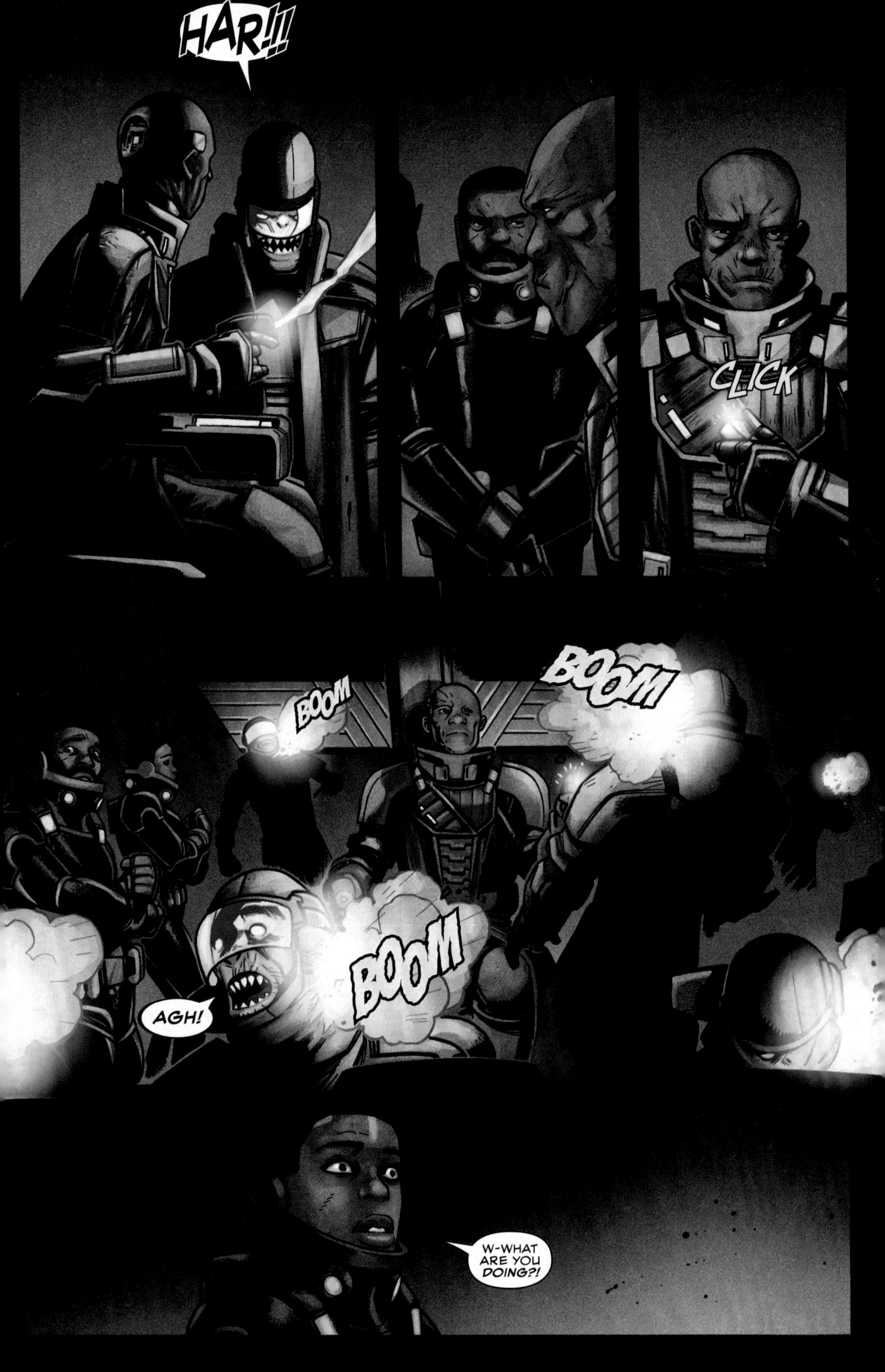
HAR!!!
CLICK
BOOM
BOOM
AGH!
BOOM
W-WHAT ARE YOU DOING?!

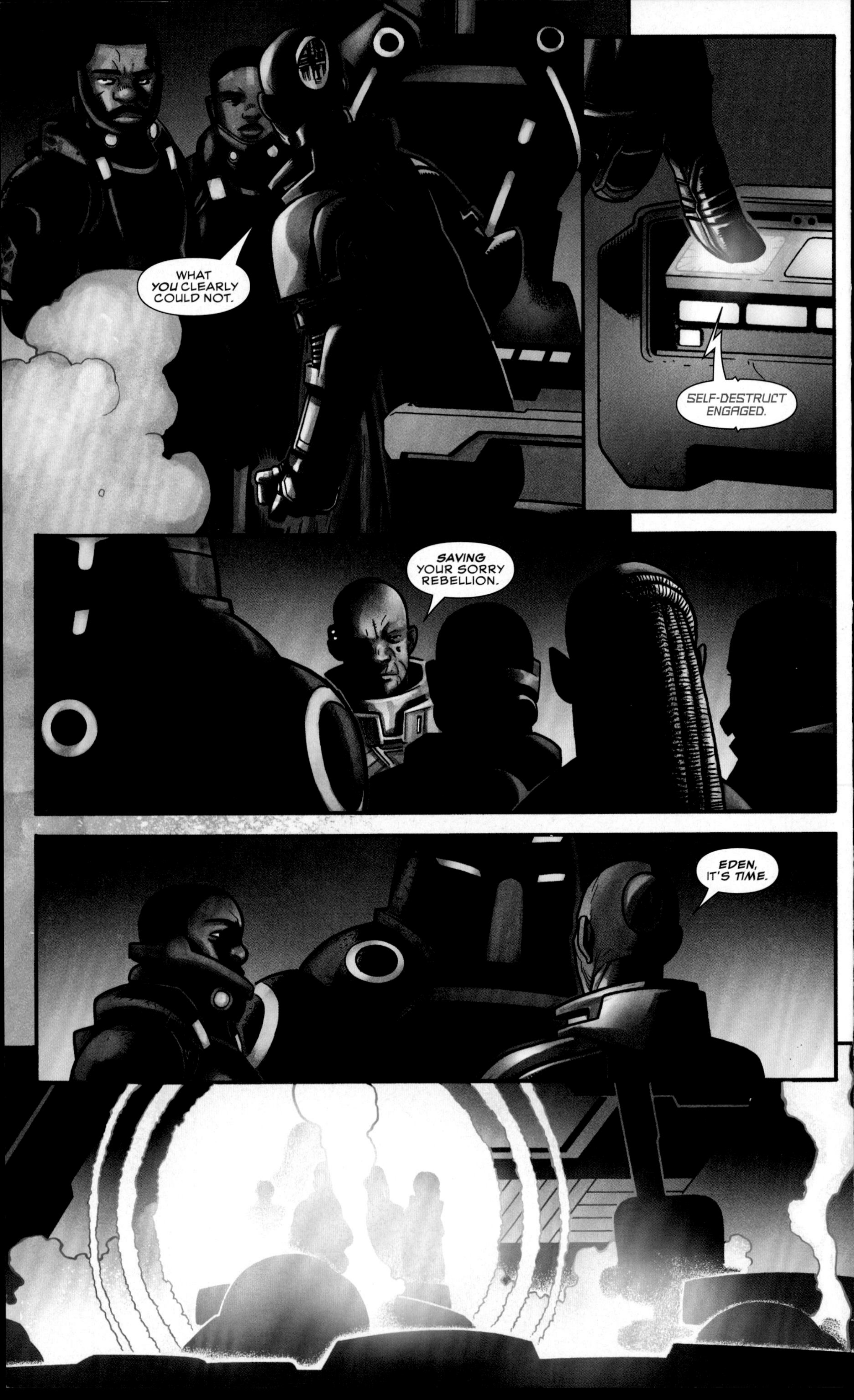
WHAT *YOU* CLEARLY COULD NOT.
SELF-DESTRUCT ENGAGED.
SAVING YOUR SORRY REBELLION.
EDEN, IT'S TIME.

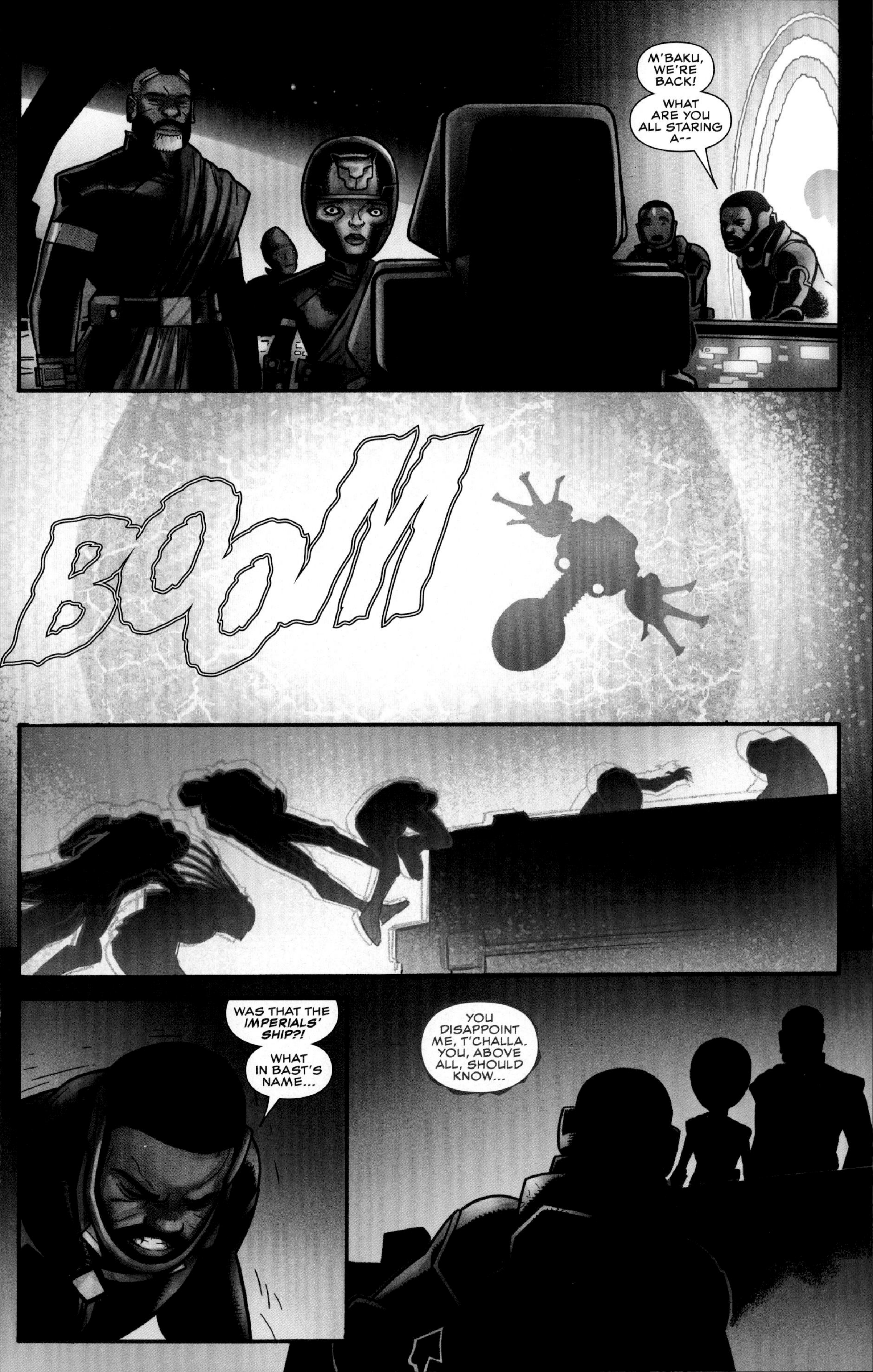
M'BAKU, WE'RE BACK!
WHAT ARE YOU ALL STARING A--
BOOM
WAS THAT THE IMPERIALS' SHIP?!
WHAT IN BAST'S NAME...
YOU DISAPPOINT ME, T'CHALLA. YOU, ABOVE ALL, SHOULD KNOW...

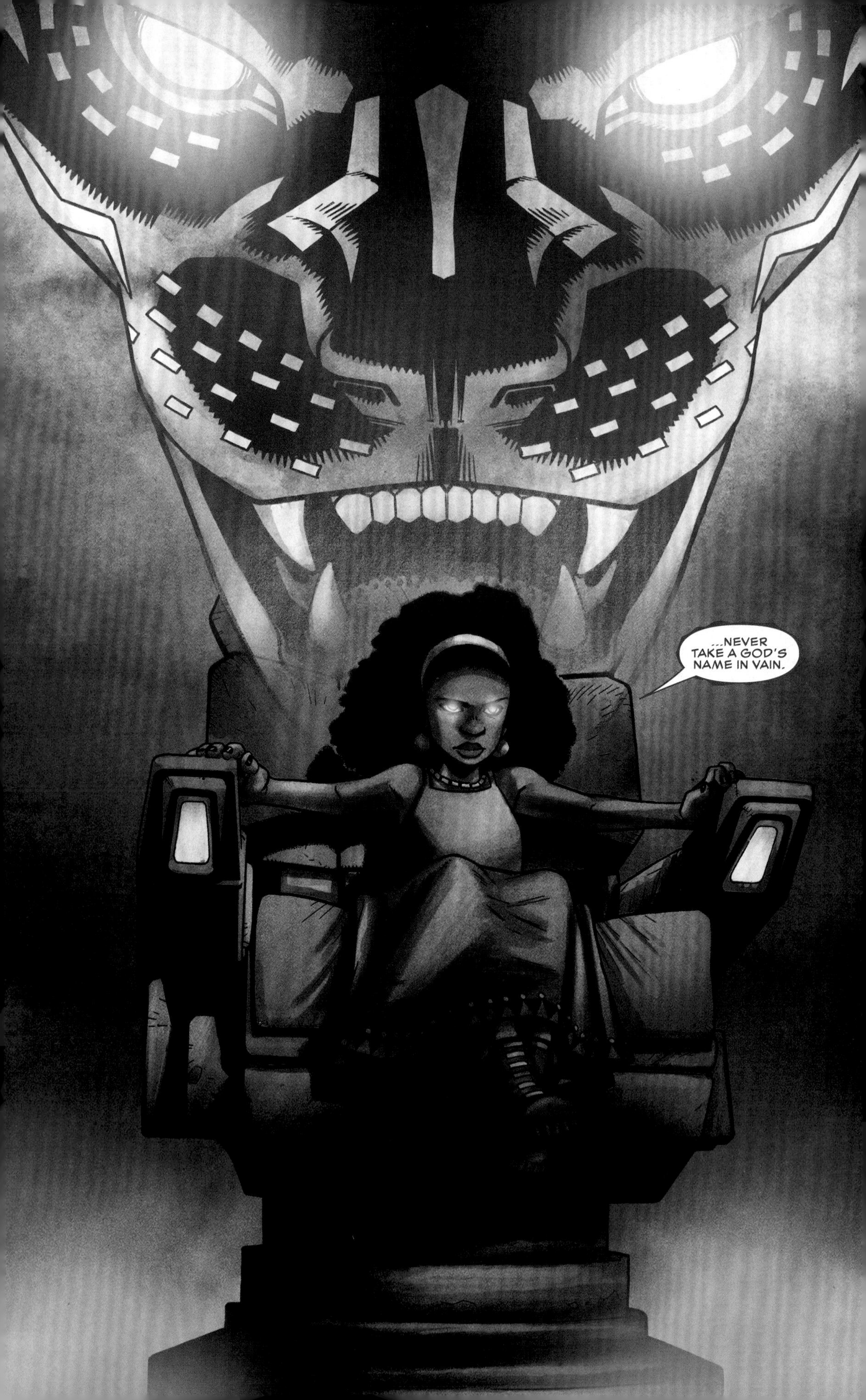
...NEVER TAKE A GOD'S NAME IN VAIN.

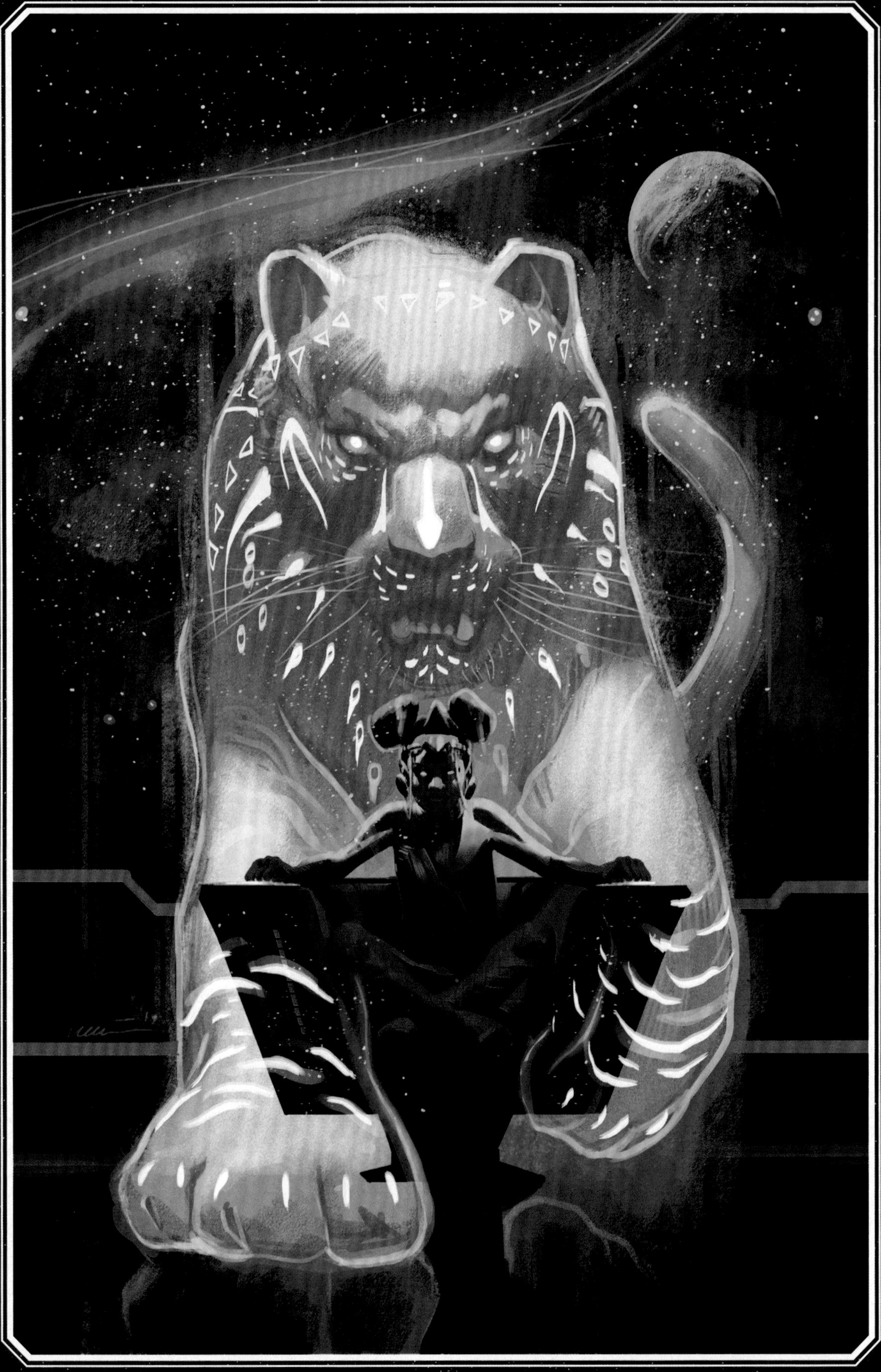

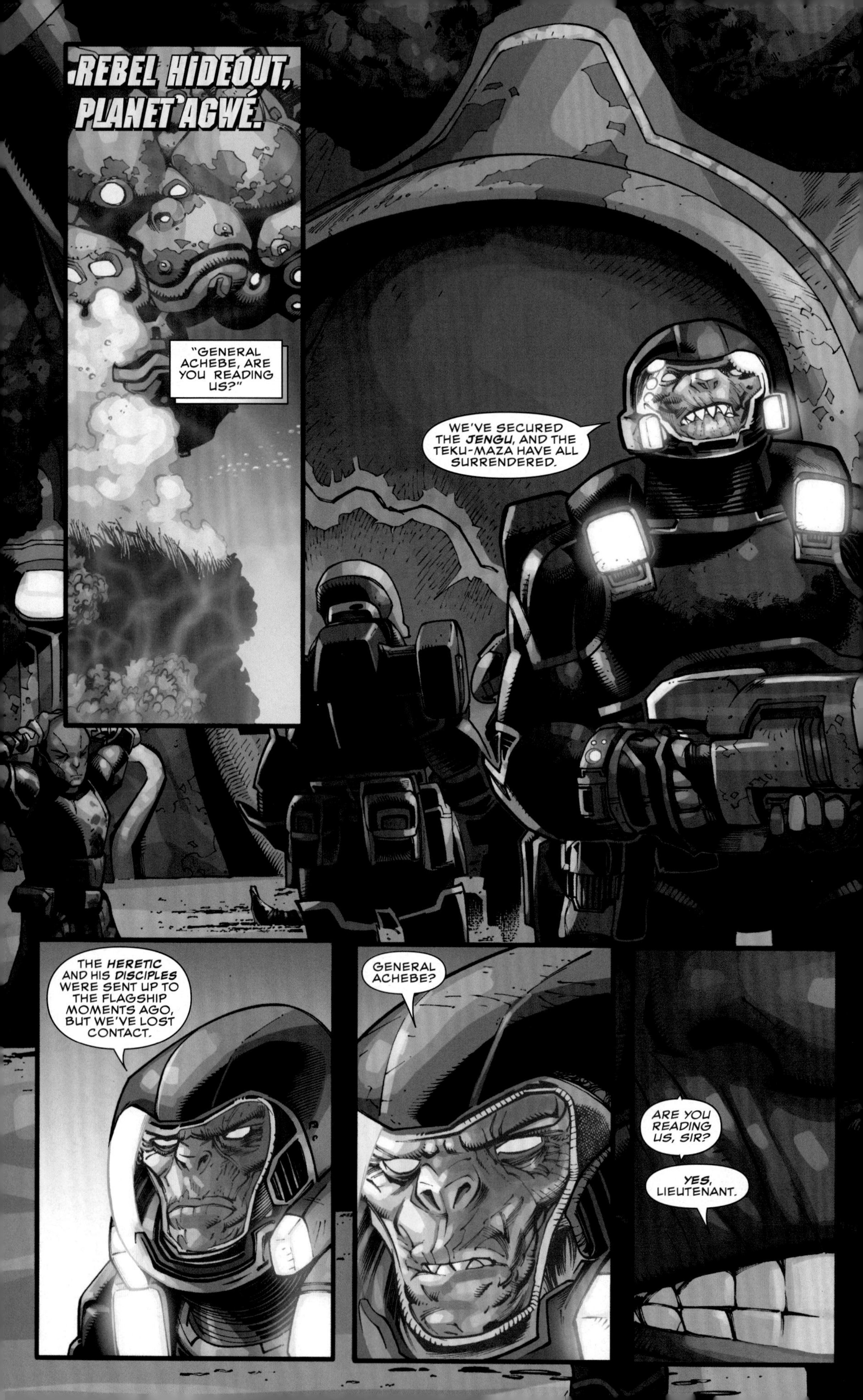

REBEL HIDEOUT, PLANET AGWÉ.
"GENERAL ACHEBE, ARE YOU READING US?"
WE'VE SECURED THE JENGU, AND THE TEKU-MAZA HAVE ALL SURRENDERED.
THE HERETIC AND HIS DISCIPLES WERE SENT UP TO THE FLAGSHIP MOMENTS AGO, BUT WE'VE LOST CONTACT.
GENERAL ACHEBE?
ARE YOU READING US, SIR?
YES, LIEUTENANT.

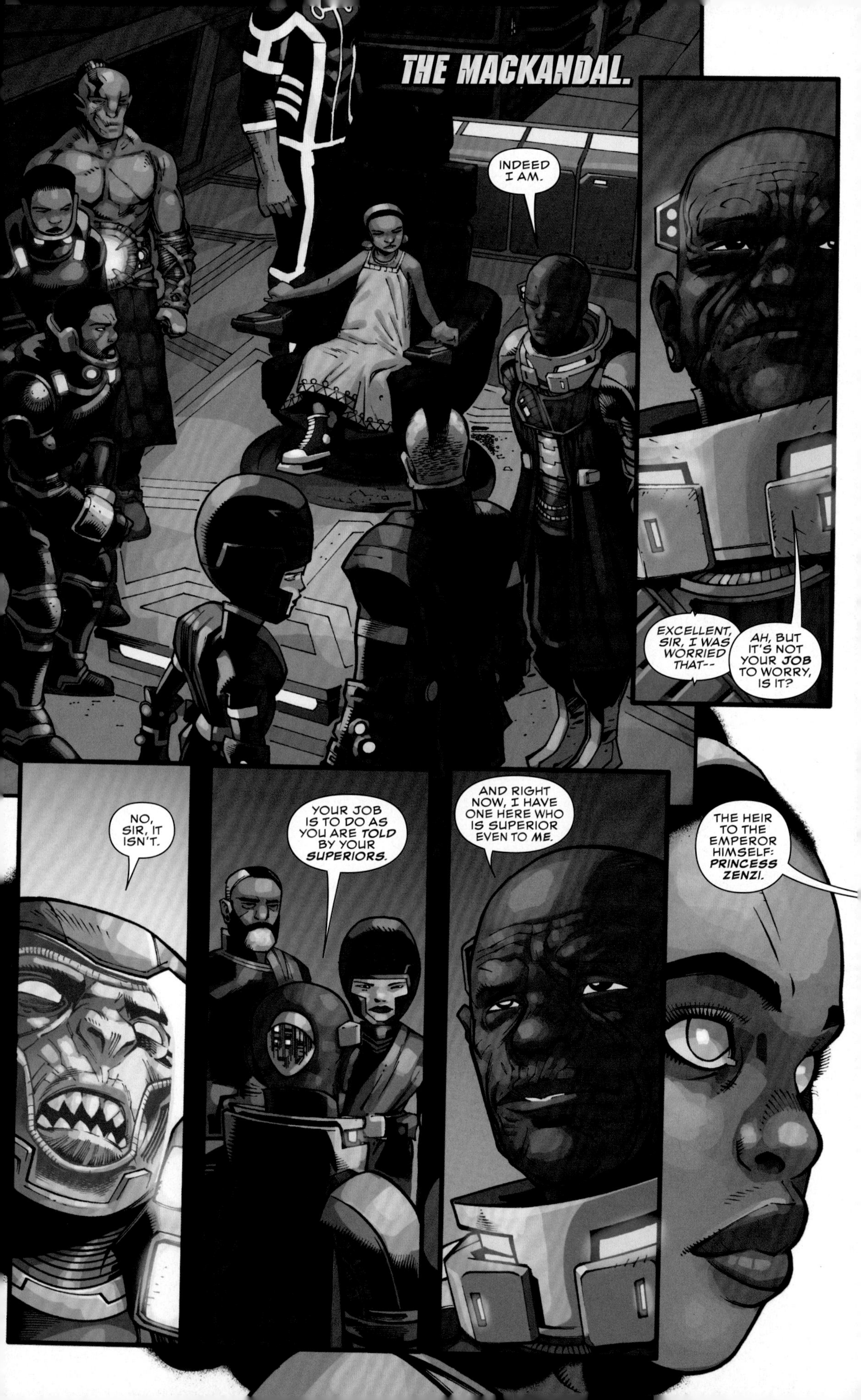
THE MACKANDAL.
INDEED I AM.
EXCELLENT, SIR, I WAS WORRIED THAT--
AH, BUT IT'S NOT YOUR JOB TO WORRY, IS IT?
NO, SIR, IT ISN'T.
YOUR JOB IS TO DO AS YOU ARE TOLD BY YOUR SUPERIORS.
AND RIGHT NOW, I HAVE ONE HERE WHO IS SUPERIOR EVEN TO ME.
THE HEIR TO THE EMPEROR HIMSELF: PRINCESS ZENZI.

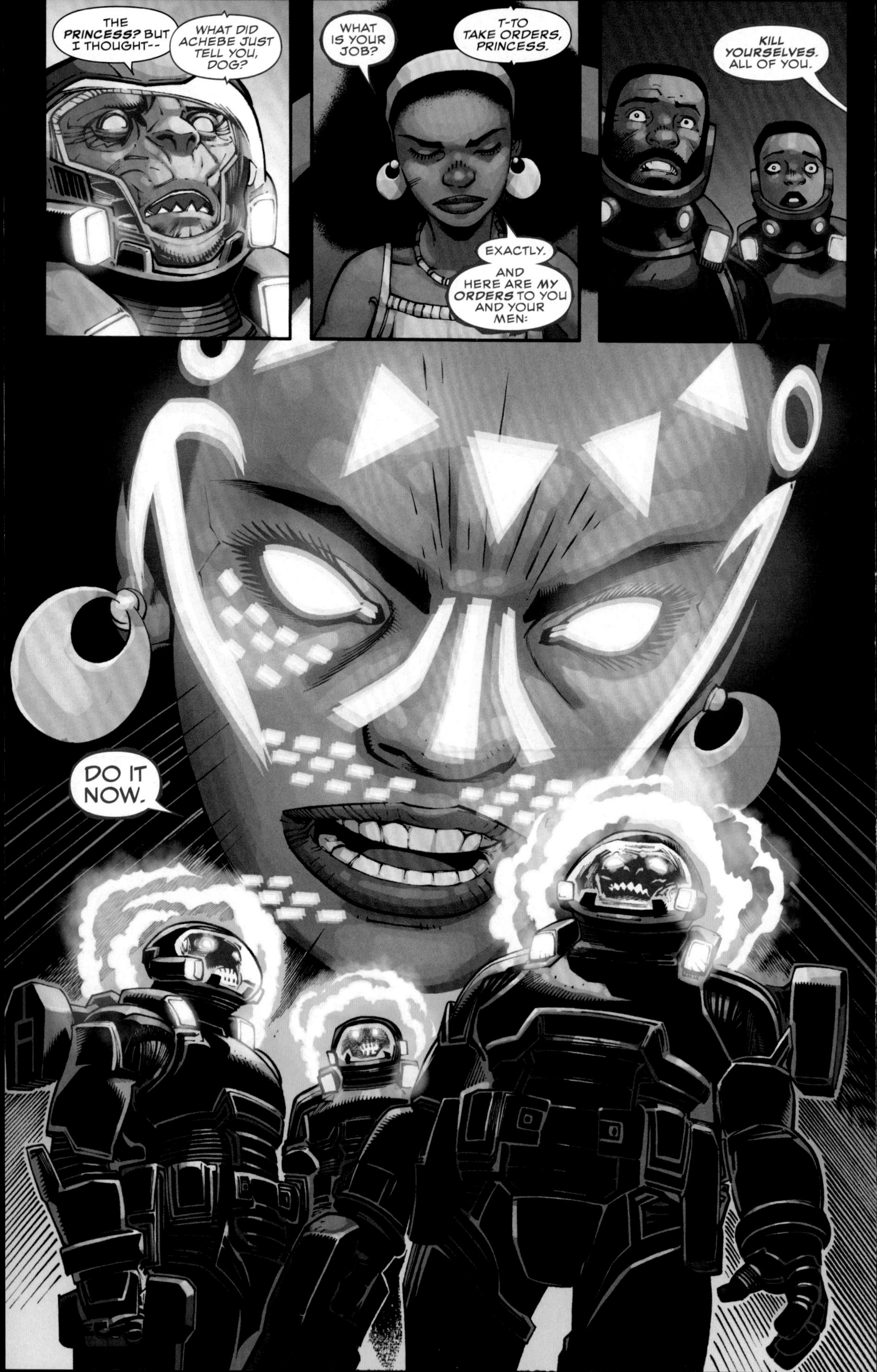
THE PRINCESS? BUT I THOUGHT--
WHAT DID ACHEBE JUST TELL YOU, DOG?
WHAT IS YOUR JOB?
T-TO TAKE ORDERS, PRINCESS.
EXACTLY.
AND HERE ARE MY ORDERS TO YOU AND YOUR MEN:
KILL YOURSELVES. ALL OF YOU.
DO IT NOW.

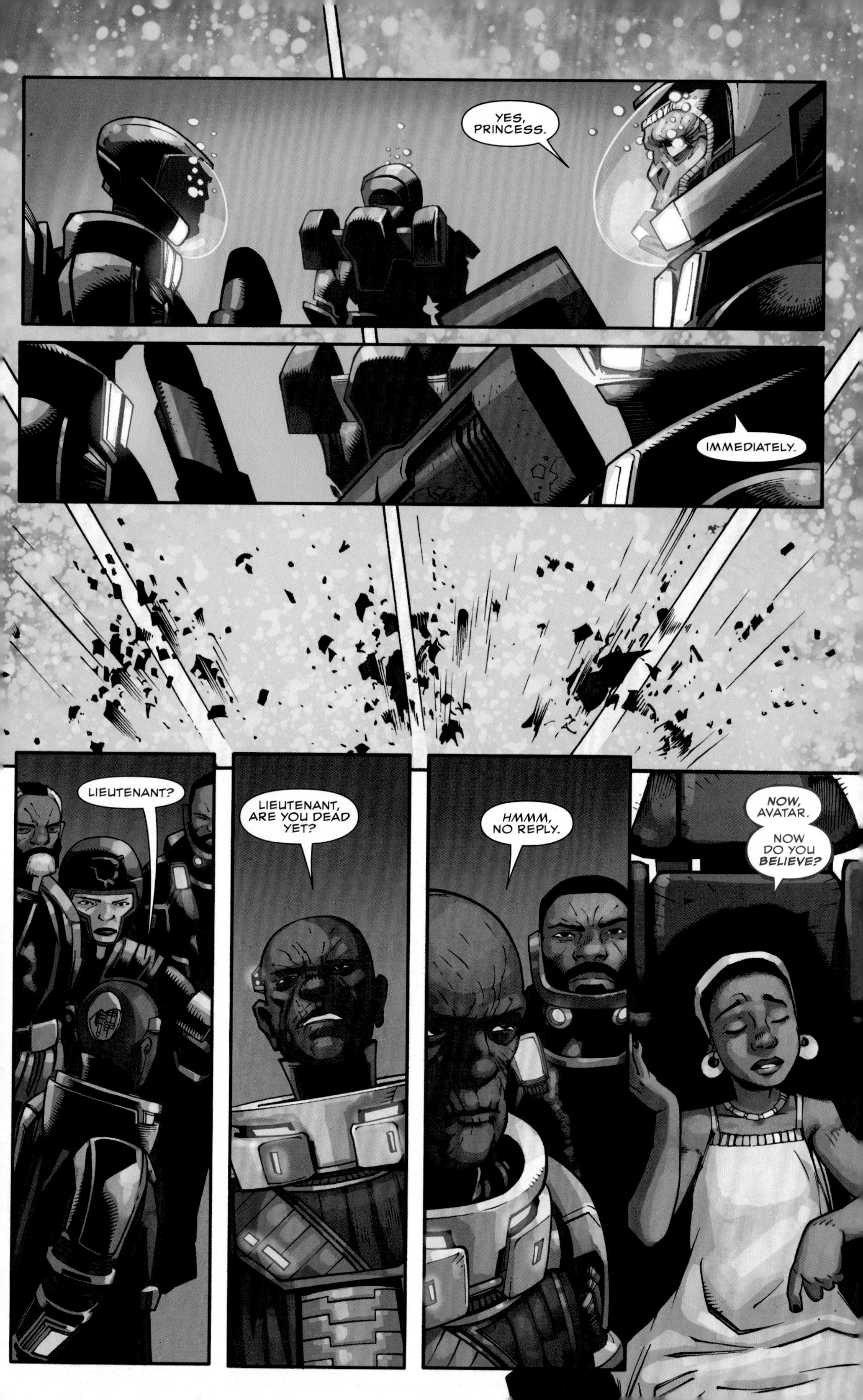
YES, PRINCESS.
IMMEDIATELY.
LIEUTENANT?
LIEUTENANT, ARE YOU DEAD YET?
HMMM, NO REPLY.
NOW, AVATAR.
NOW DO YOU BELIEVE?

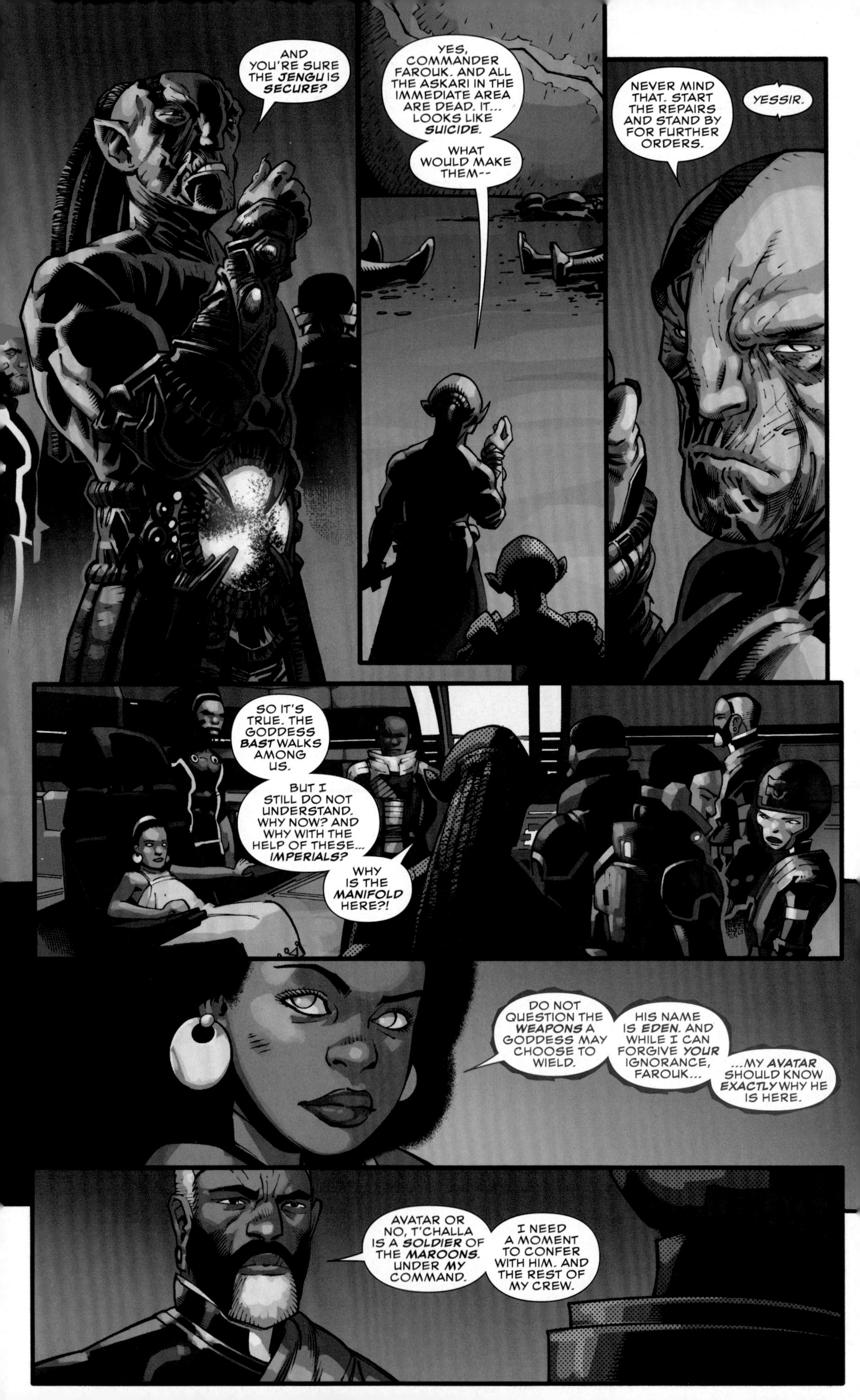
AND YOU'RE SURE THE JENGU IS SECURE?
YES, COMMANDER FAROUK. AND ALL THE ASKARI IN THE IMMEDIATE AREA ARE DEAD. IT... LOOKS LIKE SUICIDE.
WHAT WOULD MAKE THEM--
NEVER MIND THAT. START THE REPAIRS AND STAND BY FOR FURTHER ORDERS.
YESSIR.
SO IT'S TRUE. THE GODDESS BAST WALKS AMONG US.
BUT I STILL DO NOT UNDERSTAND. WHY NOW? AND WHY WITH THE HELP OF THESE... IMPERIALS?
WHY IS THE MANIFOLD HERE?!
DO NOT QUESTION THE WEAPONS A GODDESS MAY CHOOSE TO WIELD.
HIS NAME IS EDEN. AND WHILE I CAN FORGIVE YOUR IGNORANCE, FAROUK...
...MY AVATAR SHOULD KNOW EXACTLY WHY HE IS HERE.
AVATAR OR NO, T'CHALLA IS A SOLDIER OF THE MAROONS. UNDER MY COMMAND.
I NEED A MOMENT TO CONFER WITH HIM. AND THE REST OF MY CREW.

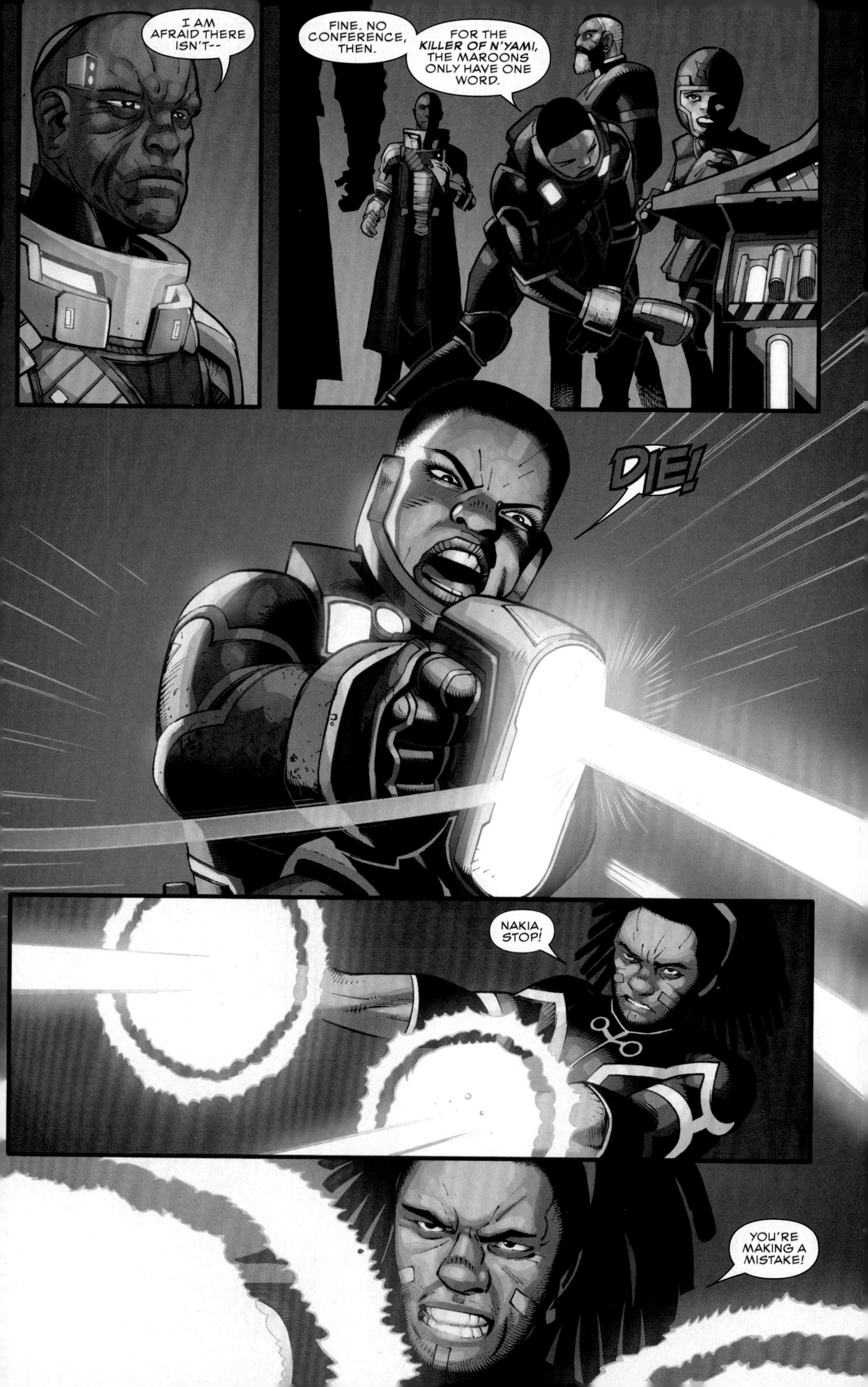
I AM AFRAID THERE ISN'T--
FINE. NO CONFERENCE, THEN.
FOR THE KILLER OF N'YAMI, THE MAROONS ONLY HAVE ONE WORD.
DIE!
NAKIA, STOP!
YOU'RE MAKING A MISTAKE!

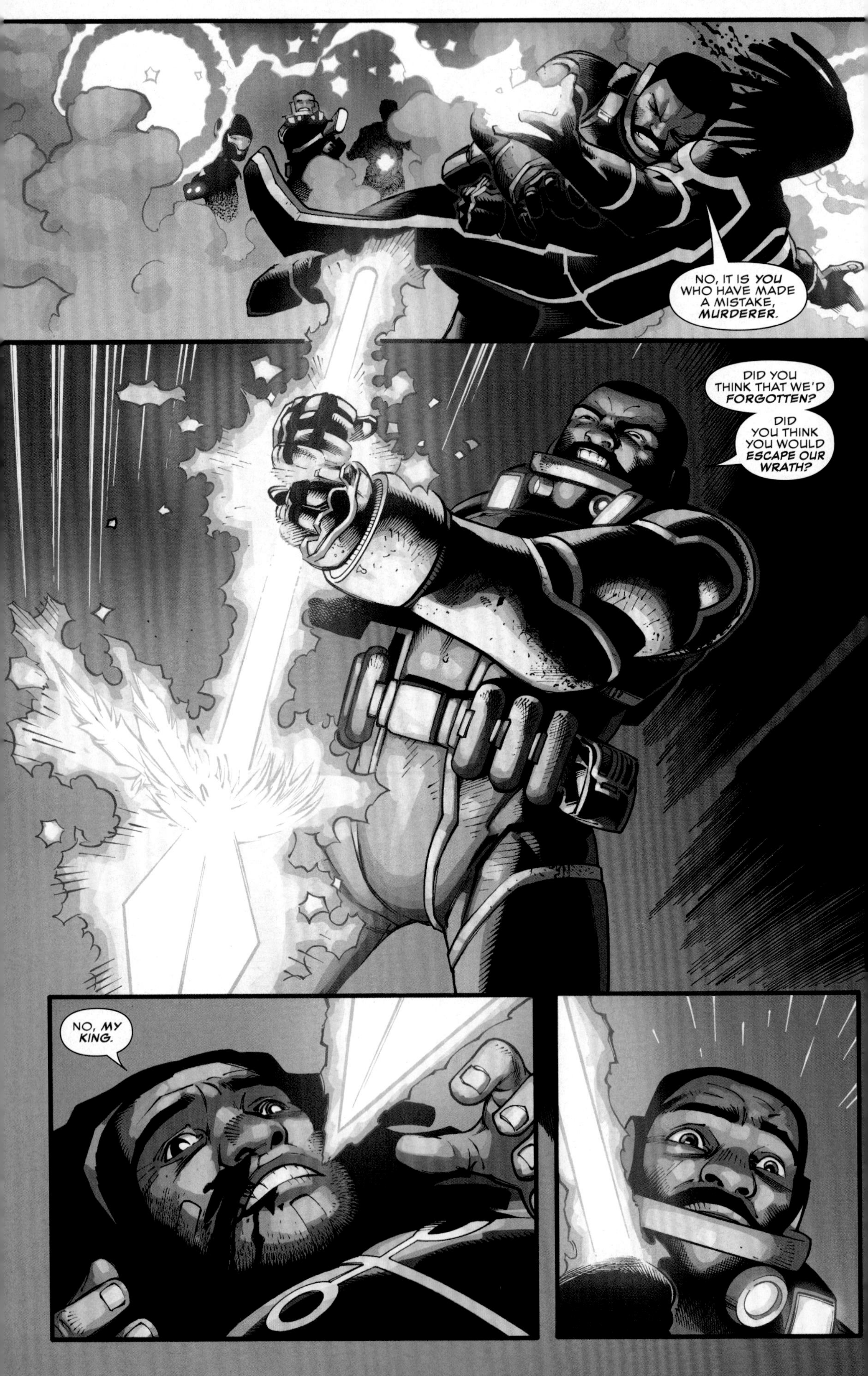
NO, IT IS *YOU* WHO HAVE MADE A MISTAKE, ***MURDERER.***
DID YOU THINK THAT WE'D ***FORGOTTEN?***
DID YOU THINK YOU WOULD ***ESCAPE OUR WRATH?***
NO, ***MY KING.***

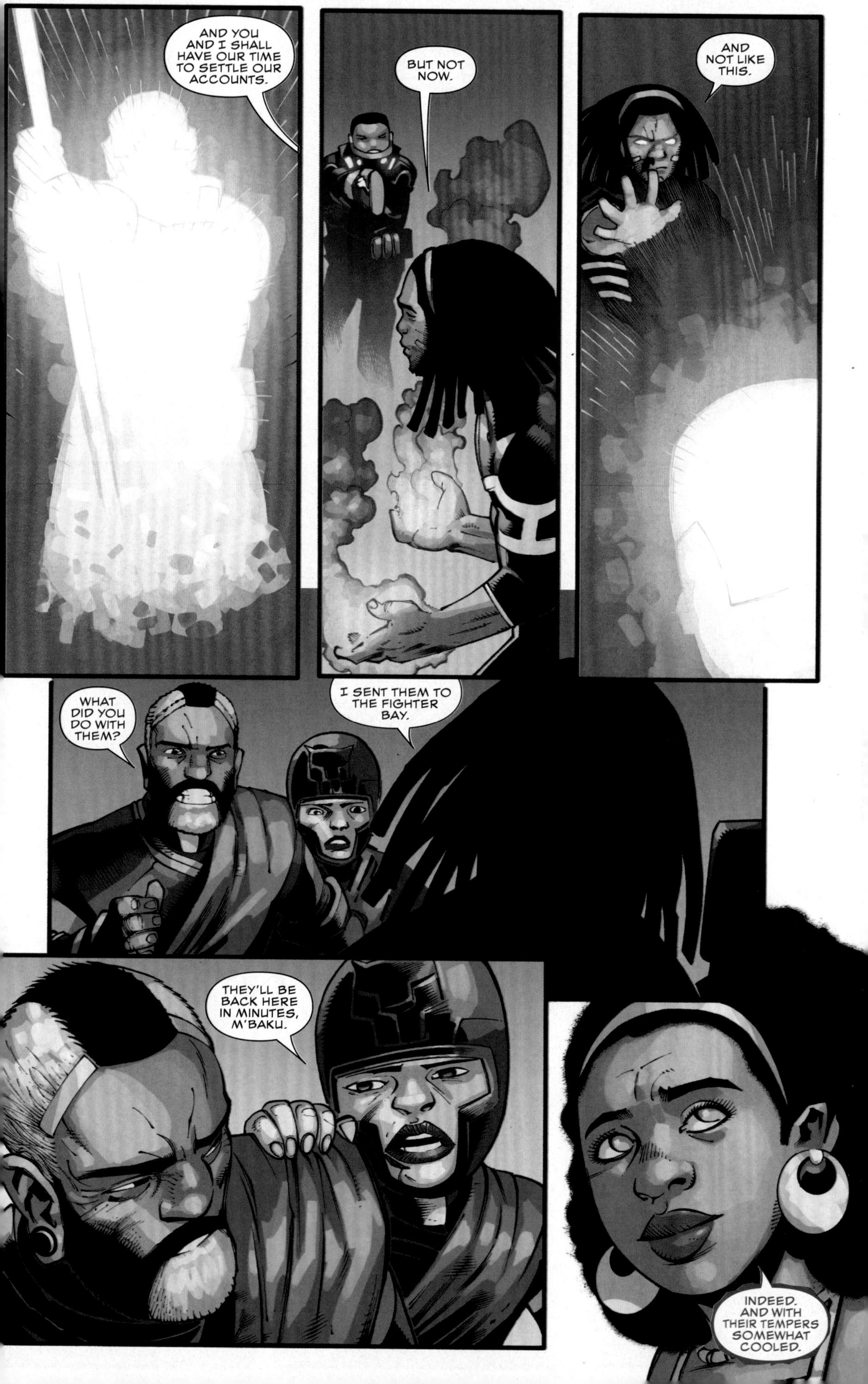
AND YOU AND I SHALL HAVE OUR TIME TO SETTLE OUR ACCOUNTS.
BUT NOT NOW.
AND NOT LIKE THIS.
WHAT DID YOU DO WITH THEM?
I SENT THEM TO THE FIGHTER BAY.
THEY'LL BE BACK HERE IN MINUTES, M'BAKU.
INDEED. AND WITH THEIR TEMPERS SOMEWHAT COOLED.

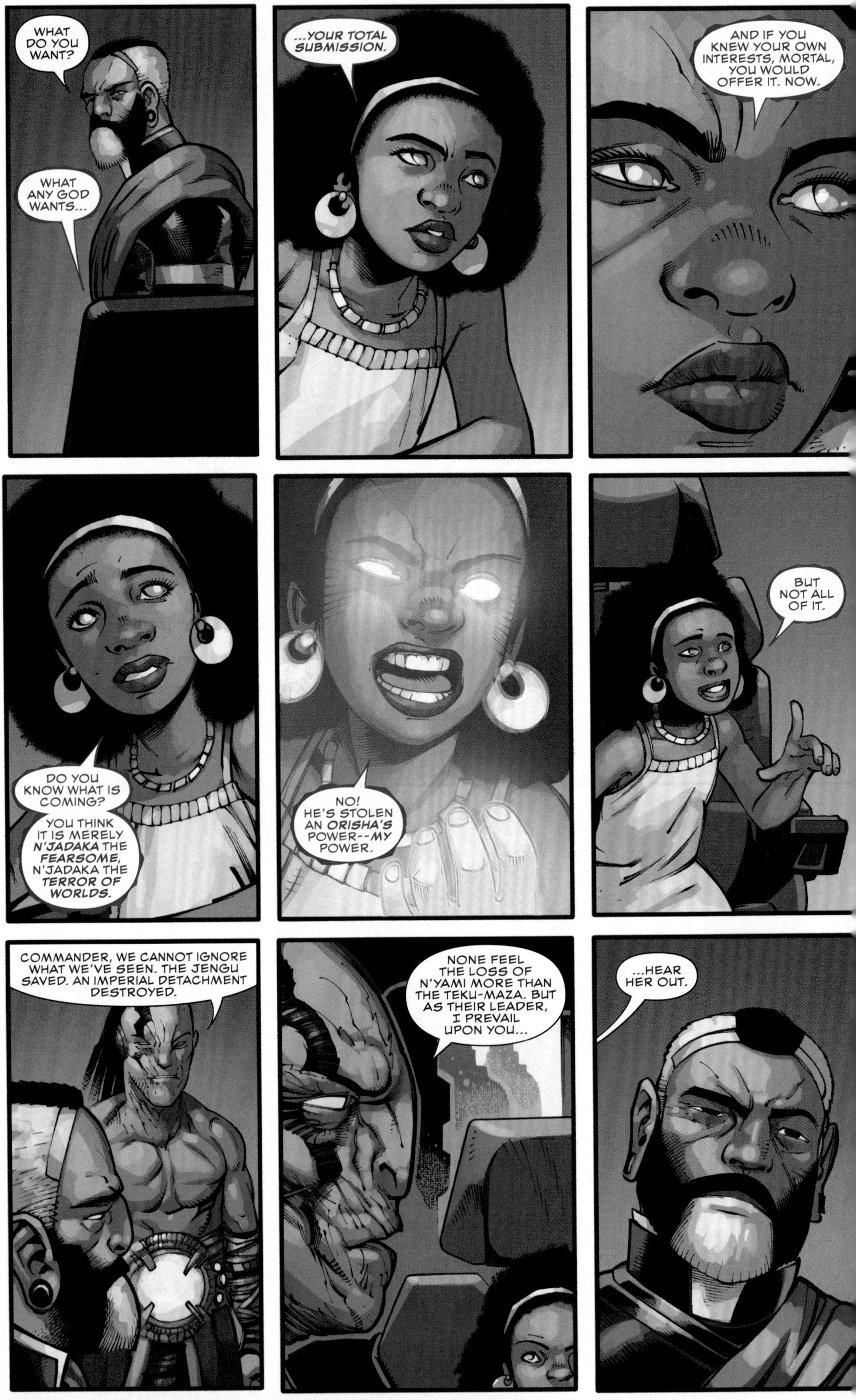
WHAT DO YOU WANT?
WHAT ANY GOD WANTS...
...YOUR TOTAL SUBMISSION.
AND IF YOU KNEW YOUR OWN INTERESTS, MORTAL, YOU WOULD OFFER IT. NOW.
DO YOU KNOW WHAT IS COMING?
YOU THINK IT IS MERELY N'JADAKA THE FEARSOME, N'JADAKA THE TERROR OF WORLDS.
NO! HE'S STOLEN AN ORISHA'S POWER--MY POWER.
BUT NOT ALL OF IT.
COMMANDER, WE CANNOT IGNORE WHAT WE'VE SEEN. THE JENGU SAVED. AN IMPERIAL DETACHMENT DESTROYED.
NONE FEEL THE LOSS OF N'YAMI MORE THAN THE TEKU-MAZA. BUT AS THEIR LEADER, I PREVAIL UPON YOU...
...HEAR HER OUT.

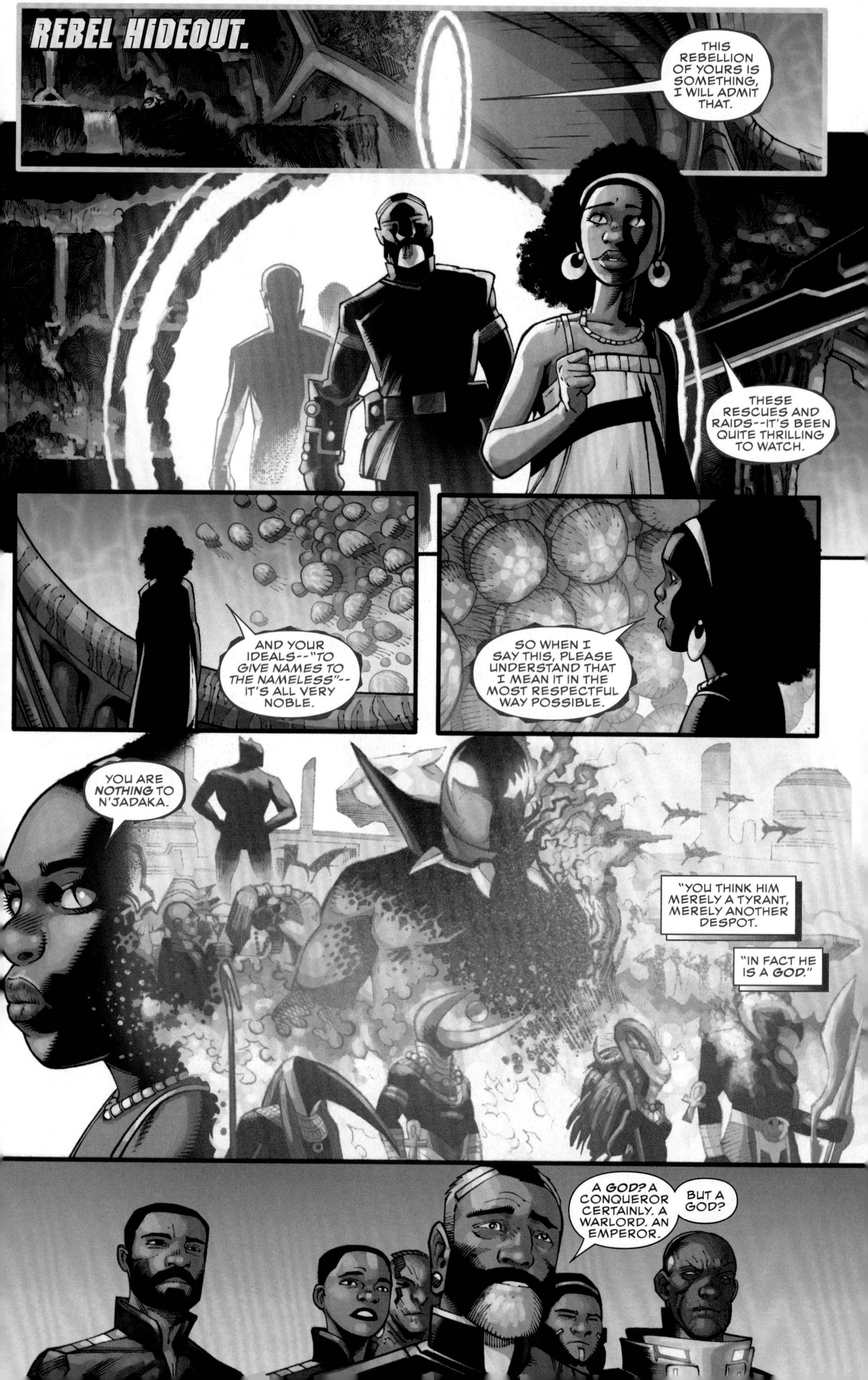
REBEL HIDEOUT.
THIS REBELLION OF YOURS IS SOMETHING, I WILL ADMIT THAT.
THESE RESCUES AND RAIDS--IT'S BEEN QUITE THRILLING TO WATCH.
AND YOUR IDEALS--"TO GIVE NAMES TO THE NAMELESS"--IT'S ALL VERY NOBLE.
SO WHEN I SAY THIS, PLEASE UNDERSTAND THAT I MEAN IT IN THE MOST RESPECTFUL WAY POSSIBLE.
YOU ARE NOTHING TO N'JADAKA.
"YOU THINK HIM MERELY A TYRANT, MERELY ANOTHER DESPOT.
"IN FACT HE IS A GOD."
A GOD? A CONQUEROR CERTAINLY. A WARLORD. AN EMPEROR.
BUT A GOD?

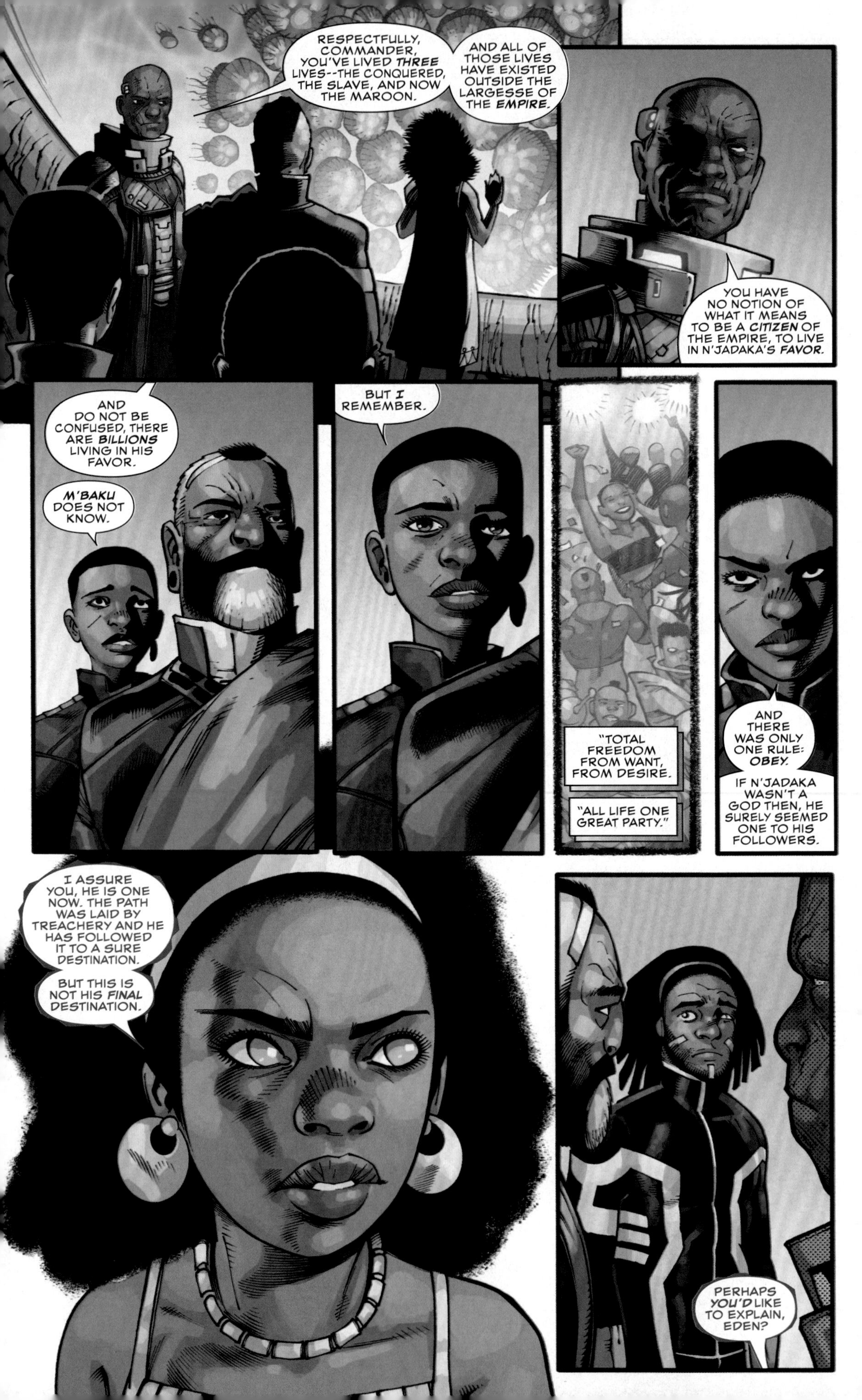
RESPECTFULLY, COMMANDER, YOU'VE LIVED *THREE* LIVES--THE CONQUERED, THE SLAVE, AND NOW THE MAROON.
AND ALL OF THOSE LIVES HAVE EXISTED OUTSIDE THE LARGESSE OF THE *EMPIRE.*
YOU HAVE NO NOTION OF WHAT IT MEANS TO BE A *CITIZEN* OF THE EMPIRE, TO LIVE IN N'JADAKA'S *FAVOR.*
AND DO NOT BE CONFUSED, THERE ARE *BILLIONS* LIVING IN HIS FAVOR.
M'BAKU DOES NOT KNOW.
BUT *I* REMEMBER.
"TOTAL FREEDOM FROM WANT, FROM DESIRE.
"ALL LIFE ONE GREAT PARTY."
AND THERE WAS ONLY ONE RULE: *OBEY.*
IF N'JADAKA WASN'T A GOD THEN, HE SURELY SEEMED ONE TO HIS FOLLOWERS.
I ASSURE YOU, HE IS ONE NOW. THE PATH WAS LAID BY TREACHERY AND HE HAS FOLLOWED IT TO A SURE DESTINATION.
BUT THIS IS NOT HIS *FINAL* DESTINATION.
PERHAPS *YOU'D* LIKE TO EXPLAIN, EDEN?

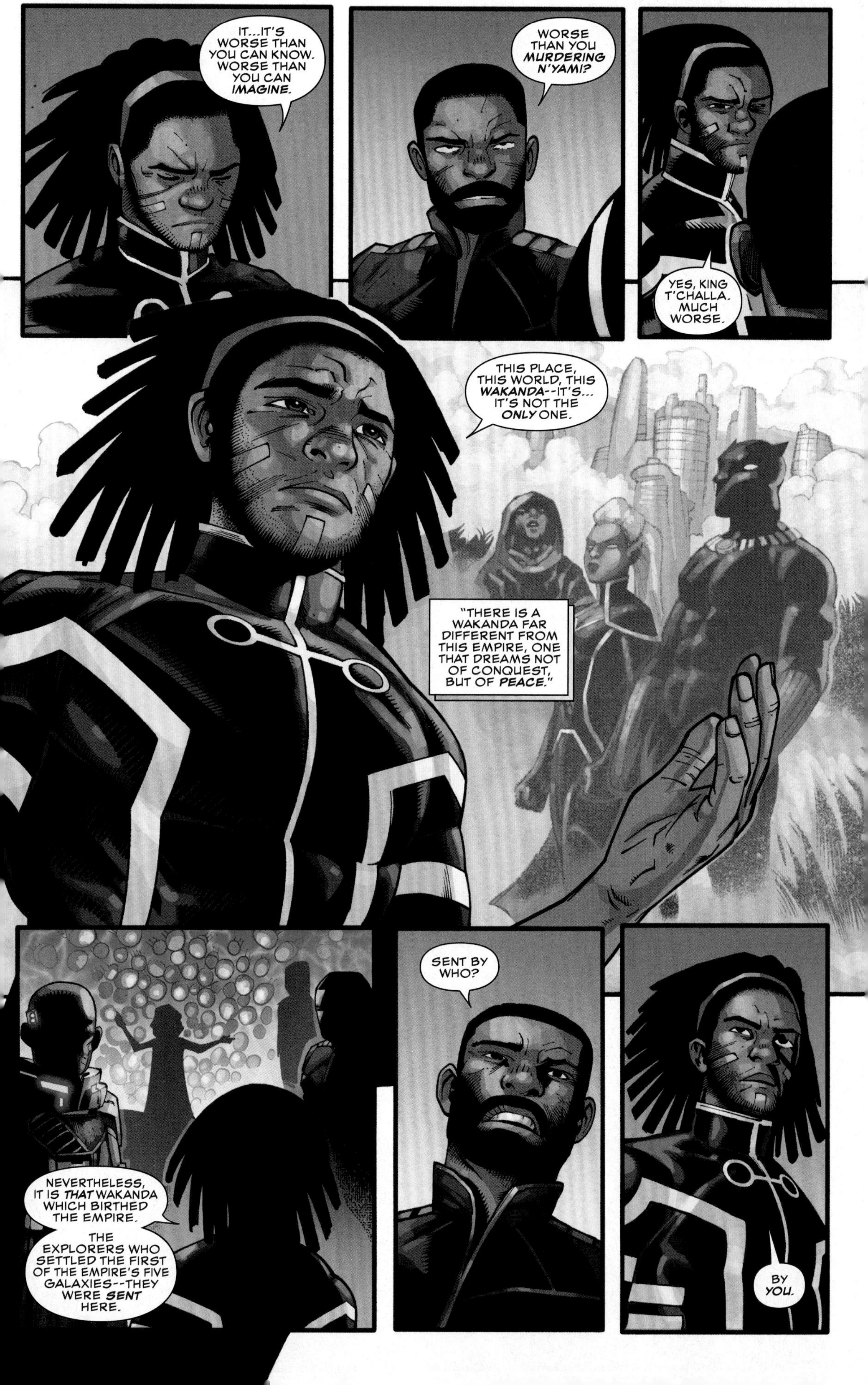
IT...IT'S WORSE THAN YOU CAN KNOW. WORSE THAN YOU CAN IMAGINE.
WORSE THAN YOU MURDERING N'YAMI?
YES, KING T'CHALLA. MUCH WORSE.
THIS PLACE, THIS WORLD, THIS WAKANDA--IT'S... IT'S NOT THE ONLY ONE.
"THERE IS A WAKANDA FAR DIFFERENT FROM THIS EMPIRE, ONE THAT DREAMS NOT OF CONQUEST, BUT OF PEACE."
NEVERTHELESS, IT IS THAT WAKANDA WHICH BIRTHED THE EMPIRE.
THE EXPLORERS WHO SETTLED THE FIRST OF THE EMPIRE'S FIVE GALAXIES--THEY WERE SENT HERE.
SENT BY WHO?
BY YOU.

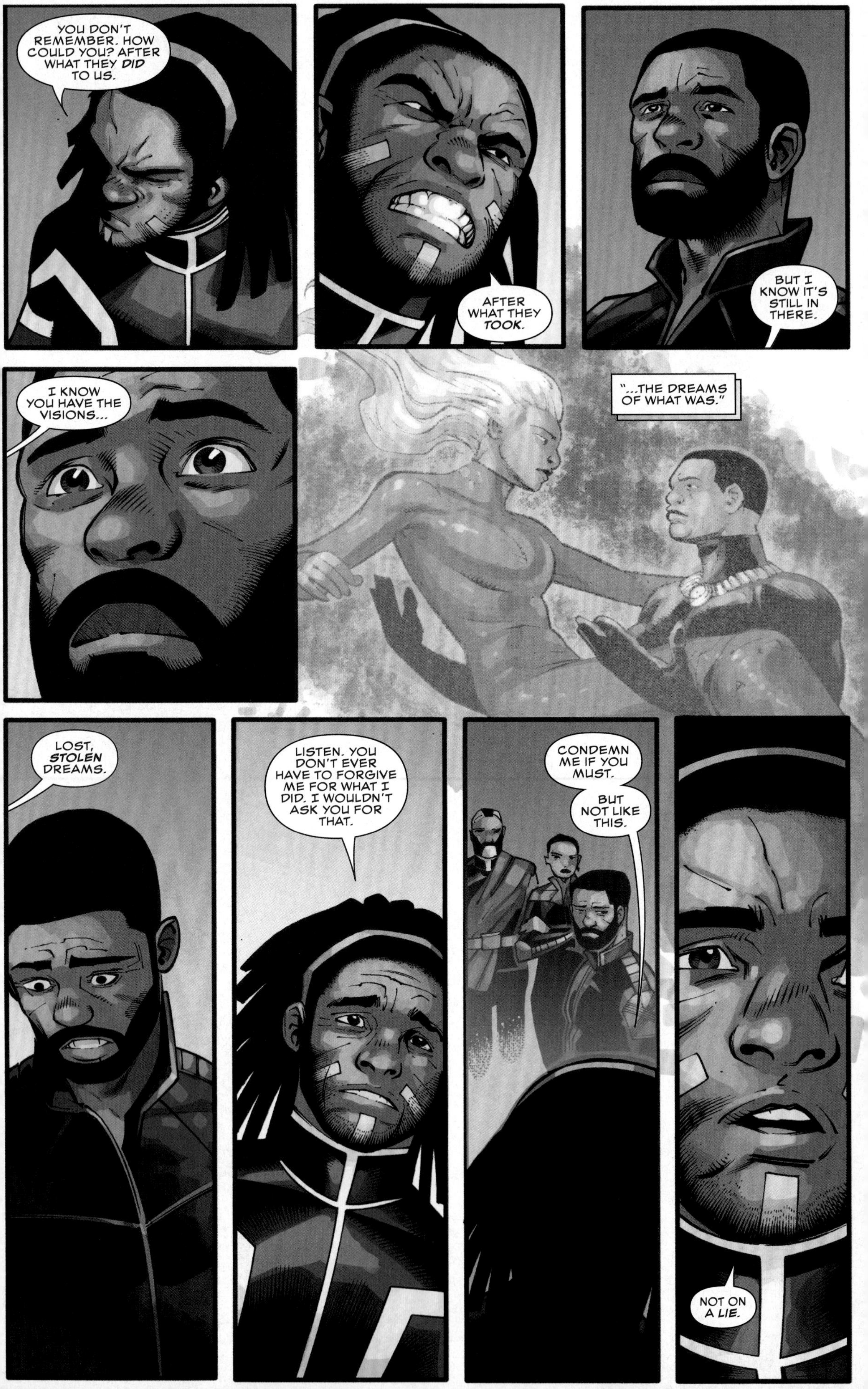
YOU DON'T REMEMBER. HOW COULD YOU? AFTER WHAT THEY DID TO US.
AFTER WHAT THEY TOOK.
BUT I KNOW IT'S STILL IN THERE.
I KNOW YOU HAVE THE VISIONS...
"...THE DREAMS OF WHAT WAS."
LOST, STOLEN DREAMS.
LISTEN. YOU DON'T EVER HAVE TO FORGIVE ME FOR WHAT I DID. I WOULDN'T ASK YOU FOR THAT.
CONDEMN ME IF YOU MUST.
BUT NOT LIKE THIS.
NOT ON A LIE.

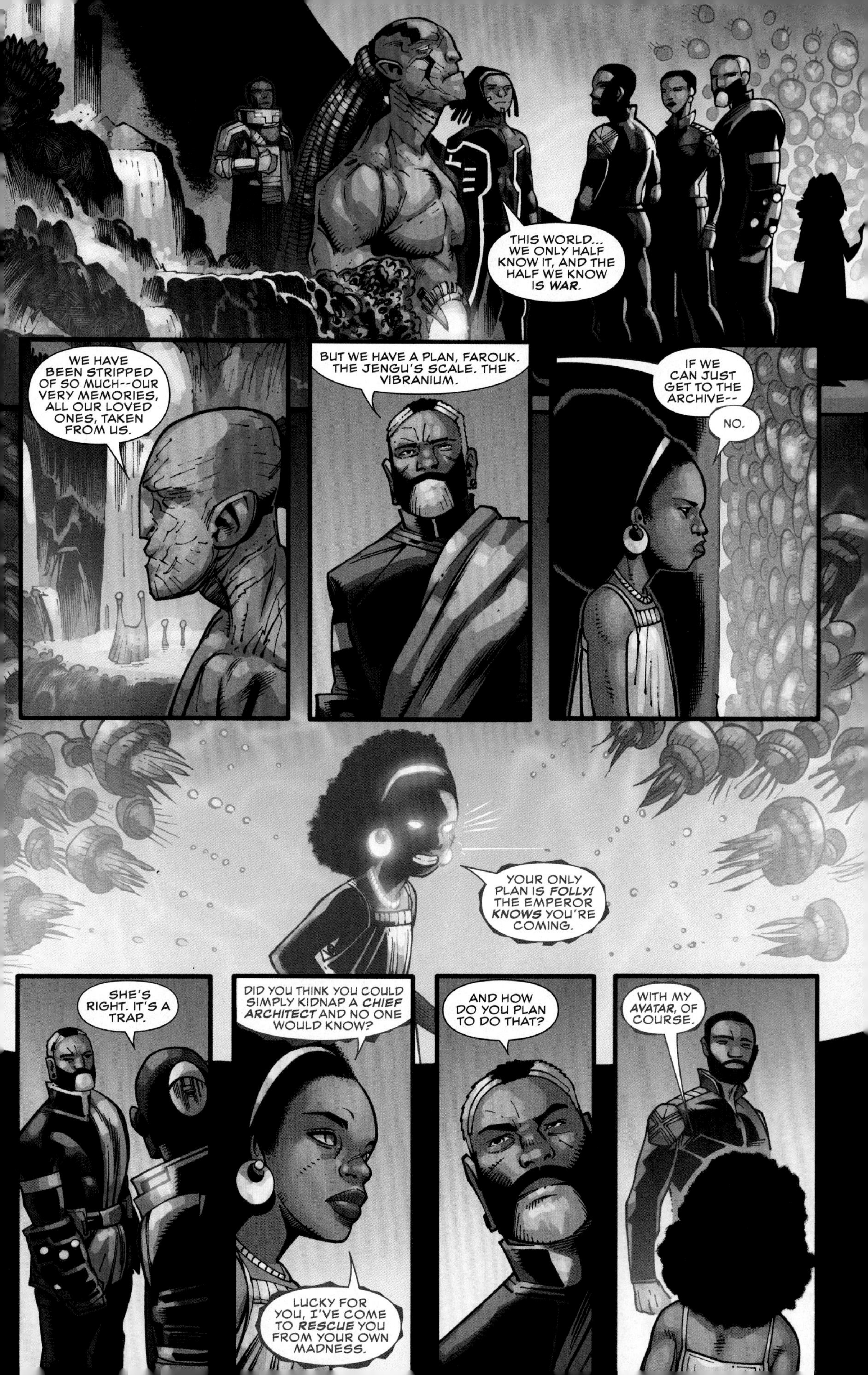
THIS WORLD... WE ONLY HALF KNOW IT, AND THE HALF WE KNOW IS WAR.
WE HAVE BEEN STRIPPED OF SO MUCH--OUR VERY MEMORIES, ALL OUR LOVED ONES, TAKEN FROM US.
BUT WE HAVE A PLAN, FAROUK. THE JENGU'S SCALE. THE VIBRANIUM.
IF WE CAN JUST GET TO THE ARCHIVE--
NO.
YOUR ONLY PLAN IS FOLLY! THE EMPEROR KNOWS YOU'RE COMING.
SHE'S RIGHT. IT'S A TRAP.
DID YOU THINK YOU COULD SIMPLY KIDNAP A CHIEF ARCHITECT AND NO ONE WOULD KNOW?
LUCKY FOR YOU, I'VE COME TO RESCUE YOU FROM YOUR OWN MADNESS.
AND HOW DO YOU PLAN TO DO THAT?
WITH MY AVATAR, OF COURSE.

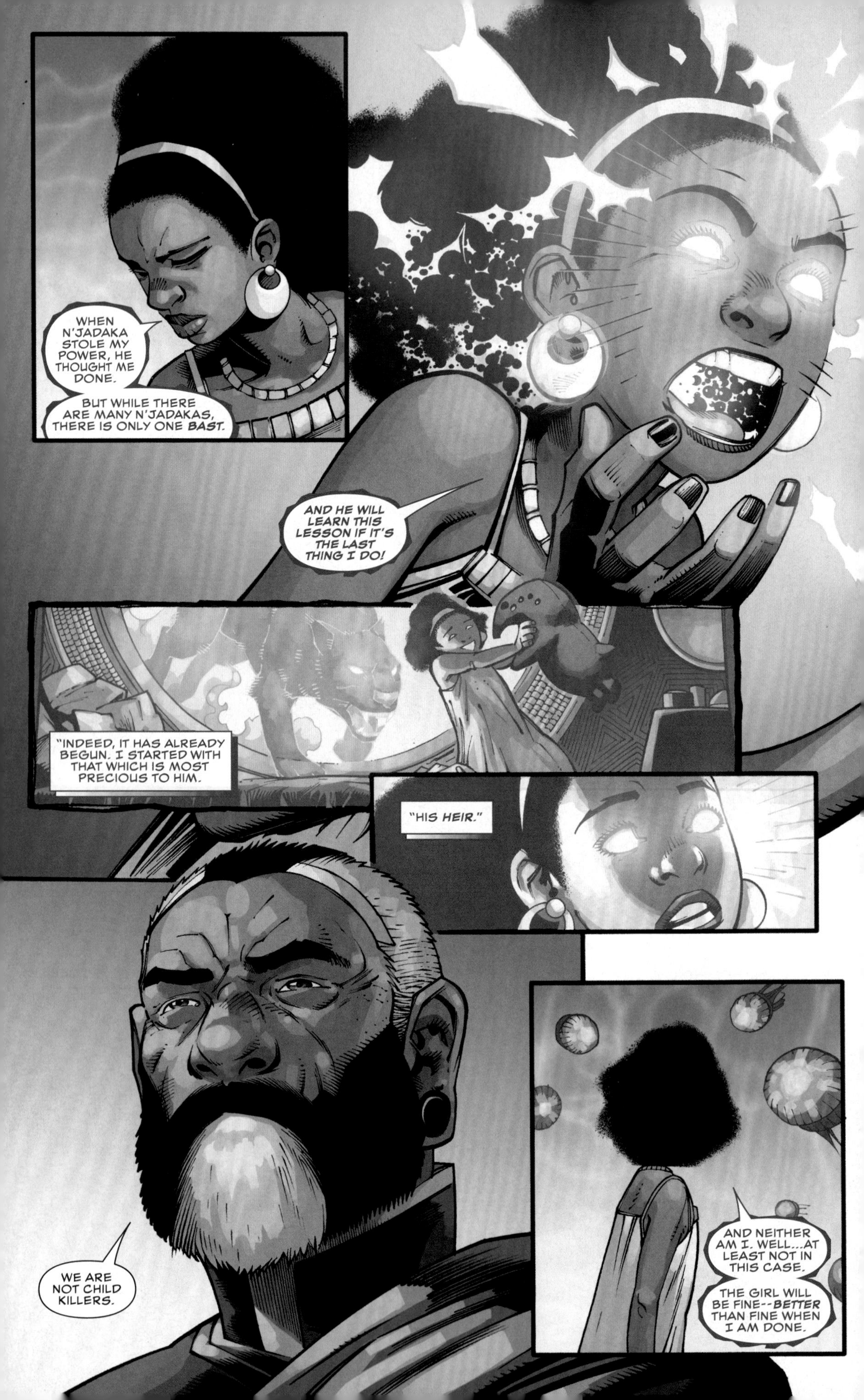
WHEN N'JADAKA STOLE MY POWER, HE THOUGHT ME DONE.
BUT WHILE THERE ARE MANY N'JADAKAS, THERE IS ONLY ONE *BAST*.
AND HE WILL LEARN THIS LESSON IF IT'S THE LAST THING I DO!
"INDEED, IT HAS ALREADY BEGUN. I STARTED WITH THAT WHICH IS MOST PRECIOUS TO HIM.
"HIS *HEIR*."
WE ARE NOT CHILD KILLERS.
AND NEITHER AM I. WELL...AT LEAST NOT IN THIS CASE.
THE GIRL WILL BE FINE--*BETTER* THAN FINE WHEN I AM DONE.

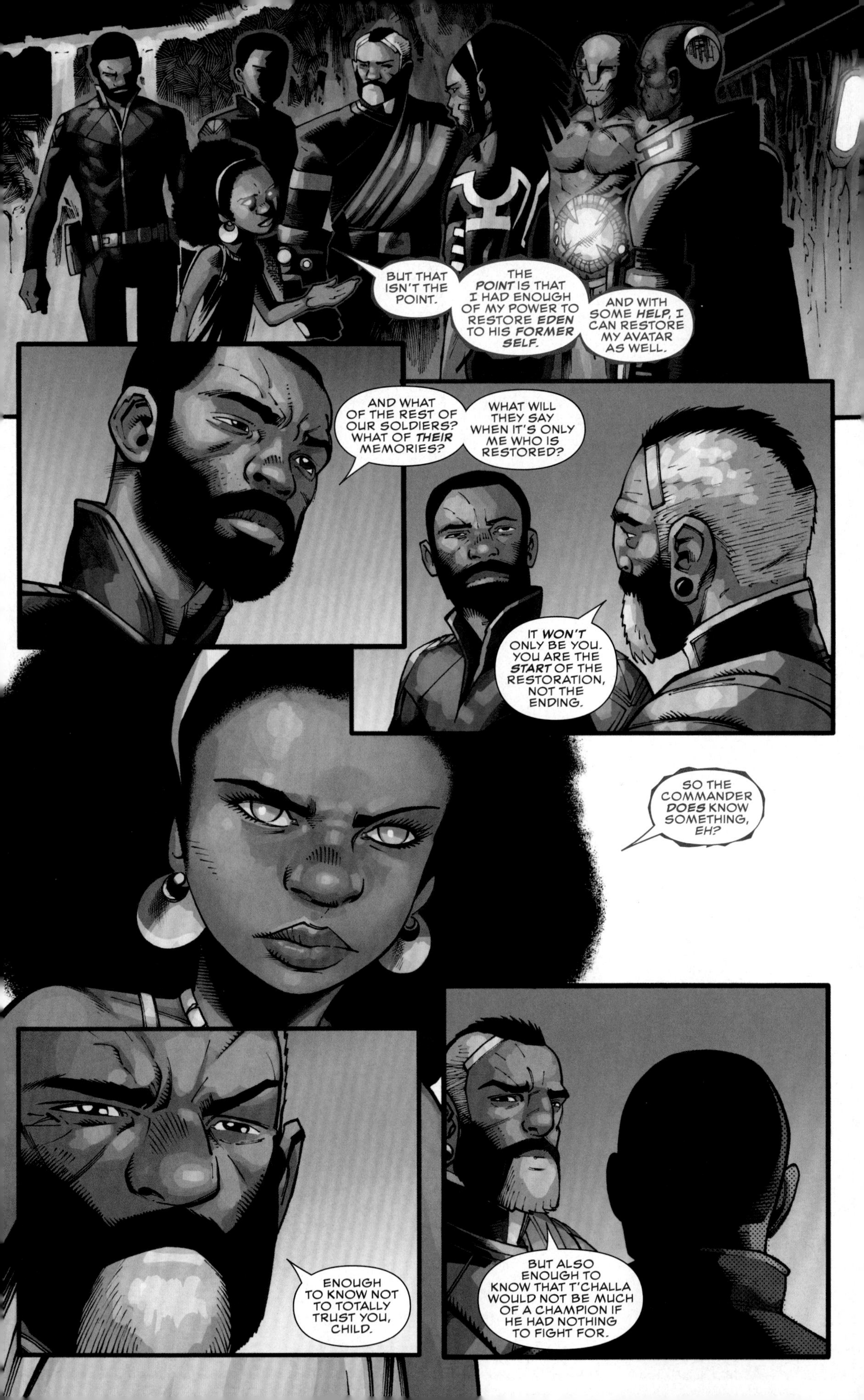
BUT THAT ISN'T THE POINT.
THE POINT IS THAT I HAD ENOUGH OF MY POWER TO RESTORE EDEN TO HIS FORMER SELF.
AND WITH SOME HELP, I CAN RESTORE MY AVATAR AS WELL.
AND WHAT OF THE REST OF OUR SOLDIERS? WHAT OF THEIR MEMORIES?
WHAT WILL THEY SAY WHEN IT'S ONLY ME WHO IS RESTORED?
IT WON'T ONLY BE YOU. YOU ARE THE START OF THE RESTORATION, NOT THE ENDING.
SO THE COMMANDER DOES KNOW SOMETHING, EH?
ENOUGH TO KNOW NOT TO TOTALLY TRUST YOU, CHILD.
BUT ALSO ENOUGH TO KNOW THAT T'CHALLA WOULD NOT BE MUCH OF A CHAMPION IF HE HAD NOTHING TO FIGHT FOR.

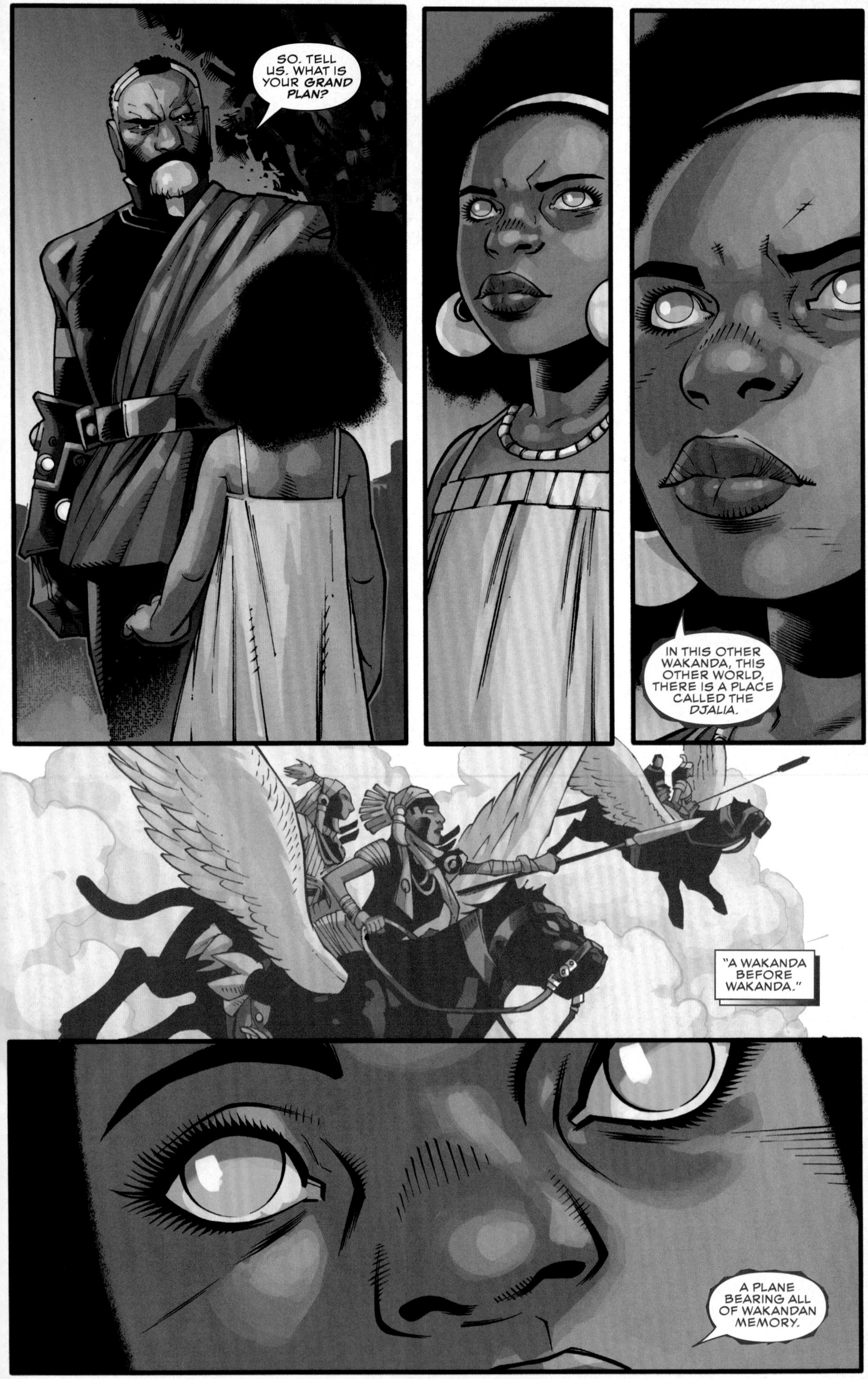
SO. TELL US. WHAT IS YOUR GRAND PLAN?
IN THIS OTHER WAKANDA, THIS OTHER WORLD, THERE IS A PLACE CALLED THE DJALIA.
"A WAKANDA BEFORE WAKANDA."
A PLANE BEARING ALL OF WAKANDAN MEMORY.

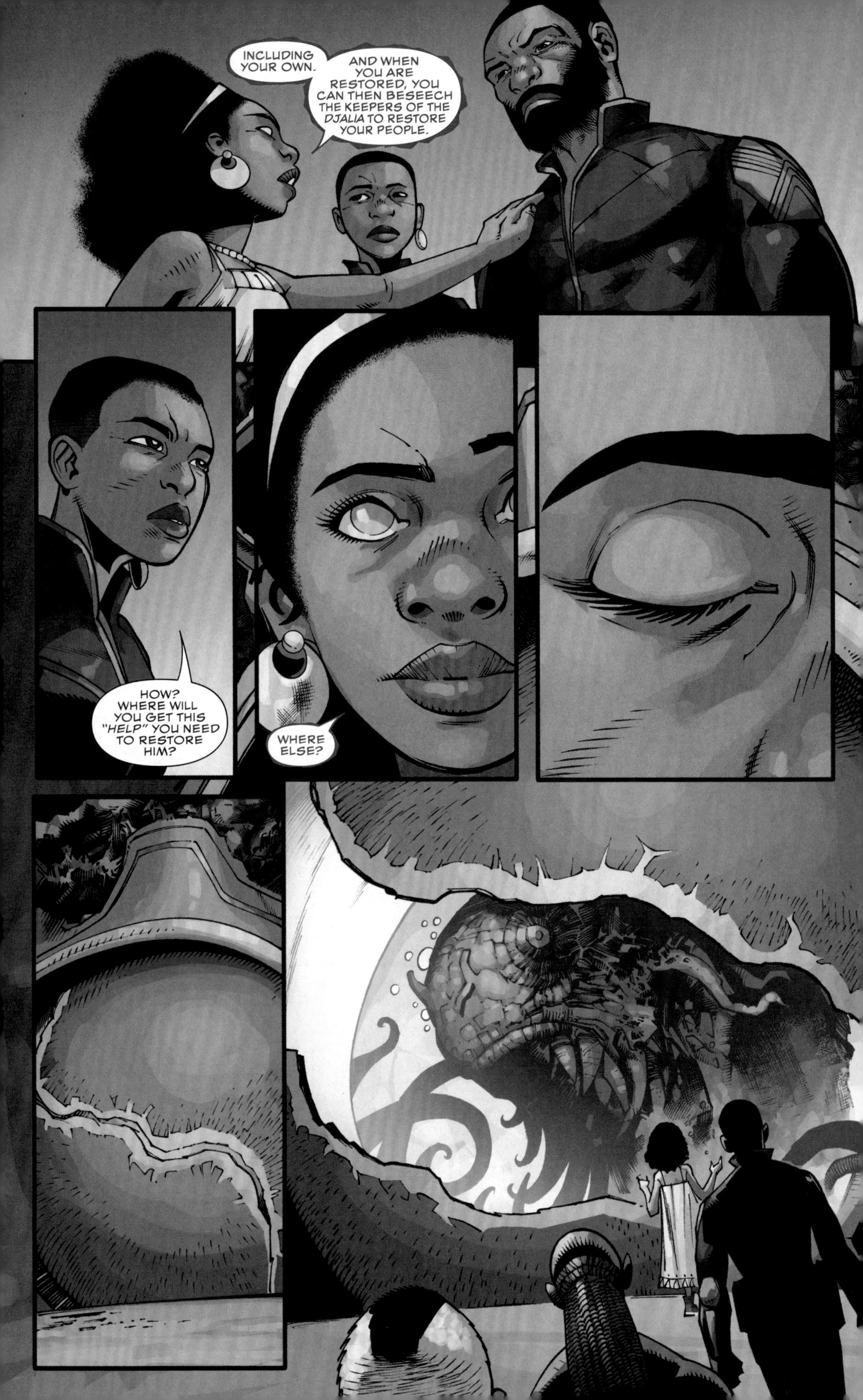
INCLUDING YOUR OWN.
AND WHEN YOU ARE RESTORED, YOU CAN THEN BESEECH THE KEEPERS OF THE DJALIA TO RESTORE YOUR PEOPLE.
HOW? WHERE WILL YOU GET THIS "HELP" YOU NEED TO RESTORE HIM?
WHERE ELSE?

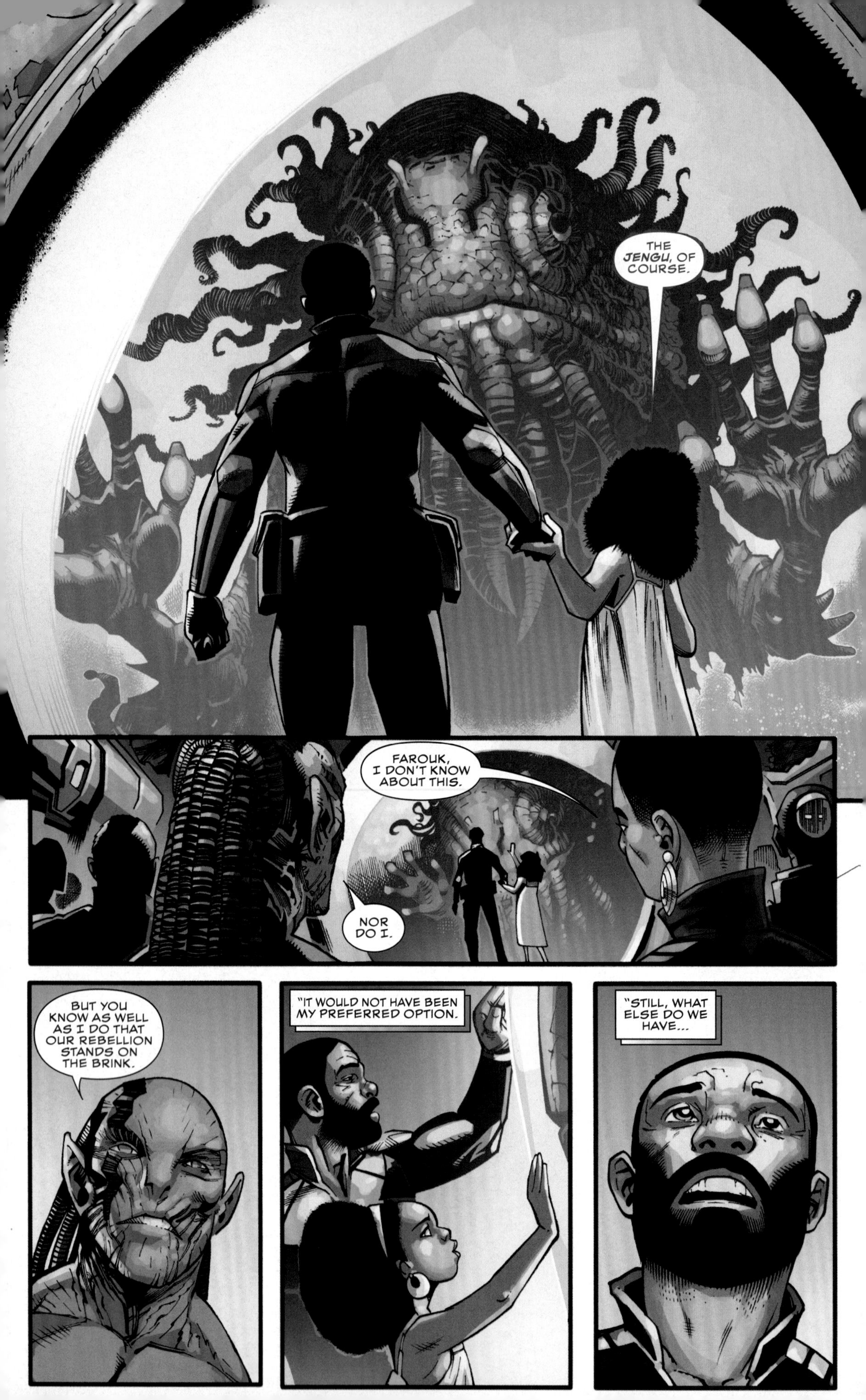
THE JENGU, OF COURSE.
FAROUK, I DON'T KNOW ABOUT THIS.
NOR DO I.
BUT YOU KNOW AS WELL AS I DO THAT OUR REBELLION STANDS ON THE BRINK.
"IT WOULD NOT HAVE BEEN MY PREFERRED OPTION.
"STILL, WHAT ELSE DO WE HAVE...

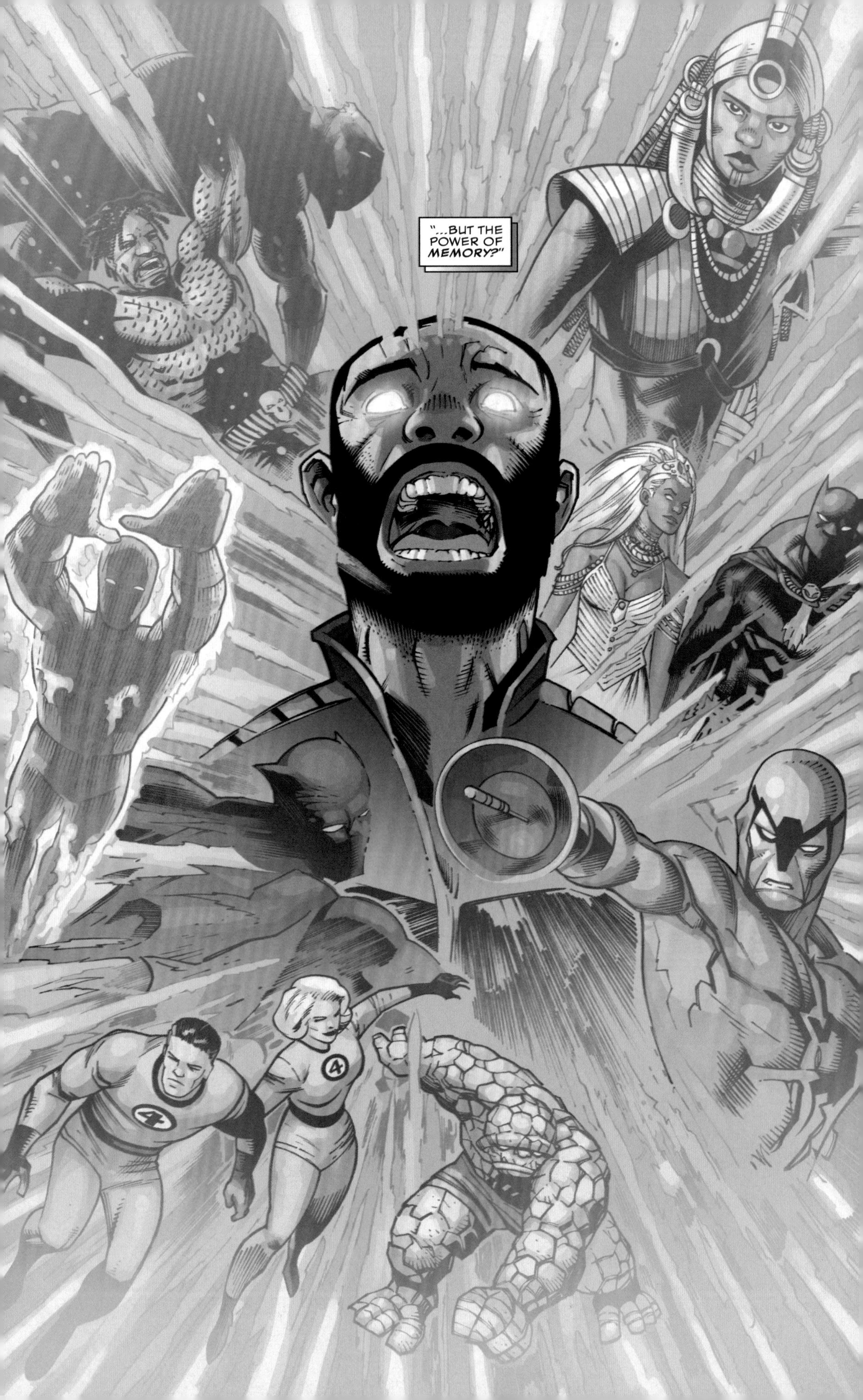
"...BUT THE POWER OF MEMORY?"

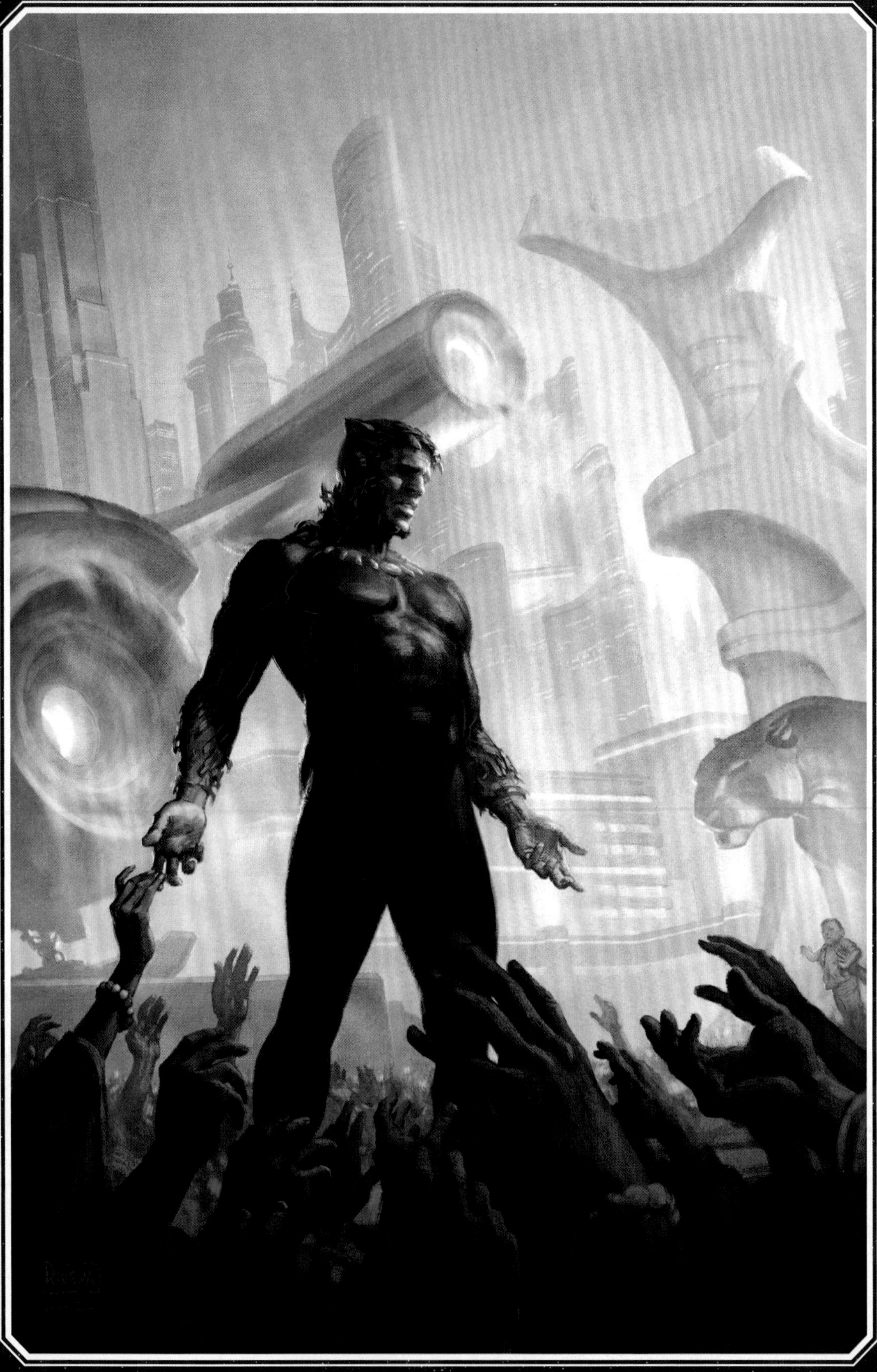

12

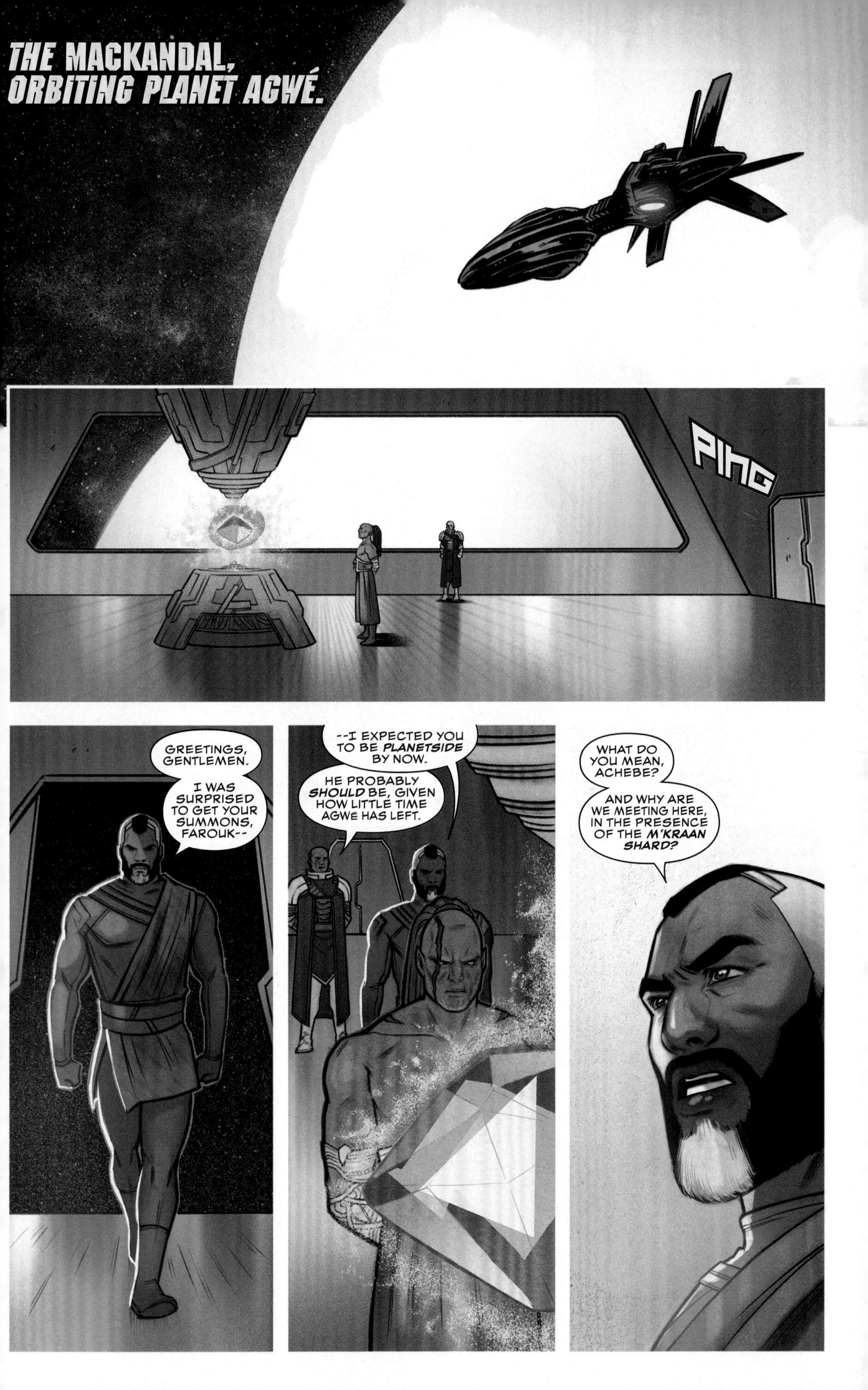
THE MACKANDAL, ORBITING PLANET AGWÉ.
PING
GREETINGS, GENTLEMEN.
I WAS SURPRISED TO GET YOUR SUMMONS, FAROUK--
--I EXPECTED YOU TO BE PLANETSIDE BY NOW.
HE PROBABLY SHOULD BE, GIVEN HOW LITTLE TIME AGWE HAS LEFT.
WHAT DO YOU MEAN, ACHEBE?
AND WHY ARE WE MEETING HERE, IN THE PRESENCE OF THE M'KRAAN SHARD?

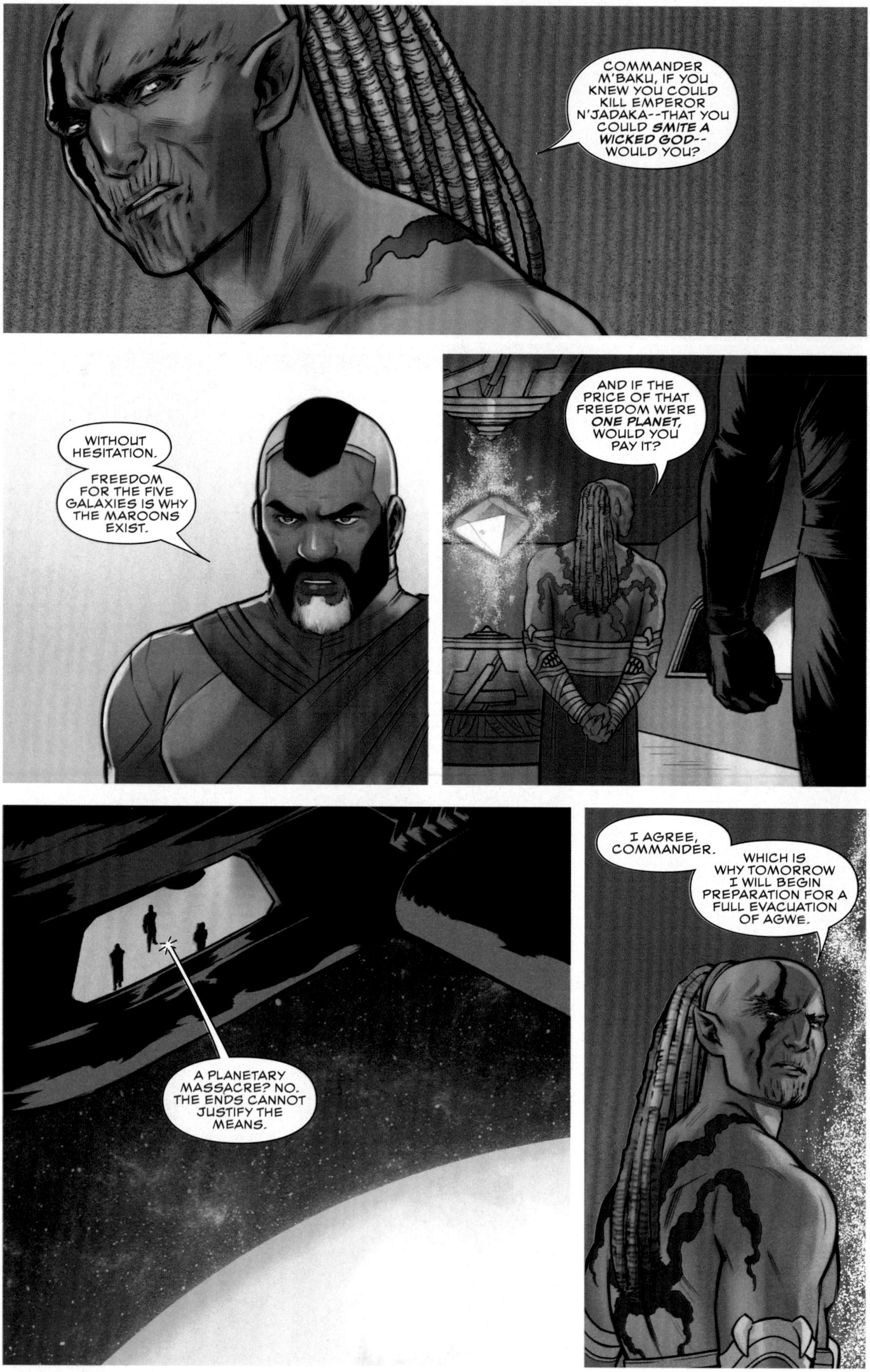
COMMANDER M'BAKU, IF YOU KNEW YOU COULD KILL EMPEROR N'JADAKA--THAT YOU COULD SMITE A WICKED GOD--WOULD YOU?
WITHOUT HESITATION.
FREEDOM FOR THE FIVE GALAXIES IS WHY THE MAROONS EXIST.
AND IF THE PRICE OF THAT FREEDOM WERE ONE PLANET, WOULD YOU PAY IT?
A PLANETARY MASSACRE? NO. THE ENDS CANNOT JUSTIFY THE MEANS.
I AGREE, COMMANDER.
WHICH IS WHY TOMORROW I WILL BEGIN PREPARATION FOR A FULL EVACUATION OF AGWE.

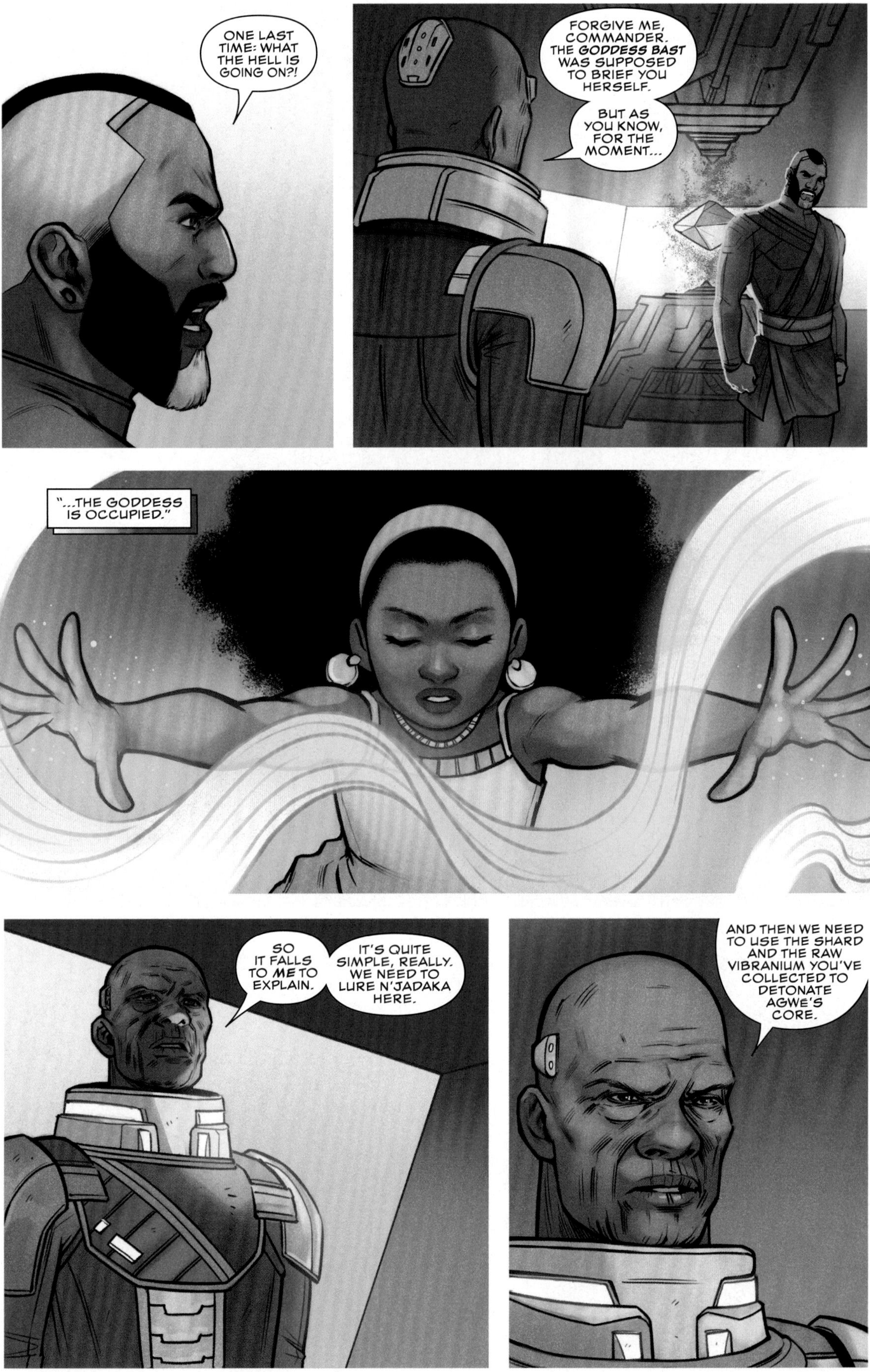
ONE LAST TIME: WHAT THE HELL IS GOING ON?!
FORGIVE ME, COMMANDER. THE GODDESS BAST WAS SUPPOSED TO BRIEF YOU HERSELF.
BUT AS YOU KNOW, FOR THE MOMENT...
"...THE GODDESS IS OCCUPIED."
SO IT FALLS TO ME TO EXPLAIN.
IT'S QUITE SIMPLE, REALLY. WE NEED TO LURE N'JADAKA HERE.
AND THEN WE NEED TO USE THE SHARD AND THE RAW VIBRANIUM YOU'VE COLLECTED TO DETONATE AGWE'S CORE.

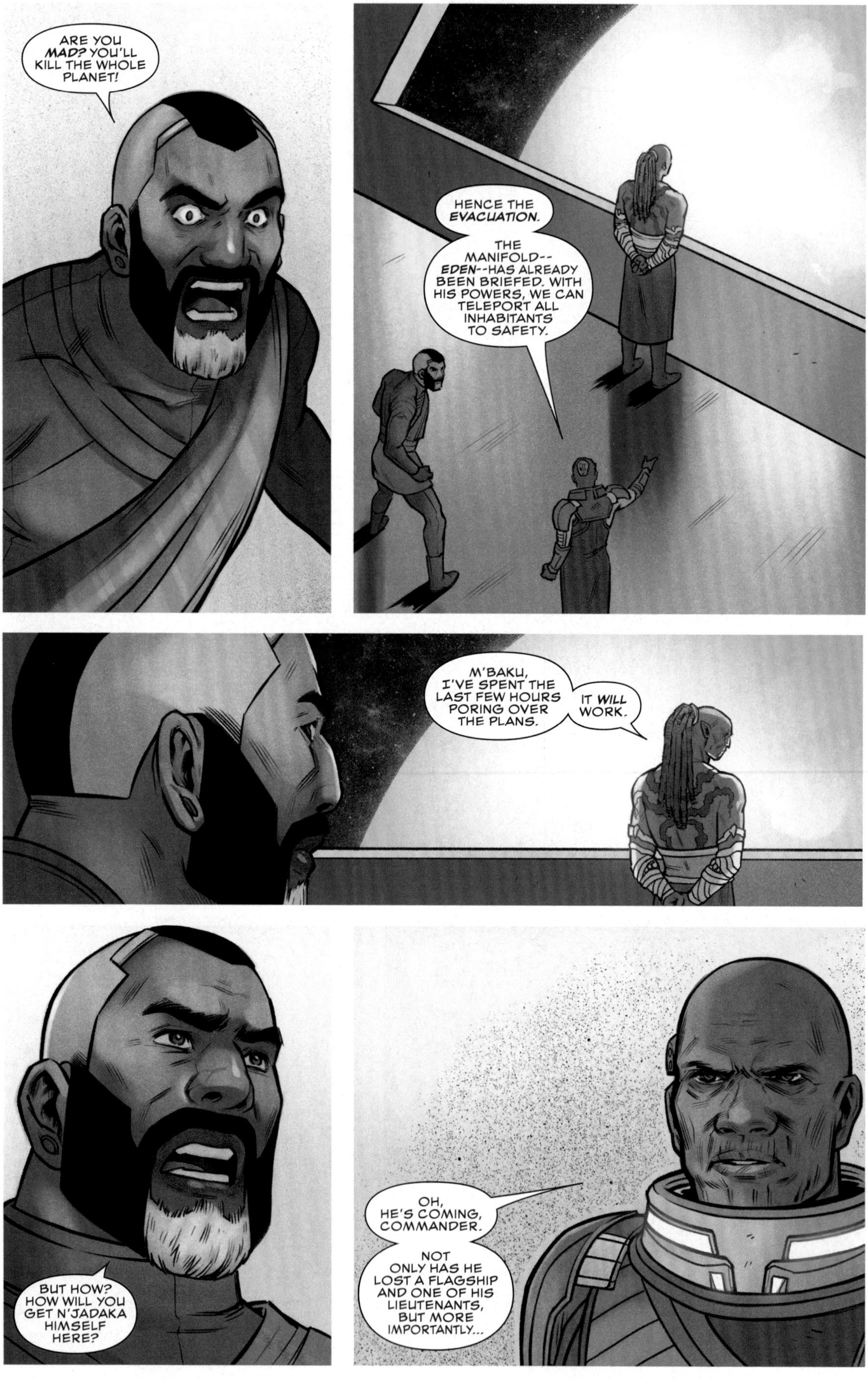
ARE YOU *MAD?* YOU'LL KILL THE WHOLE PLANET!
HENCE THE *EVACUATION.*
THE MANIFOLD-- *EDEN*--HAS ALREADY BEEN BRIEFED. WITH HIS POWERS, WE CAN TELEPORT ALL INHABITANTS TO SAFETY.
M'BAKU, I'VE SPENT THE LAST FEW HOURS PORING OVER THE PLANS.
IT *WILL* WORK.
BUT HOW? HOW WILL YOU GET N'JADAKA HIMSELF HERE?
OH, HE'S COMING, COMMANDER.
NOT ONLY HAS HE LOST A FLAGSHIP AND ONE OF HIS LIEUTENANTS, BUT MORE IMPORTANTLY...

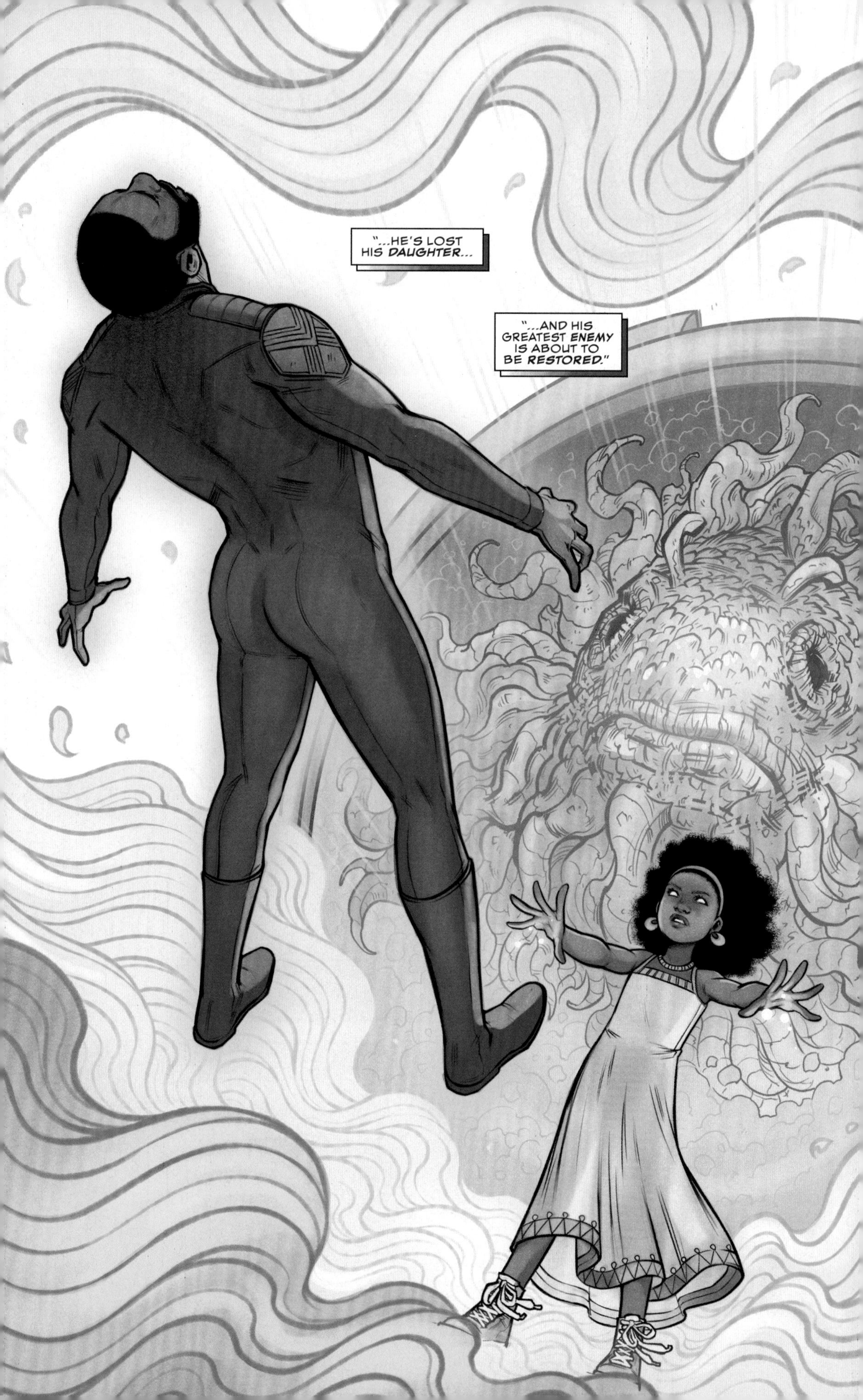
"...HE'S LOST HIS DAUGHTER...
"...AND HIS GREATEST ENEMY IS ABOUT TO BE RESTORED."

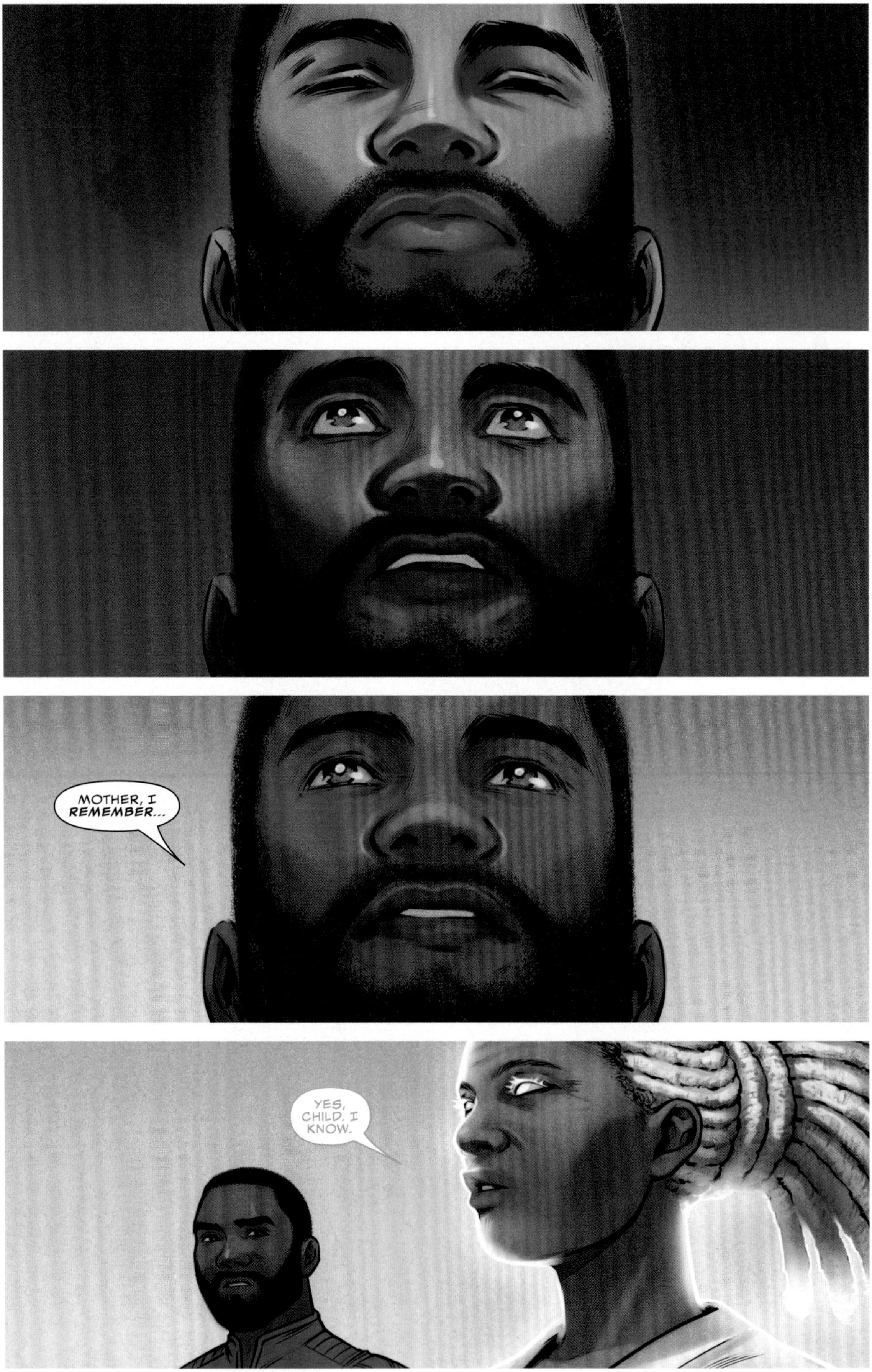
MOTHER, I REMEMBER...
YES, CHILD. I KNOW.

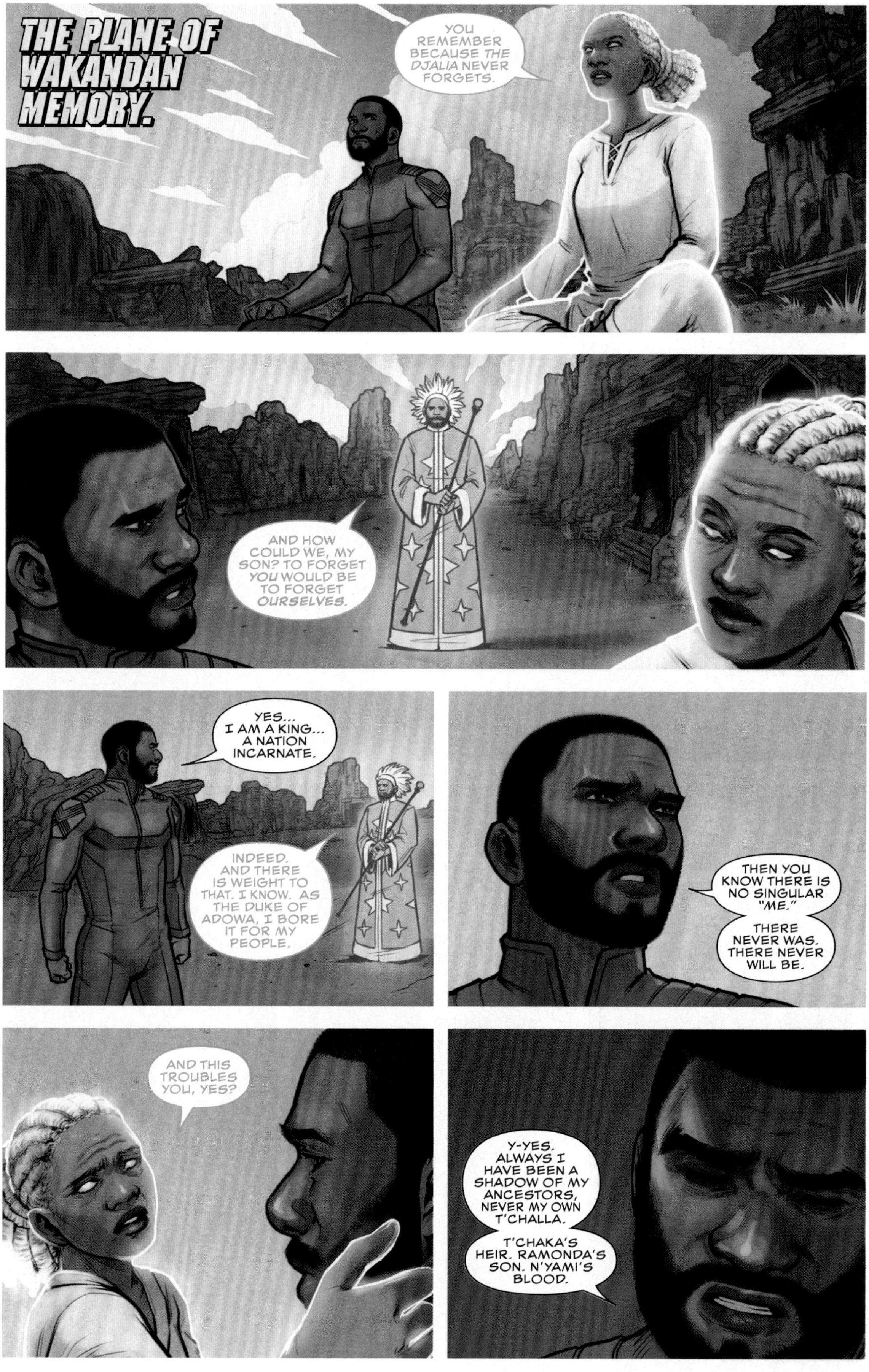
THE PLANE OF WAKANDAN MEMORY.
YOU REMEMBER BECAUSE THE DJALIA NEVER FORGETS.
AND HOW COULD WE, MY SON? TO FORGET YOU WOULD BE TO FORGET OURSELVES.
YES... I AM A KING... A NATION INCARNATE.
INDEED. AND THERE IS WEIGHT TO THAT. I KNOW. AS THE DUKE OF ADOWA, I BORE IT FOR MY PEOPLE.
THEN YOU KNOW THERE IS NO SINGULAR "ME."
THERE NEVER WAS. THERE NEVER WILL BE.
AND THIS TROUBLES YOU, YES?
Y-YES. ALWAYS I HAVE BEEN A SHADOW OF MY ANCESTORS, NEVER MY OWN T'CHALLA.
T'CHAKA'S HEIR. RAMONDA'S SON. N'YAMI'S BLOOD.

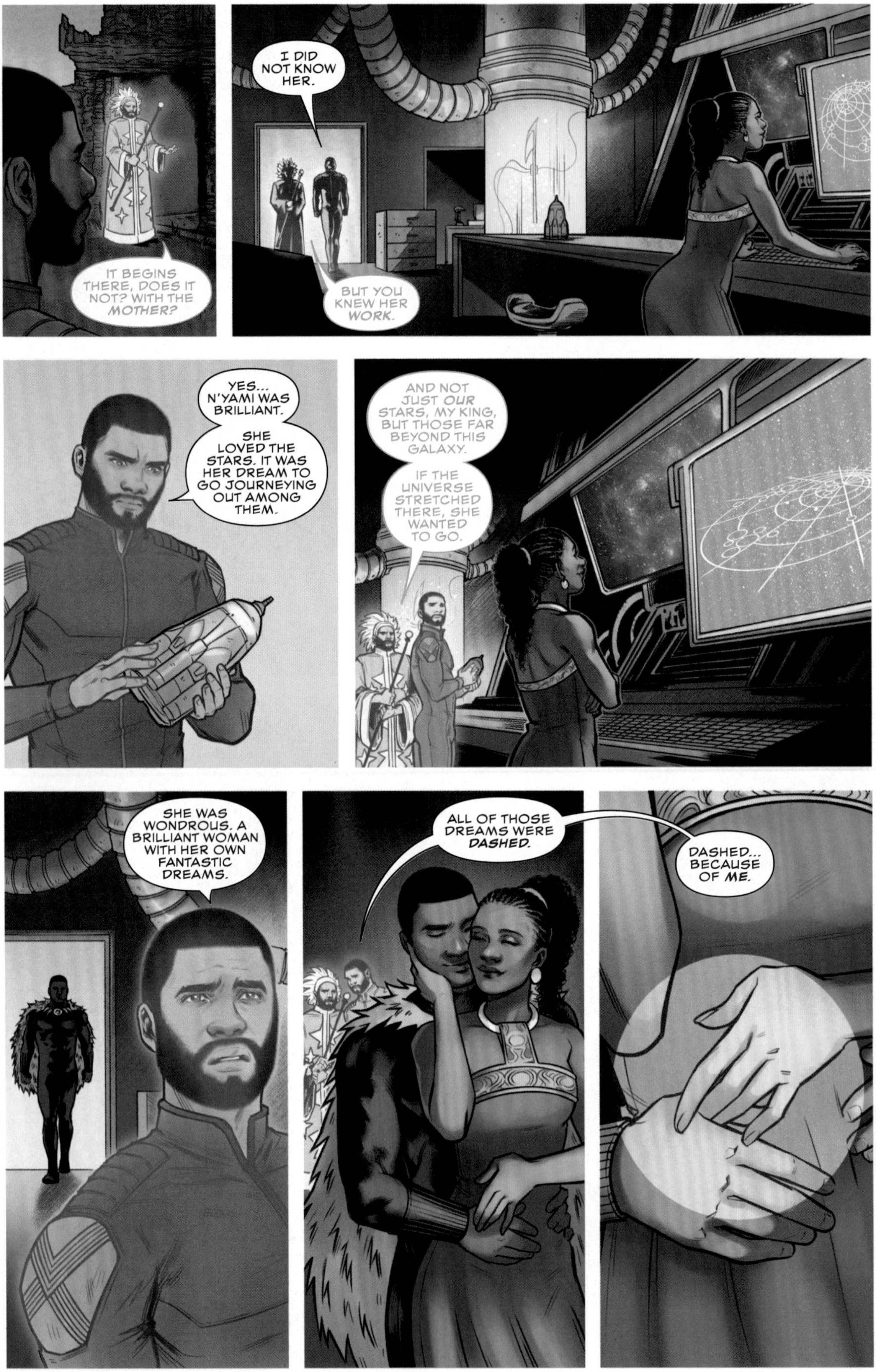
IT BEGINS THERE, DOES IT NOT? WITH THE MOTHER?
I DID NOT KNOW HER.
BUT YOU KNEW HER WORK.
YES... N'YAMI WAS BRILLIANT.
SHE LOVED THE STARS. IT WAS HER DREAM TO GO JOURNEYING OUT AMONG THEM.
AND NOT JUST OUR STARS, MY KING, BUT THOSE FAR BEYOND THIS GALAXY.
IF THE UNIVERSE STRETCHED THERE, SHE WANTED TO GO.
SHE WAS WONDROUS. A BRILLIANT WOMAN WITH HER OWN FANTASTIC DREAMS.
ALL OF THOSE DREAMS WERE DASHED.
DASHED... BECAUSE OF ME.

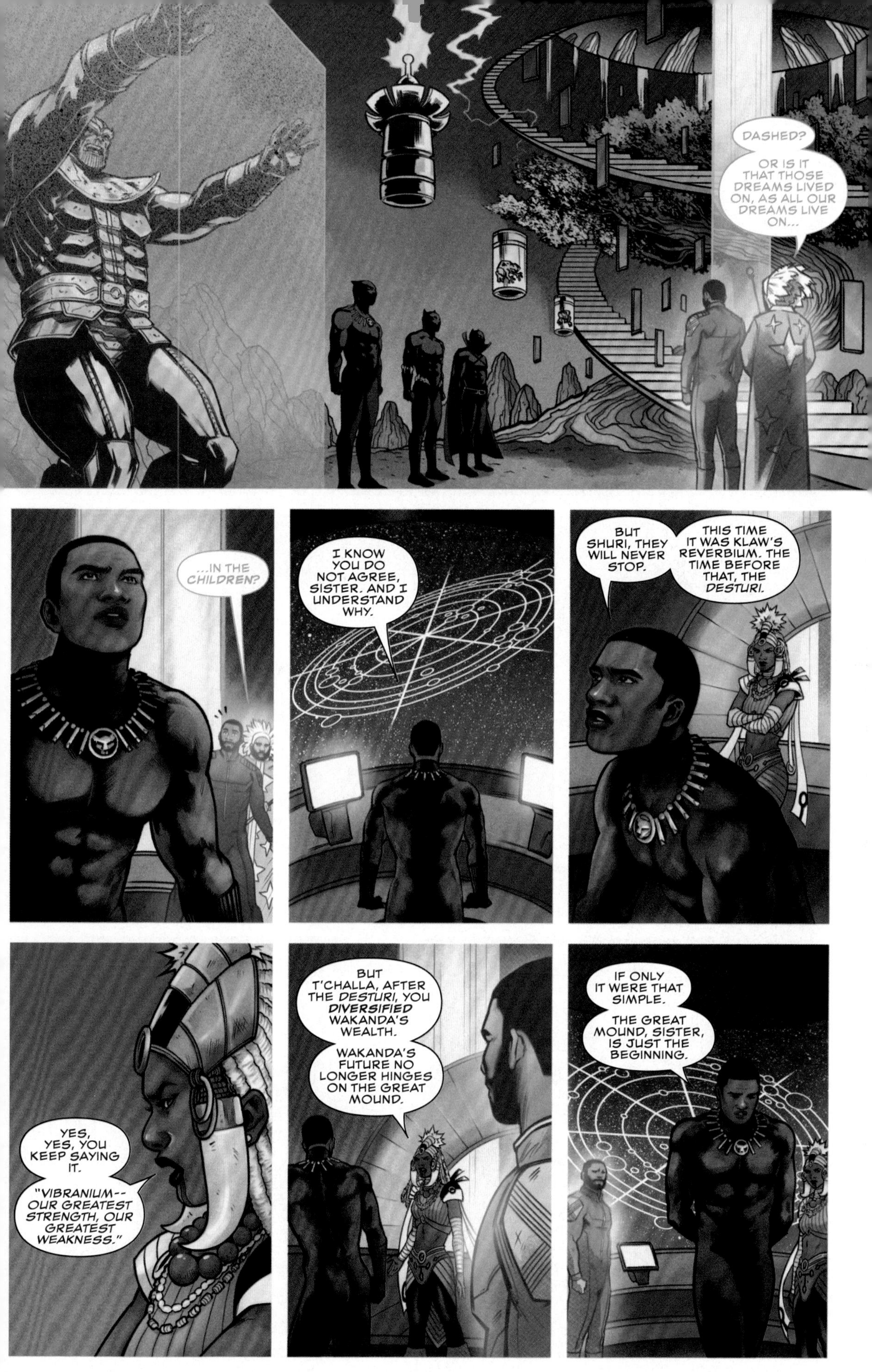
DASHED?
OR IS IT THAT THOSE DREAMS LIVED ON, AS ALL OUR DREAMS LIVE ON...
...IN THE CHILDREN?
I KNOW YOU DO NOT AGREE, SISTER. AND I UNDERSTAND WHY.
BUT SHURI, THEY WILL NEVER STOP.
THIS TIME IT WAS KLAW'S REVERBIUM. THE TIME BEFORE THAT, THE DESTURI.
YES, YES, YOU KEEP SAYING IT.
"VIBRANIUM-- OUR GREATEST STRENGTH, OUR GREATEST WEAKNESS."
BUT T'CHALLA, AFTER THE DESTURI, YOU DIVERSIFIED WAKANDA'S WEALTH.
WAKANDA'S FUTURE NO LONGER HINGES ON THE GREAT MOUND.
IF ONLY IT WERE THAT SIMPLE.
THE GREAT MOUND, SISTER, IS JUST THE BEGINNING.

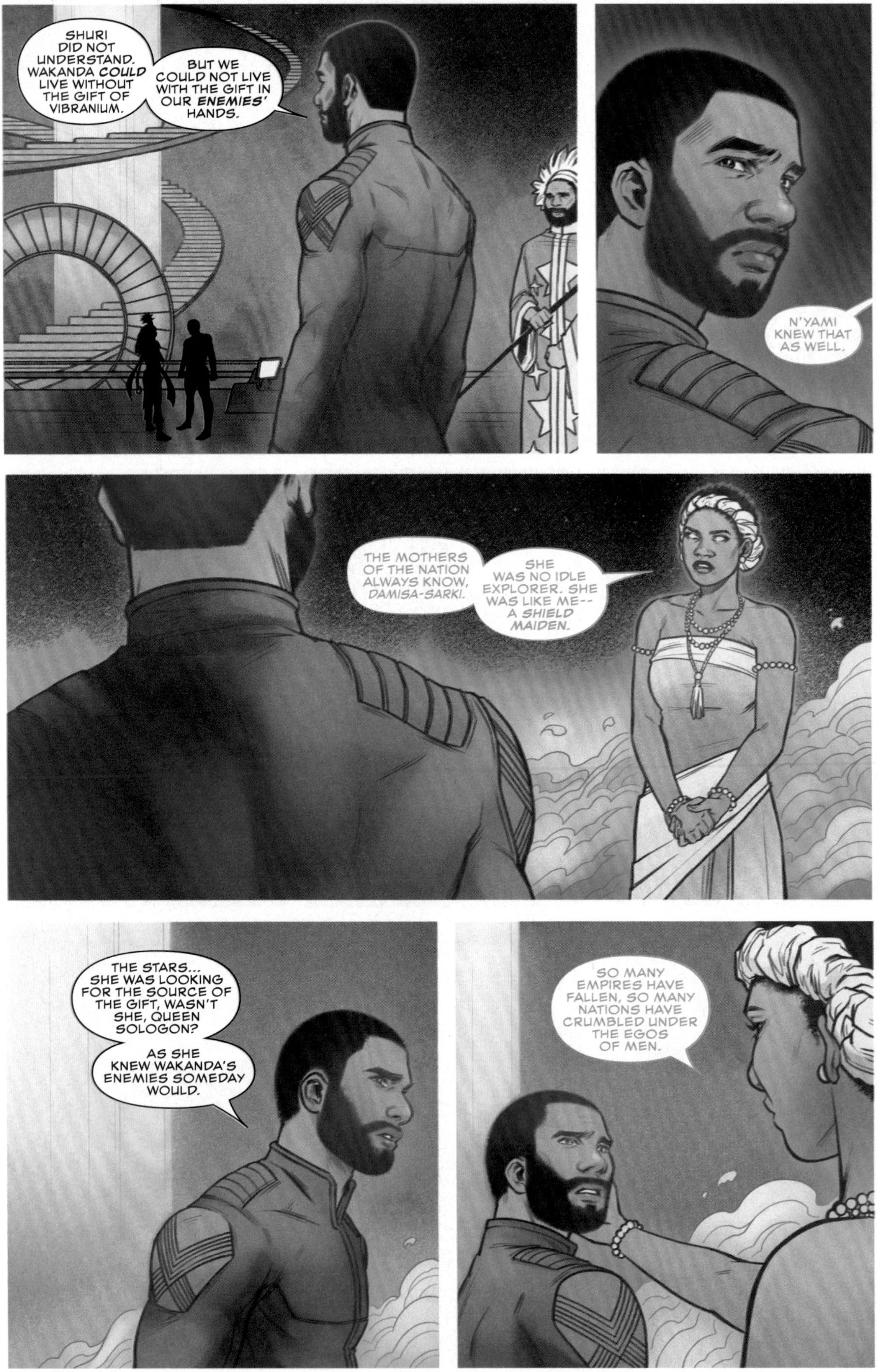
SHURI DID NOT UNDERSTAND. WAKANDA COULD LIVE WITHOUT THE GIFT OF VIBRANIUM.
BUT WE COULD NOT LIVE WITH THE GIFT IN OUR ENEMIES' HANDS.
N'YAMI KNEW THAT AS WELL.
THE MOTHERS OF THE NATION ALWAYS KNOW, DAMISA-SARKI.
SHE WAS NO IDLE EXPLORER. SHE WAS LIKE ME-- A SHIELD MAIDEN.
THE STARS... SHE WAS LOOKING FOR THE SOURCE OF THE GIFT, WASN'T SHE, QUEEN SOLOGON?
AS SHE KNEW WAKANDA'S ENEMIES SOMEDAY WOULD.
SO MANY EMPIRES HAVE FALLEN, SO MANY NATIONS HAVE CRUMBLED UNDER THE EGOS OF MEN.

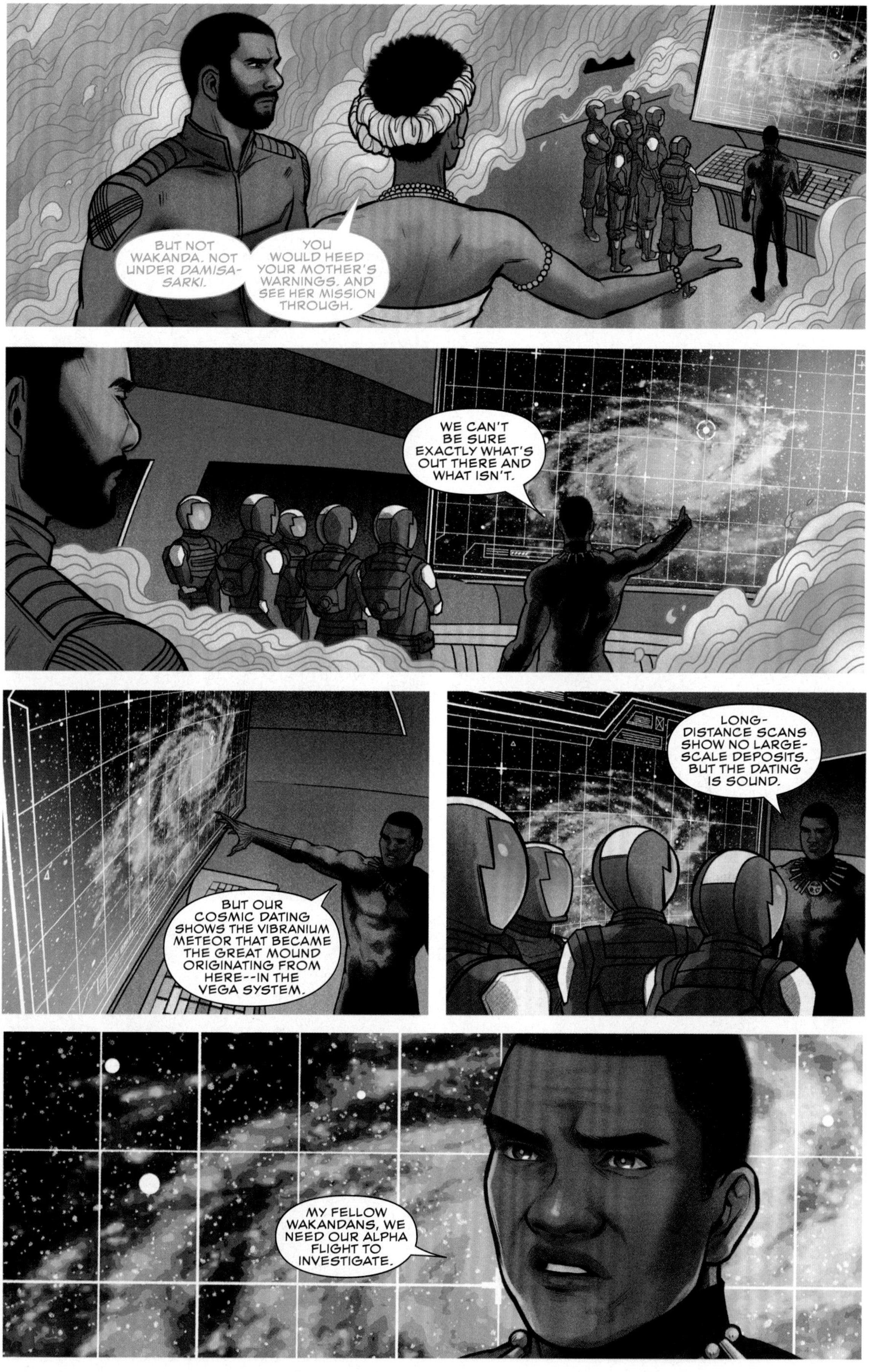
YOU WOULD HEED YOUR MOTHER'S WARNINGS. AND SEE HER MISSION THROUGH.
BUT NOT WAKANDA. NOT UNDER DAMISA-SARKI.
WE CAN'T BE SURE EXACTLY WHAT'S OUT THERE AND WHAT ISN'T.
BUT OUR COSMIC DATING SHOWS THE VIBRANIUM METEOR THAT BECAME THE GREAT MOUND ORIGINATING FROM HERE--IN THE VEGA SYSTEM.
LONG-DISTANCE SCANS SHOW NO LARGE-SCALE DEPOSITS. BUT THE DATING IS SOUND.
MY FELLOW WAKANDANS, WE NEED OUR ALPHA FLIGHT TO INVESTIGATE.

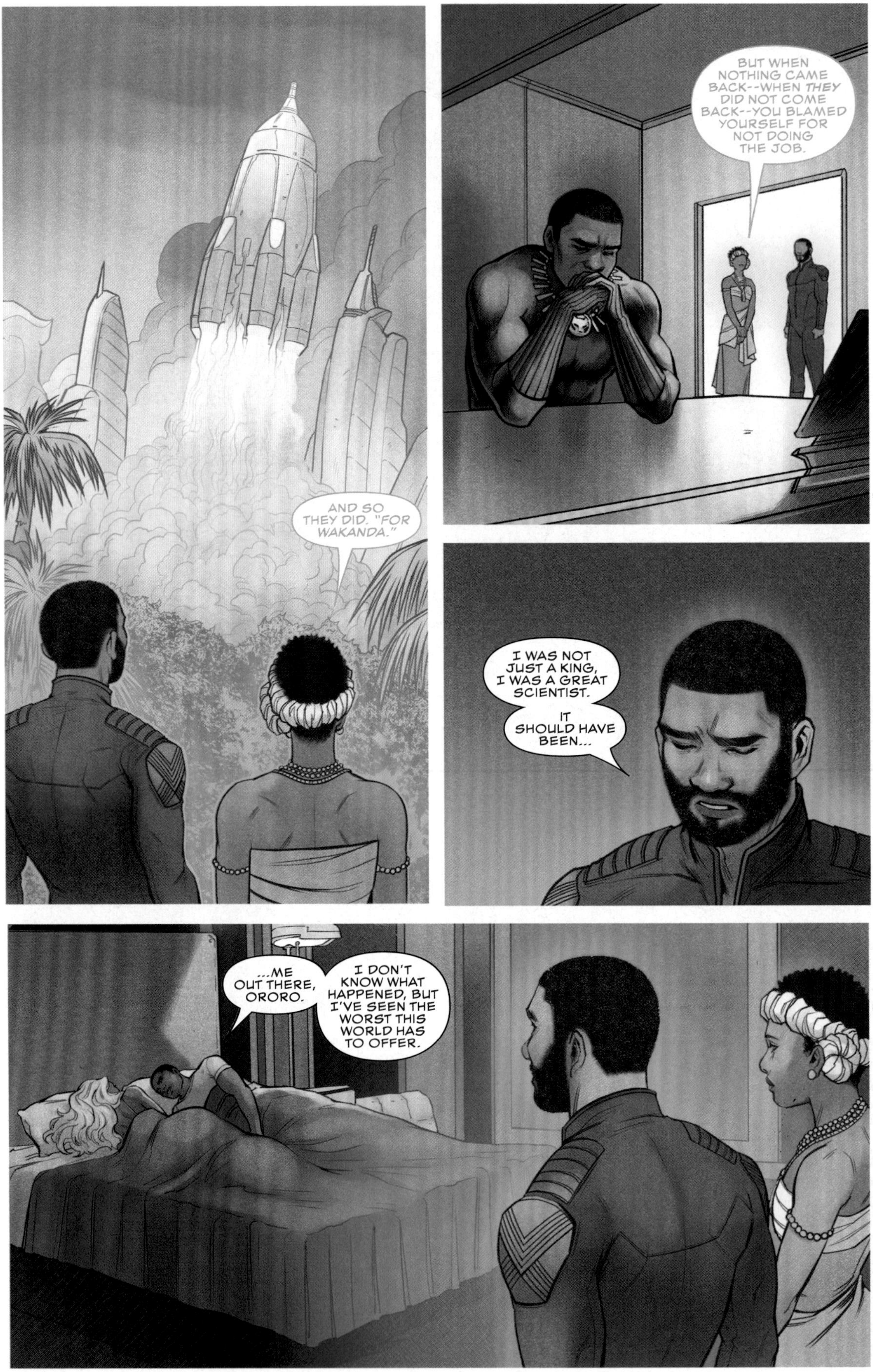
AND SO THEY DID. "FOR WAKANDA."
BUT WHEN NOTHING CAME BACK--WHEN *THEY* DID NOT COME BACK--YOU BLAMED YOURSELF FOR NOT DOING THE JOB.
I WAS NOT JUST A KING, I WAS A GREAT SCIENTIST.
IT SHOULD HAVE BEEN...
...ME OUT THERE, ORORO.
I DON'T KNOW WHAT HAPPENED, BUT I'VE SEEN THE WORST THIS WORLD HAS TO OFFER.

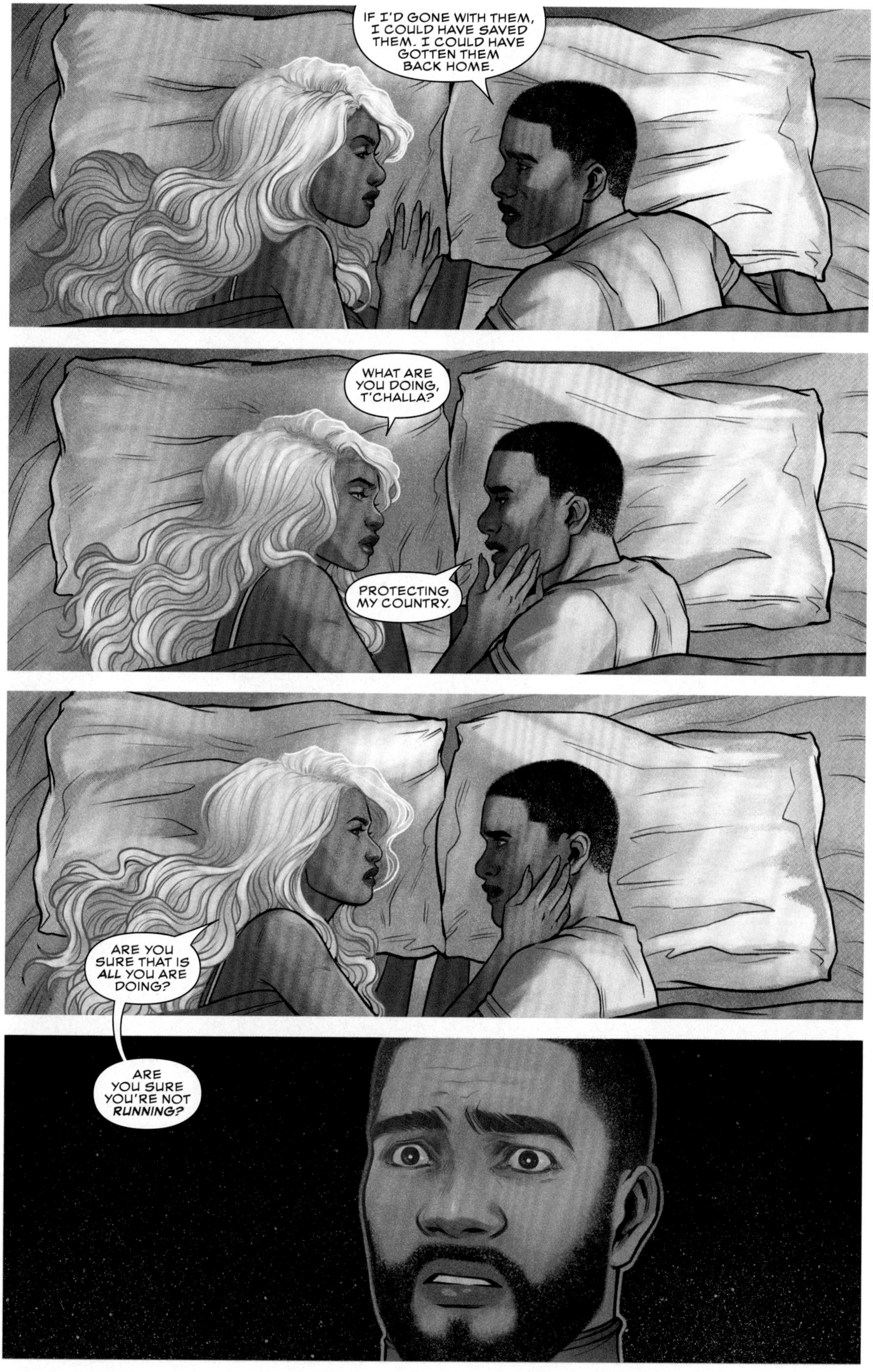
IF I'D GONE WITH THEM, I COULD HAVE SAVED THEM. I COULD HAVE GOTTEN THEM BACK HOME.
WHAT ARE YOU DOING, T'CHALLA?
PROTECTING MY COUNTRY.
ARE YOU SURE THAT IS ALL YOU ARE DOING?
ARE YOU SURE YOU'RE NOT RUNNING?

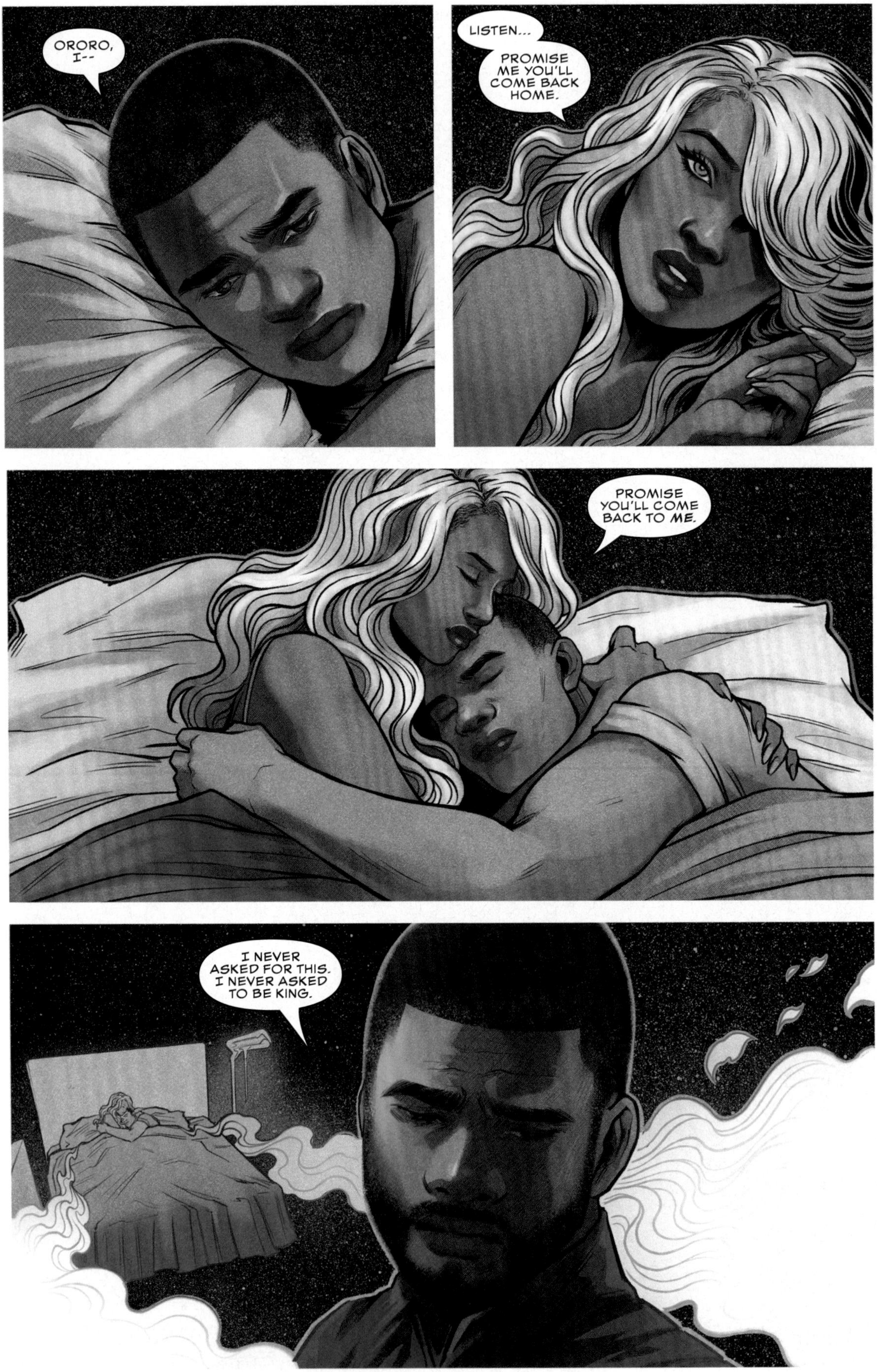
ORORO, I--
LISTEN...
PROMISE ME YOU'LL COME BACK HOME.
PROMISE YOU'LL COME BACK TO *ME*.
I NEVER ASKED FOR THIS. I NEVER ASKED TO BE KING.

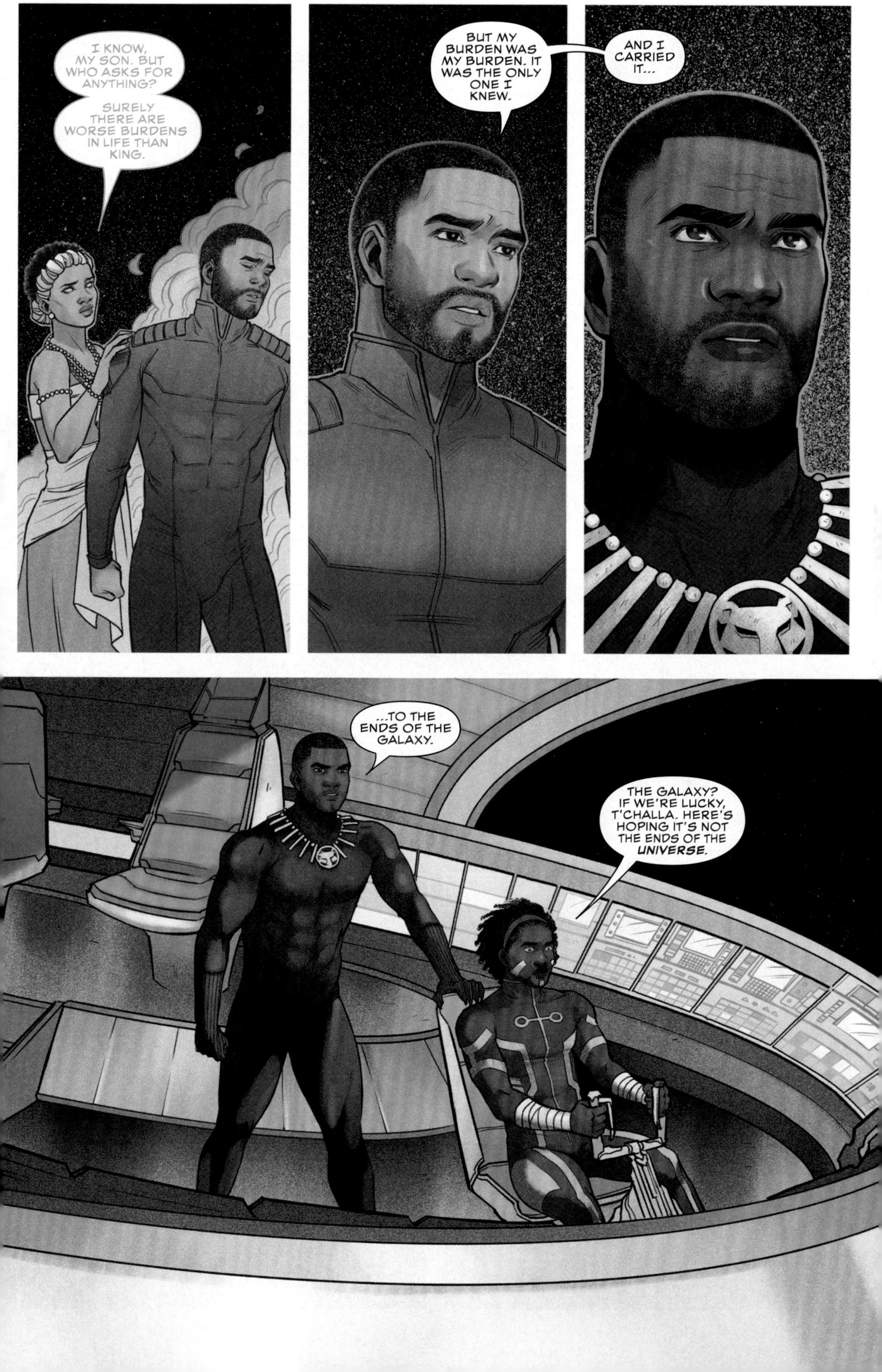
I KNOW, MY SON. BUT WHO ASKS FOR ANYTHING?
SURELY THERE ARE WORSE BURDENS IN LIFE THAN KING.
BUT MY BURDEN WAS MY BURDEN. IT WAS THE ONLY ONE I KNEW.
AND I CARRIED IT...
...TO THE ENDS OF THE GALAXY.
THE GALAXY? IF WE'RE LUCKY, T'CHALLA. HERE'S HOPING IT'S NOT THE ENDS OF THE *UNIVERSE*.

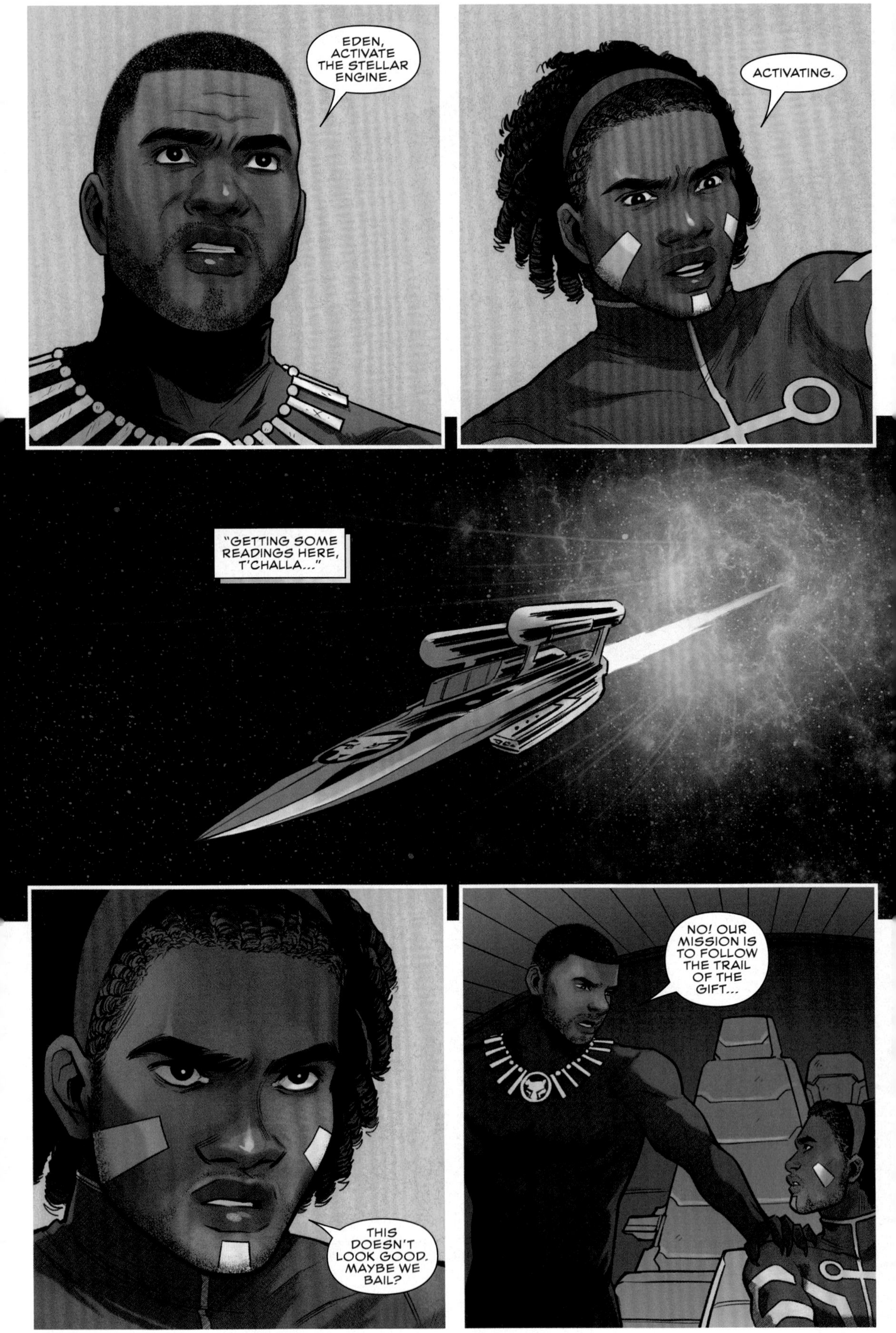
EDEN, ACTIVATE THE STELLAR ENGINE.
ACTIVATING.
"GETTING SOME READINGS HERE, T'CHALLA..."
THIS DOESN'T LOOK GOOD. MAYBE WE BAIL?
NO! OUR MISSION IS TO FOLLOW THE TRAIL OF THE GIFT...

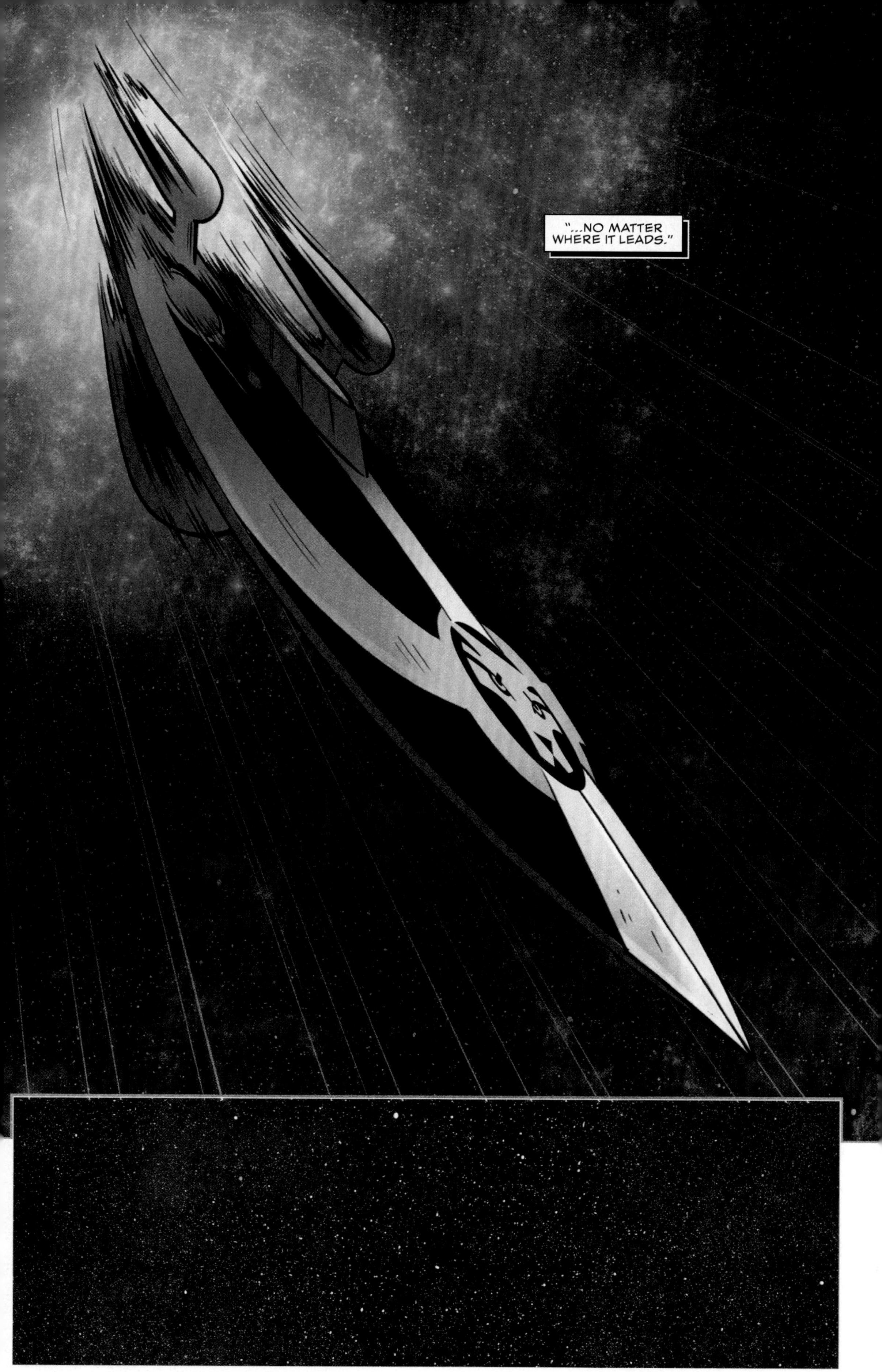
"...NO MATTER WHERE IT LEADS."

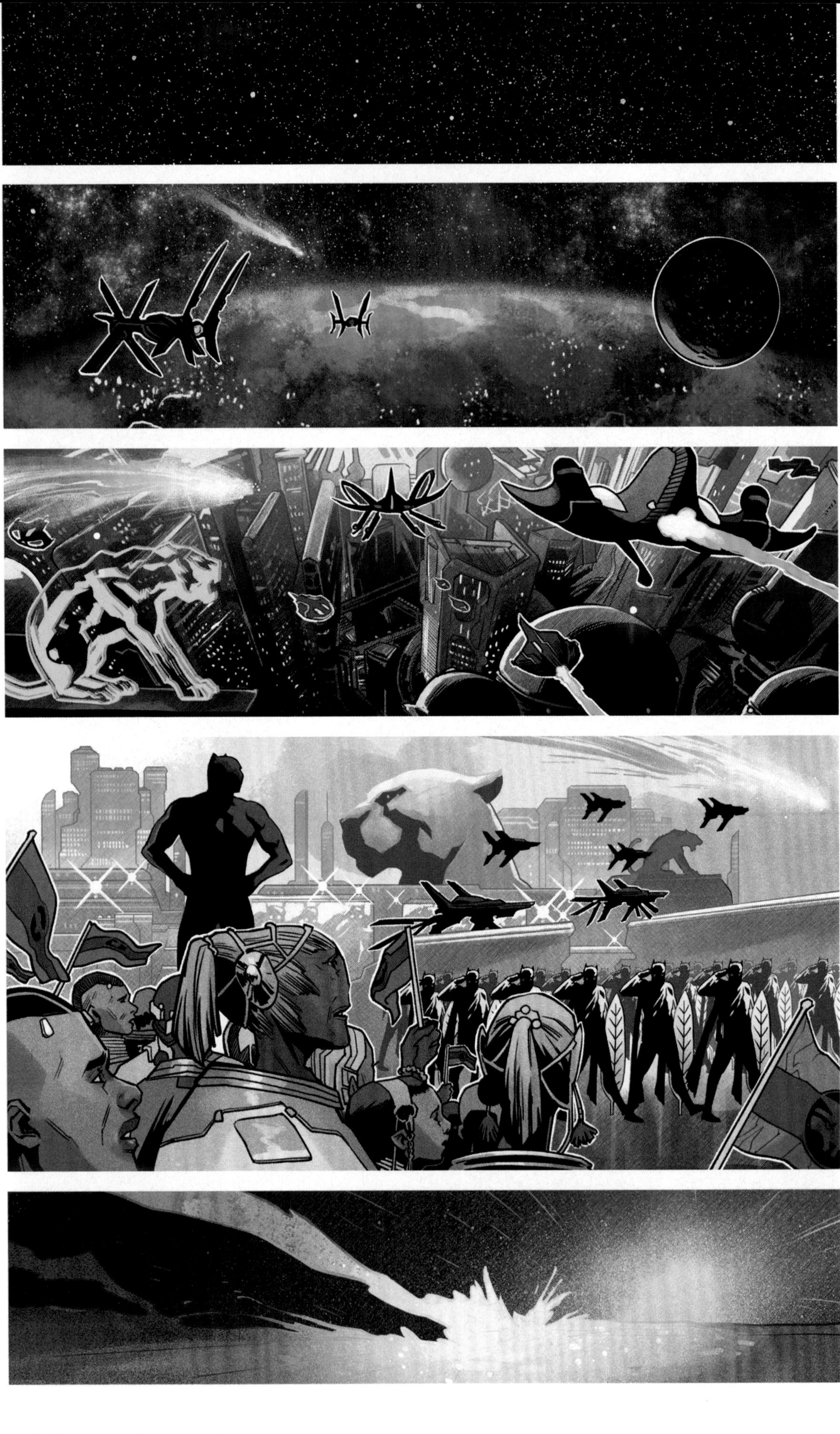

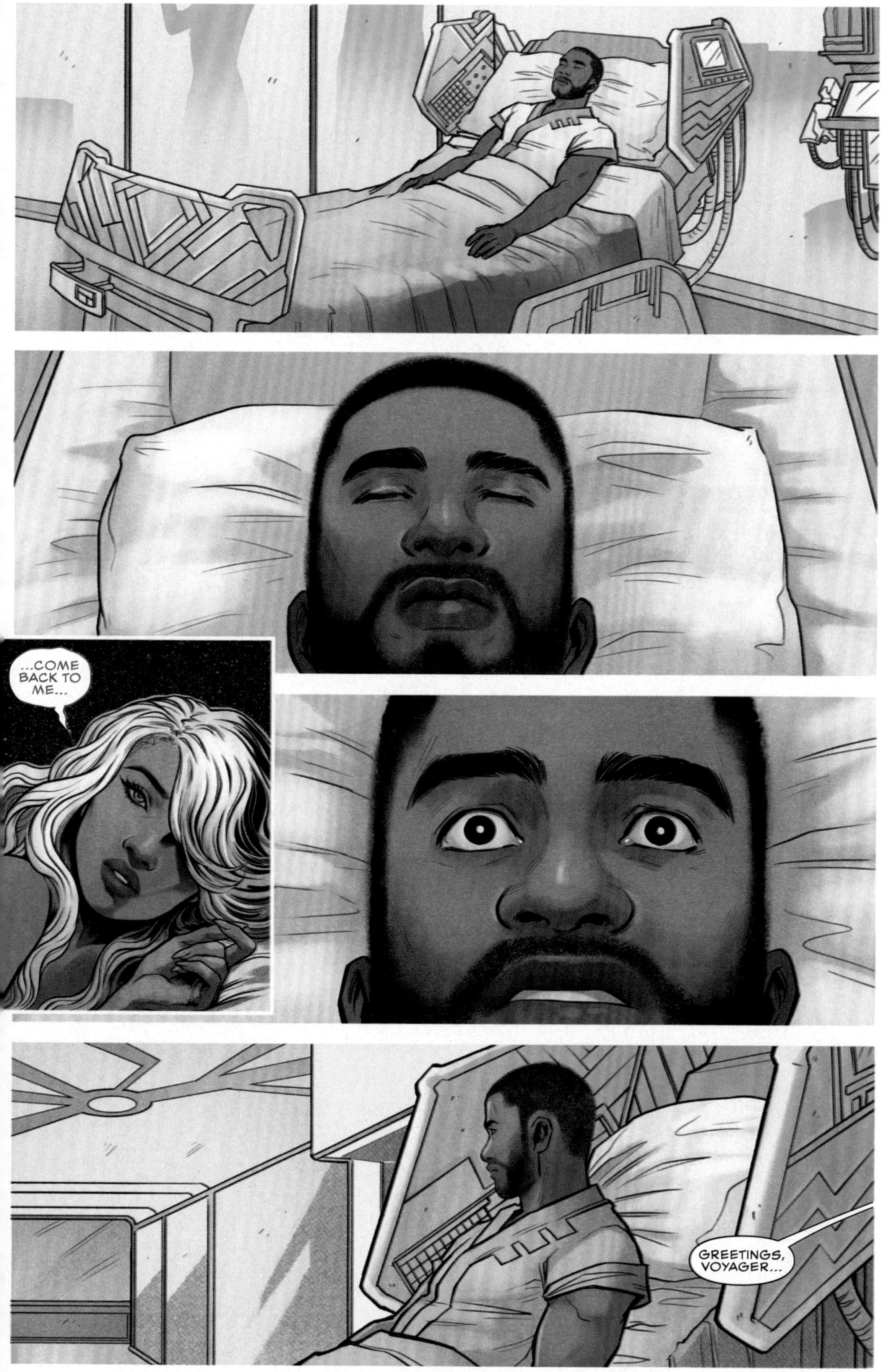
...COME BACK TO ME...
GREETINGS, VOYAGER...

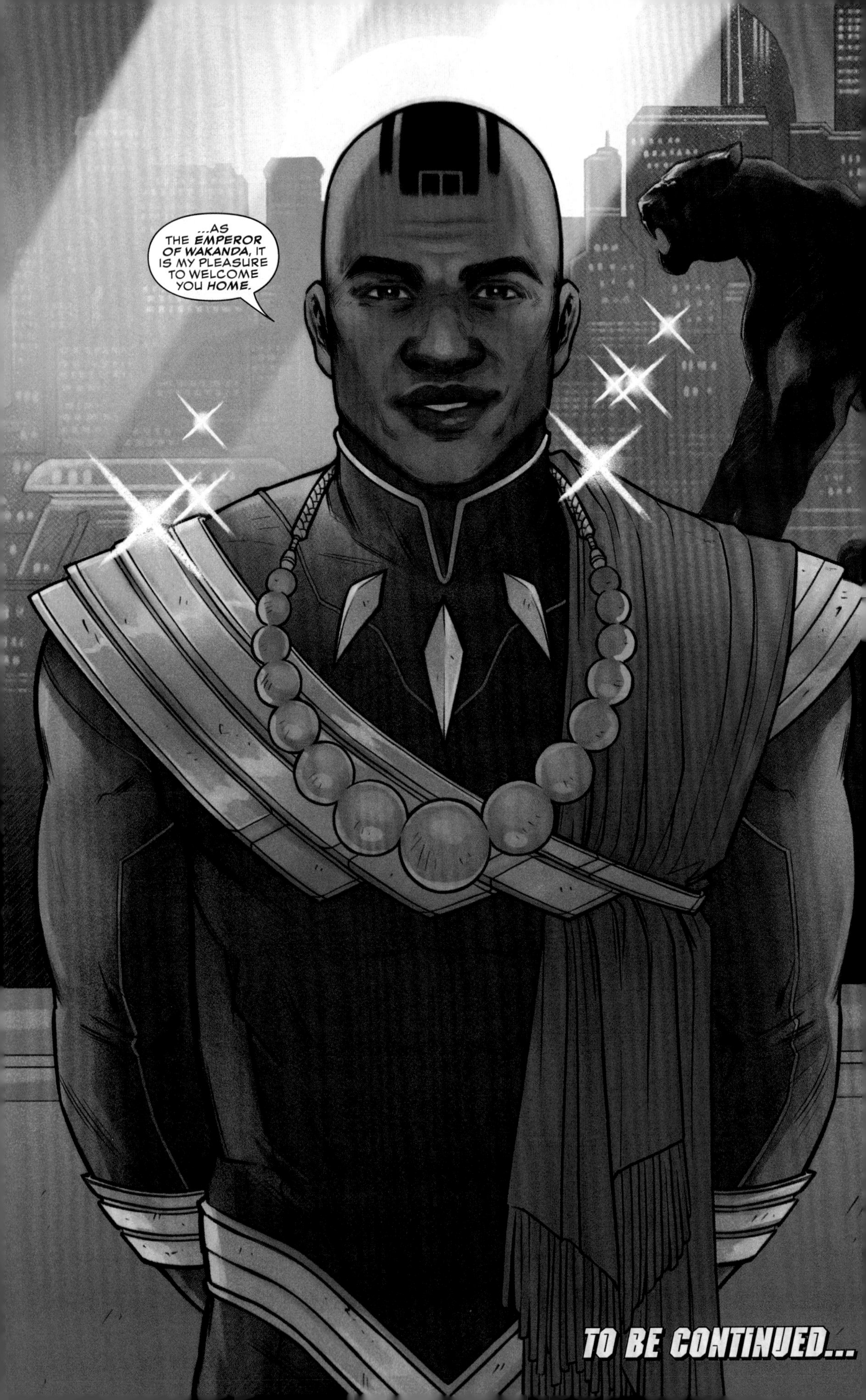
...AS THE EMPEROR OF WAKANDA, IT IS MY PLEASURE TO WELCOME YOU HOME.
TO BE CONTINUED...

IN THIS ISSUE, TA-NEHISI COATES AND JEN BARTEL DOVE INTO SOME *BLACK PANTHER* HISTORY. NEED A BIT OF YOUR OWN MEMORY RESTORED? LUCKILY, YOU DON'T HAVE TO HAVE AN ALIEN WATER CREATURE OR AN ANCIENT GODDESS-IN-CHILD-FORM. JUST CHECK OUT THESE SINGLE ISSUES AND TRADES!

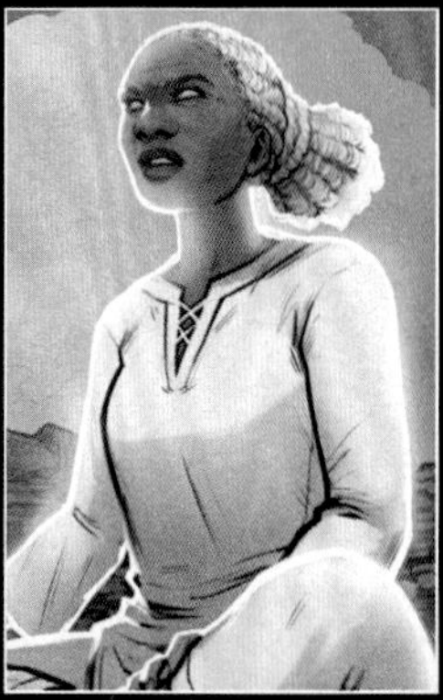

"MOTHER" GRIOT AND THE *DJALIA*

TAKING THE FORM OF QUEEN MOTHER RAMONDA, A GRIOT—A STORYTELLER AND KEEPER OF HISTORY—GUIDED PRINCESS SHURI THROUGH THE PLANE OF WAKANDAN MEMORY TO RESTORE HER TO LIFE AS THE ANCIENT FUTURE, IMBUED WITH THE POWER OF WAKANDAN LEGENDS. BLACK PANTHER (2016) #4-8.

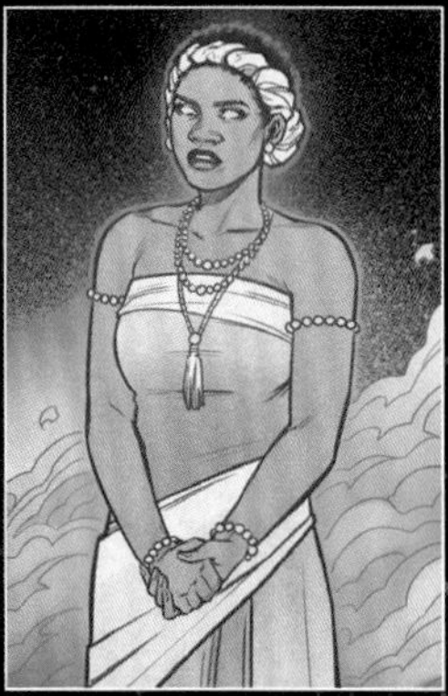

QUEEN SOLOGON

RULER OF THE BAKO, THE TRIBE THAT UNIFIED WAKANDA AND USHERED IN THE FIFTH DYNASTY, QUEEN MOTHER SOLOGON LED HER PEOPLE INTO BATTLE AGAINST AN ARMY BENT ON CONQUERING AFRICA. FROM HER, SHURI LEARNED THE LESSON THAT A "SPIRIT OF IRON MAKES SKIN OF STONE"—GRANTING HER THE ABILITY TO HARDEN HER SKIN AGAINST ATTACK. BLACK PANTHER (2016) #8.

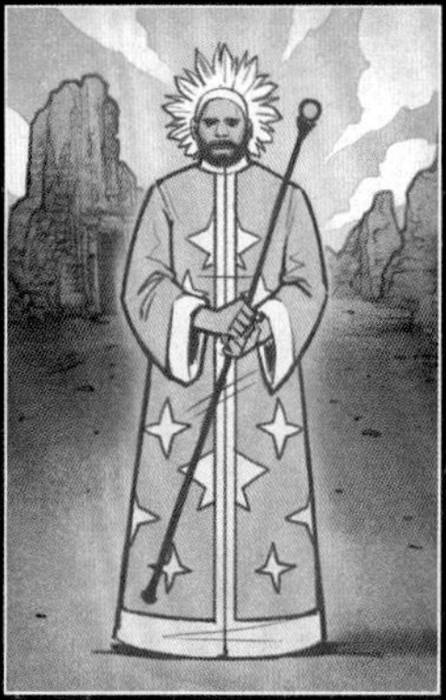

DUKE OF ADOWA

MANY GENERATIONS AGO, STRANGERS ARRIVED IN THE DUCHY OF ADOWA DEMANDING TRIBUTE. WITH NO STANDING ARMY, THE DUKE CHOSE A DIFFERENT FORM OF DEFENSE: HE MELTED INTO HIS NATION AND BECAME ONE WITH HIS OWN PEOPLE. UNIFIED, THE ADOWANS DECEIVED THE STRANGERS AND SLOWLY DESTROYED THEM. FROM THE DUKE, SHURI LEARNED THAT "EITHER YOU ARE A NATION, OR YOU ARE NOTHING." BLACK PANTHER (2016) #5.

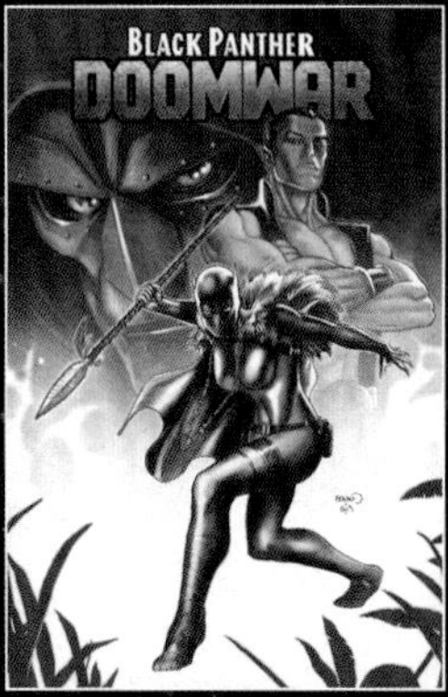
BLACK PANTHER
DOOMWAR

THE DESTURI

FOR MOST OF ITS HISTORY, WAKANDA WAS HIDDEN TO THE LARGER WORLD. BY THIS ISOLATIONISM, THEY BUILT THEIR GREAT WEALTH. BUT AFTER HIS FATHER WAS KILLED BY WESTERN INVADERS AND THE FANTASTIC FOUR DISCOVERED WAKANDA BY ACCIDENT, T'CHALLA REALIZED THE COUNTRY COULD HIDE NO LONGER AND REVEALED ITS EXISTENCE TO THE NATIONS OF THE WORLD. A SMALL GROUP OF WAKANDANS VIOLENTLY PROTESTED T'CHALLA'S DECISION, FORMING A GROUP CALLED "THE DESTURI," A SWAHILI WORD MEANING "CUSTOM" OR "TRADITION." BLACK PANTHER (2010) #7-12.

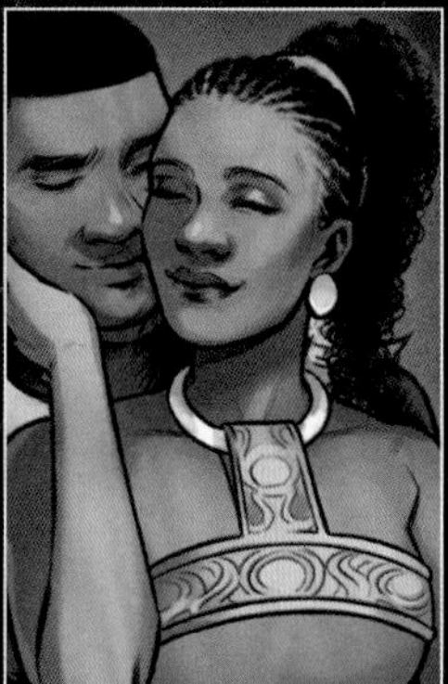

N'YAMI

A BRILLIANT SCIENTIST, N'YAMI CAME TO KING T'CHAKA'S ATTENTION THROUGH HER STUDY OF VIBRANIUM. AS QUEEN, SHE SPEARHEADED PLANS FOR WAKANDA'S EXPLORATION OF SPACE. BUT SHE CONTRACTED A RARE AUTOIMMUNE DISEASE AND DIED SOON AFTER GIVING BIRTH TO T'CHALLA. YEARS LATER, KING T'CHAKA MARRIED RAMONDA, A SOUTH AFRICAN WOMAN WHO STUMBLED ONTO WAKANDA, AND RAMONDA RAISED T'CHALLA AS HER OWN SON. THE RISE OF THE BLACK PANTHER #1-5.

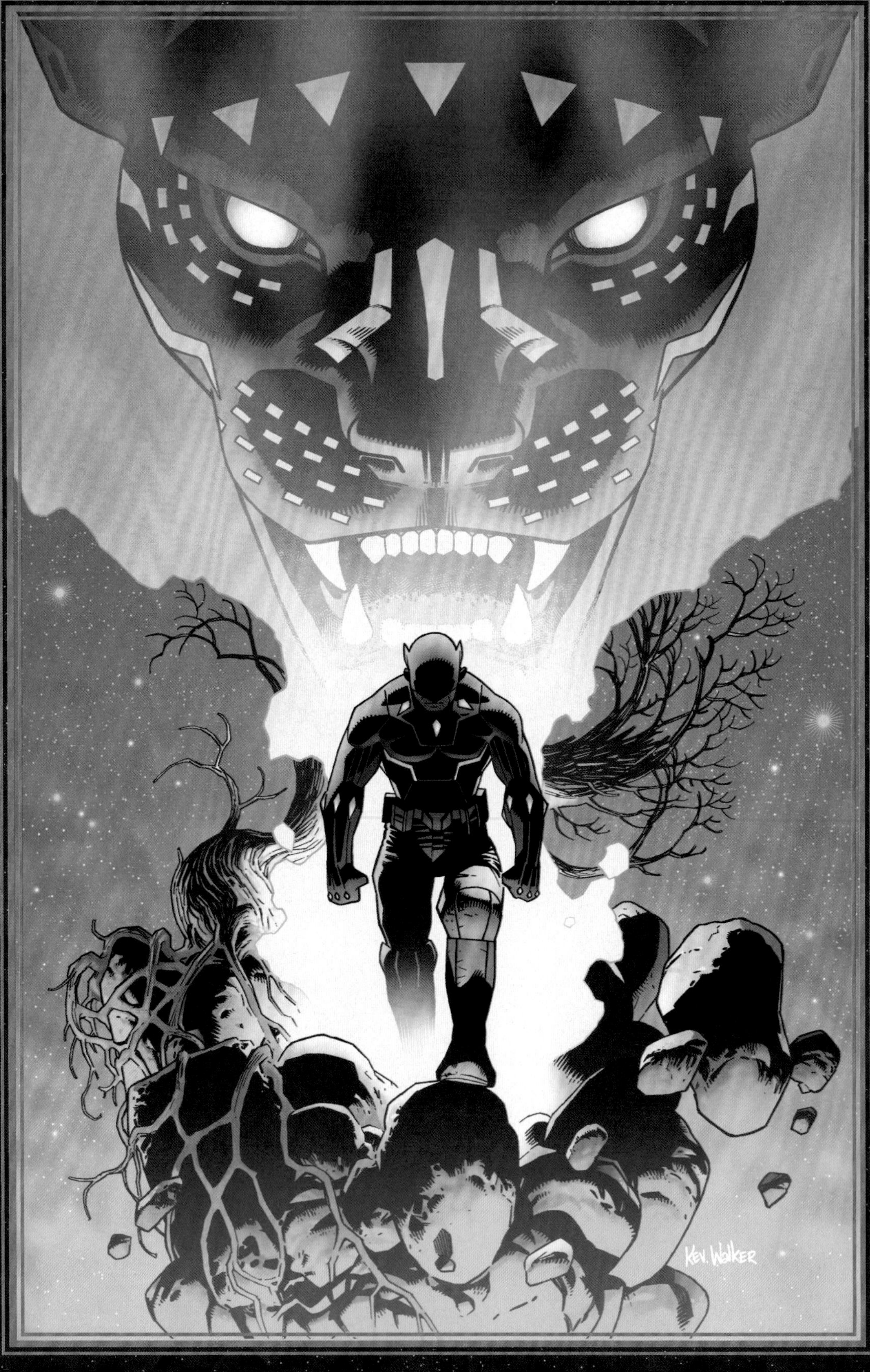
KEV. WALKER

Kev Walker

7 VARIANT

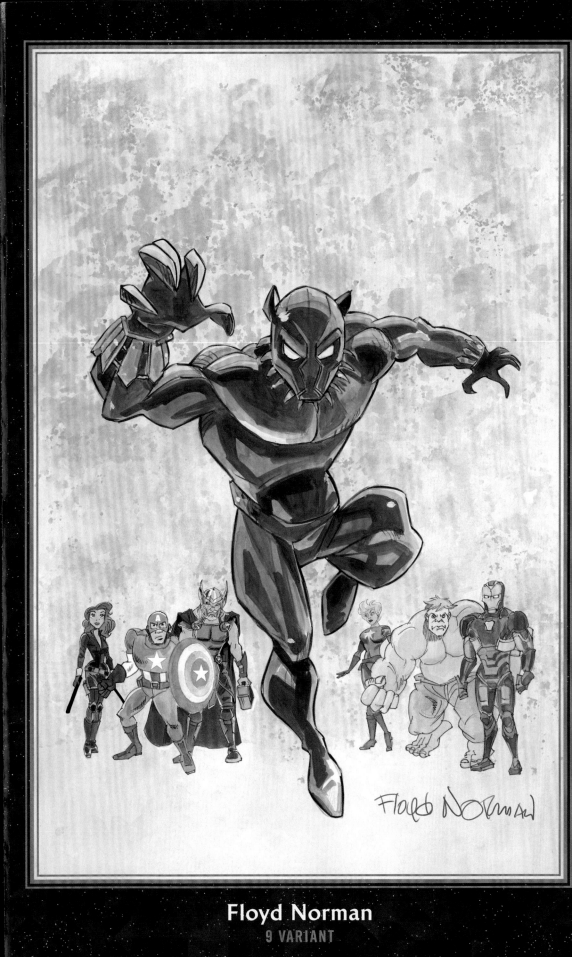

Floyd Norman
9 VARIANT

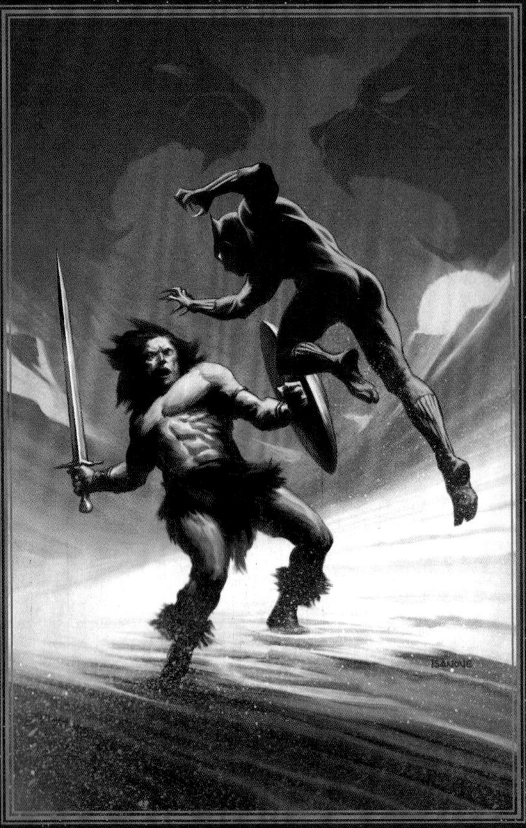
ISANOVE

Richard Isanove
7 CONAN VS. VARIANT

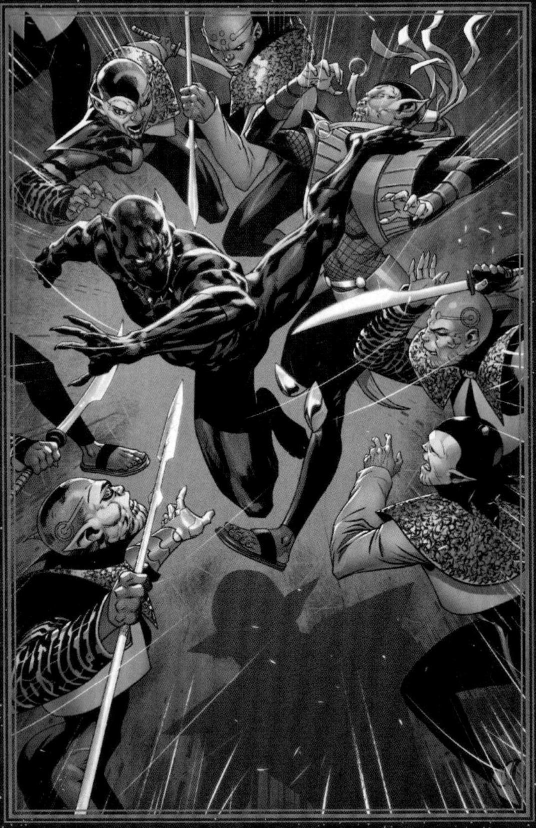

Ryan Benjamin & Nolan Woodard
9 SKRULLS VARIANT

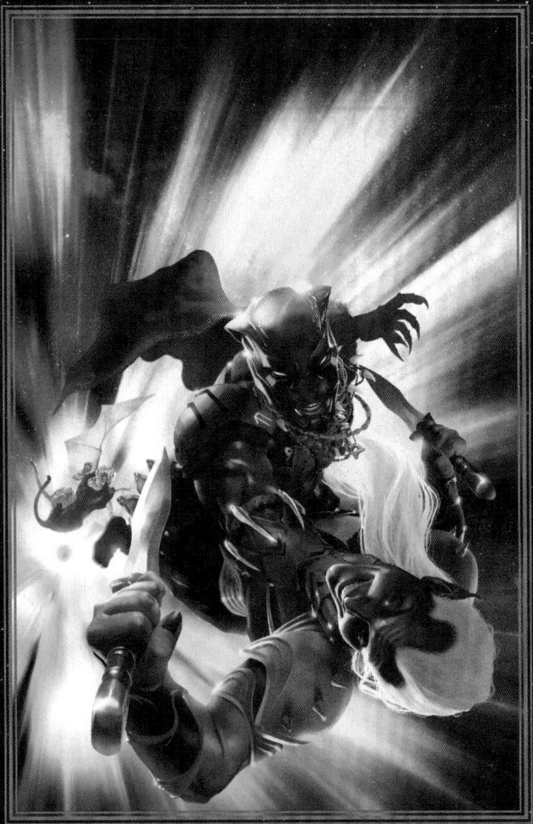

Rahzzah
11 ASGARDIAN VARIANT